THE COMPLETE BOOK ON OVERCALLS

———— ♠ ♠ ————

OTHER BOOKS BY MICHAEL LAWRENCE:

HOW TO READ YOUR OPPONENT'S CARDS
Prentice-Hall — 1973

JUDGMENT AT BRIDGE
Max Hardy — 1976

WINNING BACKGAMMON
Pinnacle — 1975

Michael Lawrence

THE COMPLETE BOOK ON OVERCALLS
In Contract Bridge

———————— ♠ ♠ ————————

with an introduction by Victor Mollo

PELHAM BOOKS

LONDON

First published in the United States of America 1979
by Max Hardy

First published in Great Britain by
Pelham Books Ltd
44 Bedford Square
London WC1B 3DU
1982

British Library Cataloguing in Publication Data
Lawrence, Michael
    The complete book on overcalls.
    1. Contract bridge
    I. Title
    795.41'53   GV1282.3

ISBN 0 7207 1411 7

Typeset by Allset
Printed and bound in Great Britain
by Billing and Sons, Worcester

CONTENTS

For Brenda who got me started . . .
For Joanna, who wouldn't let me quit.

INTRODUCTION
BY VICTOR MOLLO

Michael Lawrence is today America's most significant bridge writer and this is his most significant book.

Millions of words have been written in books and articles about bidding, and for the side which opens every step from 1♣ to 7NT has been minutely examined, codified, encapsulated in charts and tables, with gadgets and conventions laid on for every imaginable situation.

What of the other side? To the broad guidelines, much the same today as they were twenty, thirty or even forty years ago, have been added a score of conventions, some good, some bad, but the basic thinking hasn't changed. The individual player is left to improvise, to exercise his judgment pragmatically and there is little in bridge literature to help him.

It's over this vast misty area, still comparatively unexplored, that Michael Lawrence directs a powerful searchlight, probing every nook and cranny. A radical by temperament, he has no use for taboos and questions precepts which to many are sacrosanct. A conservative at heart, he insists on 'sound money', not just points or honour cards, but playing tricks all the way.

No feature of his philosophy has so impressed the critics as his advocacy of overcalls on four-card suits, and bad suits at that, when the occasion warrants. And yet, as Lawrence demonstrates, in the right context it is eminently safe. When you have length in the suit bid under you, partner must be short. So he is marked with some support for your four-card suit. It's this prospect of a fit which provides the safety margin. Meanwhile you put up a hurdle, interrupting enemy communications.

Have you three small cards in the suit bid under you? It's a gross liability. Have you three small in a suit bid by one of the opponents and supported by the other? It's an asset, for now partner will have at most a doubleton, perhaps a singleton or none. Again there's the promise of a fit.

Expectancy, the likelihood that partner will or will not have a fit, that is the cornerstone of the author's philosophy. Lawrence shows you how you can live dangerously in safety — so long as you know what makes it safe.

How do you rate an unsupported queen or knave? In the days of yore, Culbertson referred to 'plus values'. Moderns apply the point count. *Any* queen, be it in your suit or theirs, is worth two points. Of course the experienced player will discount the value of a queen in a suit bid by opponents. But is that enough? With irresistible logic Lawrence explains that such cards are 'minus values'. That queen, no use to you, would be worth a trick to opponents. Since that trick is missing, they must have another to make up for it, one that would be worth a trick to you, too. That trick you can no longer expect from partner. Your expectancy has lessened.

The ever-recurring motif of this book is locked in the phrase 'the state of the auction'. Every bid, every pass reflects the distribution and points the way ahead. As Hamlet might have said: No bid is right or wrong, but the state of the auction makes it so.

Nearly eight hundred examples illustrate every facet of the overcall and the response to it. No sequence is omitted. Here again Lawrence's approach is very much his own, differing from the accepted practice.

In textbooks examples are clearcut. There are no rough edges, no grey areas. At the table many a hand may not fit perfectly into any textbook and the player has to find not the best possible bid, but the best bid possible. Michael Lawrence doesn't shy away from these indeterminate hands. He positively welcomes them and readily admits that on occasion he wouldn't be sure of the best bid himself. His purpose is not to lay down the law — there is none — but to show the reader how to exercise his judgment, to signpost the way through the early, crucial stages of the auction. This he does remarkably well.

Having read and written so much about bridge myself, I am always happy to find something new in a book, something instructive which I had not come across before. I have found a lot in this book and I have learned a lot from it. For this I am truly grateful.

In his Introduction to the American edition Alfred Sheinwold writes: 'If you read several bridge books per year, you're already on your way to the cash register. If you read only one bridge book per year, this should be it.' I would go further and advise you to read not only this book, but those that will follow as well. What if he hasn't yet written them? When you read this one, you will know that Lawrence has a lot to give, to contribute, for he is a very unusual author, a very original thinker and a very original person. Allow me to introduce him to you.

MEET MICHAEL LAWRENCE

I first met Michael Lawrence a couple of months after he became world champion. As a member of Ira Corn's Aces he had just won the Bermuda Bowl, symbol of world supremacy, in Stockholm. That was in 1970 and Lawrence was not yet thirty years old. Earnest, shy, diffident, he never smiled and seemed very unsure of himself. After interviewing him in Ira Corn's study in Dallas, I wrote: 'All who come in contact with Michael Lawrence are conscious of a depth to his character, though what exactly is hidden in its recesses it would be hard to say. Perhaps he needs more time to mature.'

A second world championship, a long string of successes in his chosen profession, have done a lot to give Lawrence some of the confidence which he always inspired in others, yet so strangely lacked himself.

He has won all America's major cups and trophies — the Spingold, the Vanderbilt four times, the Reisinger three times, well over a hundred regional Championships. His two previous books on bridge — there's also one on Backgammon — have won wide acclaim. Once upon a time he was too shy to teach. Today he is a most successful lecturer and teacher.

His hobbies are revealing — ink abstracts, artistic leather decorations for bottles, and more recently, stained glass. Artistic, sensitive, always creative, Michael Lawrence has come a long way since those early days in Dallas. He is surely destined to go much further.

Victor Mollo

AUTHOR'S FOREWORD

Playing matchpoints with your favourite partner, you pick up some hand like the following, an ordinary eleven count.

♠ J 10 7
♡ K J 9 8
◇ Q 8 6 3
♣ A 2

Vulnerable versus not, your partner opens with one club and RHO passes. You respond one heart and partner raises to two. Deciding your hand is not quite worth a game, but certainly worth a try, you bid 2NT. Over this, partner signs off in 3 hearts, showing a minimum, but confirming four card support. Having nothing extra, you pass on the theory that it is not necessary to push to questionable games at matchpoints.

An easy hand to bid? Yes. At every stage you were able to make a useful and convenient bid. Both you and your partner had ample time to describe your hands and your final decision was well judged. Nicely bid.

Now, let's start again.

Partner bids one club as before, and RHO bids one spade. *What now?*

Let's assume for the moment that you don't play negative doubles. What are your options?

Well, your spades aren't good enough for a penalty double.

Neither can you bid one notrump without a spade stopper.

This leaves you with two hearts or two diamonds. But both have flaws. Partner will tend to play you for a five card suit, or at least a better four card suit. Assuming that you are happy with either bid, how happy are you going to be when partner raises to three? Should you pass or should you try for game?

And if you try for game, which one should it be? Very difficult.

How about a weaker hand such as the following:

♠ Q 10 3
♡ K 8 7 6 5
♢ Q 9 2
♣ 4 3

With no one vulnerable, partner deals and bids one diamond. When RHO passes you respond one heart. This hand is no bargain and, if partner shows no ambitions, you will be happy to make a part-score. But if partner has a good hand game is possible. One heart is a fine start towards whatever contract you hope to reach. Again, an easy hand.

But, what if RHO, instead of passing, intrudes with two clubs?

1♢ − 2♣ − ?

You are truly stuck.

If you pass, you have misgivings about the heart suit or perhaps the marginal diamond support. Two hearts seriously overstates the hand, and two diamonds would overstate the diamond support and would probably lose the heart suit. Awful.

Is there a solution?

If you use the negative double, you can attempt to solve the two hands in this fashion:

Hand one:

♠ J 10 7
♡ K J 9 8
♢ Q 8 6 3
♣ A 2

1♣ − 1♠ − ?

An ideal hand for the negative double: four cards in the unbid suits, sufficient values in case of a mishap.

With this hand, not much can go wrong because of your extra high cards. But partner may have doubts about introducing hearts on 7 6 4 2 and there may be some difficulty in working out whether you have a spade stopper for three notrumps. And there is always the possibility that, even if you do have a spade stopper, you may not have enough values for three no-trumps. Your hand isn't *that* good.

But the negative double did help — it's certainly better than nothing.

How does it work on the second hand?

♠ Q 10 3
♡ K 8 7 6 5
◇ Q 9 2
♣ 4 3

1◇ — 2♣ — ?

It doesn't work very well, does it?

You wouldn't like it if partner bids two spades. And you will like it even less if he bids them at the three or four level.

You hope partner will bid hearts or rebid diamonds. But you know as well as I do he's going to bid spades far too often to make a negative double work with this hand. The answer? There is none. At least, nothing perfect.

Am I trying to talk you out of the negative double? No, not at all.

What I am trying to do is to show you how hard a simple hand becomes when opponents intervene.

If you look at both hands you will note that in each case the overcall took away the one level response you would have had available. This effectively cut the amount of information you would like to have exchanged by half, or more. Very simple and very effective.

Now, if you have trouble with these rather ordinary hands just because an opponent has overcalled, is there any reason to believe that your opponents will not have the same problems if they open and you overcall?

I assure you that they will.

WHY SHOULD YOU OVERCALL?

There are several good reasons for overcalling:

1. You may buy the contract for a successful game or part-score.

2. You may get partner off to a good lead.

3. You may push opponents too high; perhaps, on occasion, at considerable expense to them.

4. You may find a successful sacrifice.

5. You may cause opponents to misjudge their hands and either miss a game (or slam) or get to the wrong game or slam. Or, for that matter, the wrong suit.

Most of these reasons are well known. They do not need elaborating. If I examined in such detail the two examples given above, it is because I wanted to emphasise as strongly as possible this one aspect of overcalling. It makes life difficult for the side that opened.

I intend to cover the entire range of hands on which I believe you should overcall. This will be done through a series of examples. General rules just don't apply in an area such as defensive bidding. Not to say that I don't believe in them. I just don't think they are adequate.

Later, I will examine the structure of responses to partner's overcall.

I will make distinctions between matchpoints and International Match Points (IMP's), Swiss teams or knockouts.

If you play both matchpoints and IMP's, we will consider whether you could make the same bid in each situation.

Part I
Overcalls

1
ONE LEVEL OVERCALLS

NO ONE VULNERABLE. RHO OPENS 1♣.

♠ A Q 10 7 6	♠ 4	♠ A K Q 9 7
♡ 4 2	♡ K Q 10 7 6 5	♡ Q 5 4
◇ K 3 2	◇ A 6 5 4	◇ 4
♣ A 10 6	♣ 3 2	♣ 10 7 6 5

♠ Q J 10 8 7 5	♠ K 4	♠ K 5
♡ 4	♡ 3	♡ A Q J 10 8 7
◇ A Q 5	◇ A J 10 8 7	◇ A J 3
♣ Q 10 7	♣ K 9 8 7 6	♣ 4 2

These hands should all be automatic overcalls regardless of the form of bridge you are playing. In all cases you have both a good suit and values approximating to an opening bid. If you feel like passing any of these hands you are being far too conservative. Also, you will find some of my ideas hard to accept.

None of these hands, however, would be worth a takeout double, intending to bid a suit later. That would be too aggressive.

In the following hand, no one is vulnerable and RHO opens 1♣.

♠ K Q 10 9 7
♡ 5 4 2
◇ K 8 3
♣ J 2

At matchpoints where overtricks are of such concern, there is much to be said for overcalling at the one level on any hand with a good suit. One spade here has almost everything going for it except that game is unlikely.

You want a spade lead.

Your overcall will take away significant room from the opponents.

It's much better for you in general to bid right away rather than to wait and so allow opponents an unimpeded discussion.

True, you may be able to balance later, but why wait? This hand is also sufficiently strong to bid 1♠ at IMP's, although that is beginning to stretch things.

IMP'S VS. MATCHPOINTS

When considering whether or not to overcall, you should realise the distinction between matchpoints and IMP's.

Matchpoints is a wild struggle where every hand is a separate battle. Winning a hand by an extra trick may be as good a result as getting 800. The worst you can do is get a zero. If, on one round you steal a trick in 2♣ and make an overtrick for +110 and get a top, and then on the next hand you go down 900 and get a zero, you have achieved an average round.

At IMP's, you may gain one IMP for your extra trick in 2♣, but you may lose 14 for your −900, and your net result is −13 IMP's. A disaster. This means that at IMP's, you must be far more conscious of safety than at matchpoints. As you will see, I recommend an aggressive stance at IMP's as well as at matchpoints, but tempered with caution.

Incidentally, there is one aspect of matchpoints which will become more and more evident as we go along. I will refer to it constantly.

Good matchpoints is rarely good bridge.

You have to learn to play badly. There are a number of things you can do which are theoretically wrong, but at matchpoints they work a high percentage of the time. And this is what matchpoints is all about. If you want to win, and to win a lot, you have to learn what works and what doesn't. And you have to be able to take the hard knocks with the rest of your results. If you can't stomach an occasional calamity, you will probably get a lot of 167's and 172½'s but you won't get many wins. You have to keep your goals in sight.

1♣: ♠ K 2
     ♡ A Q 10 9 8
     ◇ 10 7 6
     ♣ 9 8 3

One heart here is fairly straightforward. Your suit affords protection against a double and prospects for a small plus score are adequate. Overcall at IMP's as well.

1♣: ♠ A 3 2
     ♡ 7 4
     ◇ K Q J 8 7
     ♣ K 5 4

One diamond. Again it should be automatic. Good hand. Good suit. Even game is not unlikely.

On the debit side is the fact that your 1◇ overcall does not do much to inconvenience opponents.

OBSTRUCTION

You should be aware of two factors when considering an overcall. These auctions: 1♣–1♠ or 1◇–2♣ are far and away the most difficult for opponents to handle. You have effectively removed the one-level from their available responses. Very hard for them to cope. Any time responder has a few points, but not enough for a two level response, he is going to be very awkwardly placed. Some of the time he may be able to make a negative double but as you've seen, that may not work if responder's hand is unsuitable.

Conversely, 1◇ over 1♣ or 1♠ over 1♡ does little to obstruct opponents. This means that when a decision is close, you might lean toward bidding if this will prove awkward for opponents.

1♣:

♠ Q 10 8 7 4   Bid one spade. Even though the suit isn't
♡ 8   quite up to what you would like it to be, the
◇ K 7 6   rest of the hand more than makes up for it.
♣ A Q 4 2   Likewise at IMP's. Clearcut.

1♣:

♠ K 9 8 7 5   Here we begin to stretch things a bit. I might
♡ K 7 4   bid one spade on the theory that it makes
◇ J 4 2   things hard for opponents, but, even at match-
♣ Q 10   points, a pass is probably best. At IMP's this
is a clearcut pass. Your maximum is likely to
be a part-score and you could easily go for a substantial number.
Not vulnerable, even −300 could be expensive.

1♣:

♠ K Q 10 8 7   This hand has the same high cards and the same
♡ K J 9   distribution as the previous hand. But now the
◇ 4 3 2   high cards are all working in that they rein-
♣ 8 7   force each other. And your suit is now fair.
Before it was not. At matchpoints this be-
comes a reasonable overcall and even at IMP's it is an acceptable
minimum. Though you may concede a penalty, you are well
placed to contend for a part score. And you do want a spade
lead. Again, the quality of your suit is a major consideration
when making an overcall on a minimum.

1♣:

♠ J 8 7 4 2   One spade. This falls into the category of
♡ 8   hands with good values but no particularly
◇ A K 3   good bid. Some good hands afford no con-
♣ A J 4 2   venient way to enter the auction. But, when
you have a good hand which includes a five
card suit, even a bad five card suit, it may be possible and even
desirable to overcall. Even at IMP's, an overcall could be clearcut. Look at your potential. If partner has as little as any four
spades, you can probably made a part score and game is not
unlikely opposite something like this:

♠ A 10 5 3
♡ Q 9 7 6 4
◇ 10 2
♣ Q 5

Even if partner has as little as:

♠ 10 3
♡ J 9 7 6 4 2
◇ 6 5 2
♣ Q 5

nothing terrible is likely to happen, while opponents can surely make game.

1♣:

♠ 9 6 5 4 2   Again one spade. Your offensive potential
♡ A 3   makes this worth an overcall at matchpoints
◇ A Q 8 7   or IMP's. Any time you feel that a moderate
♣ K 2   fit could have a future, you should bid.
Note that when you overcall with bad suits, you are doing so only at the one level. And if the suit is bad, the rest of your hand is good. You need an opening bid or powerful distribution to take the risk. Also, your high cards should be aces and kings.

1♣:

♠ 8 7 6 4 2   This hand is too dangerous for an overcall.
♡ K J   Your suit is bad and opposite a weak dummy
◇ K Q 7   you could find yourself having to lead away
♣ K J 5   from all those kings and jacks. If, at match-
points you want to overcall 1♠, well OK. This is the kind of bad bid you may make at matchpoints. It may work.

But at IMP's, never.

1♣:

♠ 8   One heart. Could your suit be worse? Hardly,
♡ 6 5 4 3 2   but, if you accepted some of the earlier
◇ A Q 3 2   examples, you should be right at home with
♣ A K 4   this one. In terms of offence, you have an
excellent hand. If partner can suggest a game, you should be happy to accept, your trump suit notwithstanding.

This is an important hand. It goes against widely accepted notions and yet much is at stake here. Passing can lead to all sorts of bad results. I intend to spend quite some time on this example.

First, there is the obvious objection that partner may get off to a bad lead. This is true. He may lead a heart from doubleton king or queen and this may not be good for your side. But for this to occur requires a number of things to happen. One of these is that partner has to be on lead. And that is not necessarily going to be so. One of the results of your overcall could be that your side will play the hand. In those cases where partner is on lead you will frequently find that the doubleton king or queen does not cost a trick. The opening bidder on your right may well have the ace, so your partner's king would be dead in any case. Perhaps there was no good lead for your side. It's possible that, if left to his own devices, partner would lead something with no future anyway. Admittedly, on the actual hand, you would prefer a club or a diamond, if that were partner's natural choice. But if opponents end up in NT, your partner might well lead a spade which would do you no good at all.

Let's say that LHO does bid 1NT and is raised to 2NT or 3NT. Let's say partner leads the doubleton K of hearts and everyone gets a good laugh as dummy on your right puts down Q J 10 of hearts and declarer takes the ace. This looks bad, but it may well be that this is the only lead to defeat them. You have all sorts of entries and may be able to establish your hearts. Now, if partner had led a spade from Q 10 8 7 2, his lead would also give declarer an extra trick, but in that case there would be no chance to recover.

The next obvious objection is that you may be doubled. This can happen and once in a while it will happen. I won't try to tell you one heart is entirely safe, because it's not. But then nothing is safe. Some people open a short club on 8 6 2 and I can't believe that is safer than overcalling one heart on 6 5 4 3 2.

It's difficult to argue this point. A big penalty is hard to ignore. But I would overcall one heart at IMP's even vulnerable. The benefits are so substantial that the occasional penalty is worth the price.

There is also the possibility that even though you could have been badly punished, opponents fail to catch you. Or, perhaps one of your opponents decides not to stand the double. Or, perhaps you escape into diamonds, or, for that matter, into clubs, spades, or notrumps. You will be surprised how seldom you get penalised heavily for overcalling on a hand such as this. Admittedly, I am asking you to accept this on trust. But if you have the proper outside values necessary to overcall when the suit is so bad, you will be doing quite well.

What happens when partner doesn't like hearts and bids something else? What happens when partner doubles opponents, expecting you to have good hearts?

Let's see. If you bid 1 heart and the bidding continues:

$$1\clubsuit - 1\heartsuit - 1NT - 2\clubsuit$$

Do you like your hand? You should. It is outstanding, aside from lack of spade support. Partner is probably short in hearts, or he would have raised your overcall. This means that your bad heart suit is not a liability at all. Now your high cards are all working and partner will be delighted to see dummy. However, if your hand were:

♠ 8
♡ K Q J 4 2
◇ K 7 6
♣ K 5 4 2

then it would not be nearly as useful in a spade contract. If partner had a singleton heart, he would have to get in, set up the hearts, get in again and somehow get to dummy to enjoy the heart tricks. The actual hand has ready-made tricks.

If partner should decide to double the opponents, your hand will not be a disappointment at all. You have excellent defensive strength. A Q and A K. If partner doubles something and it makes, partner should either have a better hand for the double or else the defence wasn't so hot. You need to make no apologies for the overcall. You had your values.

And, finally, if partner raises hearts, you should be pleased. One of the purposes of overcalling is to find a fit and arrive at a good contract. A raise from partner is good news indeed.

I repeat that this hand is clearly worth a bid, at any vulnerability and at any form of the game, including IMP's. It's even possible that you might do some further bidding with it. But, more on that later.

1♣:

♠ 8 2
♡ A J 3
◇ 8 7 6 4 2
♣ A K 10

Pass or one diamond. Experience has shown that there is not much future in overcalling with a bad minor as opposed to a bad major. It does little to obstruct opponents. Here you have a good hand so you could overcall, but, with anything less, you ought to pass. Perhaps later you can re-enter the auction.

There is one more area, or style, of overcalling which properly used can be truly devastating. There is very little literature on it, so, for the most part, people are unfamiliar with it. Which is certainly to my advantage. Quite frankly, I would prefer my opponents not to know too much about it.

Perhaps this is why no one has bothered to discuss it in print. Anyway, here goes . . .

2

OVERCALLING ON FOUR CARD SUITS

Every now and then, you will find yourself with a goodish hand and your RHO opens the bidding. Feeling that you should take some action, but finding nothing convenient, you pass and later discover that you had a game or partial though neither you nor partner were able to enter the auction. Certainly there are hands with which you would open the bidding but with which you can't compete after an opening bid. Such problems can often be solved by overcalling on a four card suit. Generalities are rarely helpful. So, instead, the usual examples.

With no one vul., RHO opens 1◇:

1◇:

♠ K Q 10 9   Bid one spade. A prerequisite for overcalling
♡ 4 2   on a four card suit is that it should be a very
◇ A Q 6 5   good suit. Partner is going to raise you when-
♣ K 5 4   ever possible and three small should be
                  adequate support if his hand qualifies other-
wise. Responder should not have to be worried about the quality
of your overcalls.

1◇:

♠ 8 2   One heart. If the possession of five cards in
♡ A Q 10 7   the suit opened bothers you, forget it. Your
◇ 10 7 6 5 4   length in diamonds plus opener's length assures
♣ A Q   you that your partner (and LHO) are also
                  short. This means your partner is likely to
have heart support. The length in diamonds therefore is not a
minus but, rather, an asset. Perhaps the two hands are something
like this:

♠ A 9 7 6 4
♡ J 8 3
◇ 3
♣ 7 6 5 2

♠ 8 2
♡ A Q 10 7
◇ 10 7 6 5 4
♣ A Q

With a diamond lead and a heart return, you should make between seven and nine tricks. Not bad considering that dummy is not all that good. If dummy had a fourth heart, ten tricks would be possible and if you found dummy with five of them, game would depend on winning either the club or heart finesse. With the opening bid on your right, game should be nearly a cinch.

Now, if game is on opposite:

♠ A 8 4 2
♡ J 9 5 4
◇ 3
♣ J 9 4 2

it would be nice to bid it. Or, if you can't get to game, at least get to hearts. Making 170 is better than being −110 or −90. If you don't bid 1♡ right away you will never get to four hearts or to hearts at all, for that matter.

1◇:

♠ K Q J 9
♡ A 2
◇ 4 3
♣ J 8 7 4 3

One spade. This hand may appear similar to the one before, but it isn't. The points are the same. The distribution is the same. The hand contains a good four card suit and a crummy five card suit. Neither hand contains a singleton.

The difference? It is in the auction. In the previous hand the opening bid was in your weak five card suit. This suggested that your partner would have substantial distributional support for your four card suit. Even if you found him with no high cards, you were assured of some kind of fit.

In this hand, however, the opening bid was in one of your doubletons. Therefore, even though it's correct to bid one spade, you do so in the hope, rather than the expectation, that partner can provide some sort of fit. If the worst comes to the worst, you will probably take three spade tricks and the ace of hearts. But my estimation is that you will seldom get less than five tricks, even opposite nothing. There are many hands with five card suits on which nearly everyone would overcall, yet end up taking fewer tricks.

1◇:

♠ A Q 8 6 2   This hand, if doubled in a one spade overcall
♡ A Q 3   could conceivably take only two tricks. While
◇ 4 2   two tricks is, admittedly, unlikely, the possi-
♣ 9 7 3   bility of taking three or four is very real. And
                 yet, nearly everyone would hasten to bid
one spade on this hand, and hasten equally quickly to pass the
hand just being discussed with K Q J 9 of spades. For my part,
I would be quite pleased to hold

♠ K Q J 9
♡ A 2
◇ 4 3
♣ J 8 7 4 3

and overcall one spade at matchpoints, rubber bridge, IMP's, or,
for that matter, board-a-match.

There is another aspect to consider. If you overcall one
spade, you must be prepared to lose the club suit. There is no
way you can ever hope to get the clubs mentioned without
partner assuming, rightly, that you have as many or more spades
than clubs.

Such hands are inflexible. Either you don't mind at all, or
you bid one spade and then subside. It is true that you may bid
again. You may accept a game try if you have a maximum, or
if partner bids notrump, there are hands on which you could
raise. Perhaps, once in a while, your partner will bid your side
five card suit. But, for the most part, once you've overcalled,
you will take no more voluntary action.

Some conventions might be useful: Michaels, Hi-Lo cue bids,
Astro cue bids, etc. Should you be using the right one at the
right time, all will be well. If not, consider the overcall. Far
better to describe some of your hand than none at all.

You may wonder why overcalling on four card suits is so
effective. Apart from the usual reasons, a four card suit overcall
must be good by definition, so it is certainly a suit you want
partner to lead. The fact that you have such a good suit suggests partner would not have high cards in it and left to himself
it might not occur to him to lead it. Furthermore, you may put
opponents off notrumps. They may credit you with a longer

suit and decide on a part-score when three notrumps is cold.

Having only a four bagger works out favourably when partner leads it, and you find yourself taking two or three tricks against a suit contract. Each opponent, holding three or even four small may have been hoping his partner to be short. When this happens, you will occasionally find opponents getting too high in the wrong suit. It's not bad when your opponents miss a game; but when you can manoeuvre them into the wrong game and beat it, when another game — usually 3NT — is cold, it's even better.

By now, if you've not been convinced that overcalling on four card suits is a good thing, done properly, do this: first, review the two hands at the introduction of this chapter. Then, during the next session or two you play, note the ease or difficulty you experience when your opponents overcall.

If you are convinced it's right to compete, consider this: it is a fact that most people do not compete on four-card suits. If a partnership decided to do so, it would compete on from one to three or four hands more per session than previously. My experience suggests that, in general, my matchpoint results are excellent where these overcalls have been used. Out of ten times, I would expect two or three tops, four very good results, an average or two, and, perhaps, one bad result. At IMP's, bad results just don't happen. At worst you will score a small plus like 70 or 90 instead of 110 or 130. At IMP's, you don't worry about such trifles.

So, if you give these methods a try, you will be well placed. At least until everyone else learns as well.

Some more examples in the same vein. This time you are not vul. vs. vul. and your RHO opens one heart.

1♥:

♠ K Q 10 8   Don't get carried away. This is a takeout
♡ 3 2   double, not a one spade overcall.
◇ A J 4 3
♣ K 6 5

1♡:

♠ A 2   Pass. Overcalling at the two level requires a
♡ 10 8 6 5 4   five card suit. Two clubs, good suit and all, is
◇ A 2   just a bit rich.
♣ K Q J 8

1♡:

♠ K 10 9 7   This is the kind of hand on which a theore-
♡ A 9 5 4 2   tically unsound bid of one spade could work
◇ 4 2   well. It's the sort of 'bad' bid you can get
♣ K 3   away with at matchpoints, but definitely not
                IMP's. Bear in mind that you are trading
heavily on the expected fit because of your heart length.

Even though you don't take much room away from
opponents by your one spade overcall, look what might happen.
Compare these three auctions:

1. 1♡—Pass—1NT—Pass
   2♣—?
2. 1♡ —Pass—1NT—Pass
   Pass—?
3. 1♡—1♠—Pass—2♠
   ?

In auction one, opponents have probably found their best fit
and whether or not your side balances, they can judge what to do.

Likewise, in auction two. If you bid 2♠ now it is somewhat
dangerous, although probably correct.

In auction three, however, you kept opponents from a smooth
exchange, and at the same time you reached the two level,
finding a fit of which you couldn't be certain on the previous
auction.

1♡:

♠ A K Q 9   After a heart opening you should come in
♡ 8 7 2   with one spade at matchpoints, but only at
◇ Q 4 3   matchpoints. You would have preferred
♣ 10 9 7   the opening bid to be one club, instead of one
                heart, because you would have deprived
                opponents of far more bidding room.

1♡:

♠ Q J 4 2
♡ 8 7 6 5 3
◇ K 10
♣ K 2

Again, at matchpoints, one spade should be both safe and effective. The reason you shouldn't try this at IMP's is that it could be expensive. At matchpoints, this is not serious if you score some victories, however small,

but IMP scoring requires caution, and cautious one spade is not.

1♡:

♠ Q 9 8 7
♡ 8 7 6 4 2
◇ K J 3
♣ A

This shows you the degree to which you might stretch things. At matchpoints, one spade is not as silly as it may seem. It's a bad bid, but you may well get away with it. Remember that you would never try this unless you had

reason to expect a fit, i.e. your heart length.

1♡:

♠ Q J 9 7
♡ 8 6 5 4 2
◇ A
♣ A J 10

With this you are getting close to a minimum one spade at IMP's. At matchpoints, for sure. At IMP's, this is reasonably safe. You have four or more likely tricks and you may score an incredible game now and then. Give partner

♠ K 8 6 4 2
♡ J
◇ 10 8 6 3
♣ Q 9 3

and four spades is possible. And you will be able to grab quite a few part-score swings.

♠ 10 8 6 3
♡ Q 2
◇ K Q 6 3
♣ 9 6 4

With this dummy, you can probably make two or, on a good day, three spades. At the same time they can make three diamonds in spite of dummy's impressive trump holding.

1♡:

♠ K J 8 7   Pass is probably best. With no reason to expect
♡ 4 2   a fit, it is too dangerous to attempt any action.
♢ A K   If you must bid something, I suppose one
♣ Q 6 4 3 2   spade is best, but I don't care for it. Be sure
                   you understand why this hand is a pass when
it is actually better than the last three examples.

1♡:

♠ K Q 10 5   One spade is reasonable at matchpoints. Hold-
♡ 8 6 4 2   ing four hearts is not as great an inducement
♢ A J 3   for you to bid as holding five hearts would
♣ 7 6   be, but it does suggest a fit is possible. Don't
                   try this one at IMP's.

1♡:

♠ K Q J 3   This is probably a better double than it is a
♡ 8 7 6   spade bid. If partner has four spades, he will
♢ A J 4   bid them. If not, the odds favour his holding
♣ K J 5   a five card minor. At matchpoints or at IMP's,
                   this hand is too good to pass. Try a double.

3
VULNERABILITY

So far, we have, by and large, ignored vulnerability. It hasn't been important. What I've been trying to do is to present a style of overcalling and to give you an idea of what works. If you have been able to accept my ideas to this point, you should have no trouble judging when to bid or not to bid according to vulnerability changes.

Since it is more expensive to go down vulnerable than not vulnerable, you need a better hand for your vulnerable overcalls, as a few examples will show.

VULNERABLE OVERCALLS — ONE LEVEL

With everyone vulnerable, the auction proceeds:

1♡:

♠ A J 10 8 7
♡ 4 2
◇ K J 3
♣ Q 9 7

This is a reasonable one spade call. Hardly a bargain. If you wanted to pass at IMP's, no one would argue with you.

1◇:

♠ Q 10 8 7 5
♡ K 2
◇ 4 2
♣ A K 10 6

One spade. Again, not too wonderful. I would do this at IMP's but would be a bit nervous.

1♣:

♠ 8 7 6 5 4   One spade. Not everyone will agree, but this
♡ A K 3   is not a bad hand for one spade. The first two
♢ 4   hands have better suits, but offer little chance
♣ A Q 6 5   of game unless partner has a mallet. Here the
                 chances of game are substantial if partner has
the right minimum. It follows that this is a compulsory overcall
at IMP's as well. The chance of game makes it well worth the
risk.

1♢:

♠ K J 9 8 7   One spade. Good potential for game opposite
♡ 4   a fit. More likely, you will be able to raise the
♢ A 10 7 6 5   auction to two or three spades, forcing
♣ J 3   opponents to make the last guess.

1♢:

♠ 8 2   Clear cut 1♡ bid at matchpoints. Also, for
♡ A J 10 8   that matter, at IMP's. There's no way you will
♢ A Q 6 5 3   get hurt in 1♡ and if partner raises, you should
♣ 5 2   have more than enough.

1♡:

♠ K 10 9 7   One spade is reasonable, but the suit is just
♡ A J 8 6 3   about as bad as you would ever have vulner-
♢ 3   able. The reasons you would overcall are the
♣ A 4 2   fit implication (5 hearts) and your good hand,
                 comprised of aces rather than kings, queens,
etc. I admit I would bid 1♠ at IMP's but without much enthusiasm.

1♢:

♠ Q 9 8 7   Pass. Now and then, a one spade bid might
♡ 4   work, but the suit is too threadbare. When
♢ A 10 9 8 7   you overcall on four card suits vulnerable
♣ A J 3   they should really be something like:

A K Q 7
A K J 8
A Q 10 7
A J 10 8
K Q J 8
K Q 10 7
K J 10 9

While you might sneak in a weaker suit on occasion, the rest of your hand should make up for it.

4

TWO LEVEL OVERCALLS

After the somewhat complex considerations of overcalling at the one level, the discussion of two level overcalls is going to be a breeze. Comparing one level and two level overcalls is like comparing night and day.

Why is this so?

First is the simple fact that overcalling at the two level means contracting for eight tricks rather than seven. This means you need extra values to give you a shot at taking that extra trick. So, right away, all those weakish hands which qualified for one level overcalls are eliminated.

Overcalling at the two level requires a good suit, so all those hands with K 8 6 4 2 or J 10 6 3 2 or 8 7 6 3 2 are eliminated.

Overcalling at the two level guarantees your suit will be at least five cards or longer. So all those nice four card suits are eliminated.

So, what's left? What's left are good hands with good suits. There just isn't the room for tactical actions that there is at the one level.

This does not mean that there is no flexibility at all. Given the basic premise that a two level overcall shows a good hand and a good suit, various manoeuvres are available.

TWO LEVEL OVERCALLS NOT VULNERABLE

Opener's bids are shown on the right:

1♠:

♠ 10 6
♡ A Q J 9 6
◇ A 10 4 2
♣ Q 3

This is a very reasonable 2♡ call at match-points. It's typical of the risk you are willing to take. Game is not too likely but you do have good chances for a part score. In IMP's, a 2♡ call would be much more dangerous. While it's true that you have the same chances of a plus score, your reasonable expectancy is plus 110 or 140 or perhaps a small set by defeating opponents. However, your potential minus is enormous. Opposite something like:

♠ K J 5 4
♡ 8 3
◇ J 8 3
♣ K 6 4 2

it could cost three hundred easily. And it could be worse. Dummy has two trumps. Sometimes it has only one. Repeating, in matchpoints, you are concerned with "how *often* can I get a plus score?" whereas at IMP's you are concerned with "how *big* is my potential plus score? How big is the risk?"

1♡:

♠ 8
♡ K 10 7 3
◇ K Q 9 8 2
♣ K 5 4

Two diamonds here. Once again there is the consideration that you hold length in opener's suit. Whereas, three cards is a very poor hold-ing, particularly Q x x or worse, four and five card holdings are good and excellent respec-tively and should encourage you to bid whenever possible. This point is so important that I would feel more comfortable bidding with this hand than on the one before which may have appeared stronger. Stronger perhaps, but safer, no. This hand, while not likely to produce a game, just barely qualifies for a call at IMP's as well. One other point is that your overcall has stolen the one level. There remains an unbid major suit and you have made it difficult for opponents to identify it.

As I mentioned earlier, these two auctions are very hard for opponents to counter.

$$1\diamondsuit - 2\clubsuit$$
$$1\clubsuit - 1\spadesuit$$

These calls take up an entire round of bidding. Compare them with 1♠—2♣.

This call takes only the 1NT response away. Had responder wanted to bid hearts or diamonds, he can do so still with no loss of bidding room.

$$1\heartsuit - 2\clubsuit$$

This call takes away both the one spade and one notrump responses. If responder wishes to mention spades, he must either bid 2 spades, or employ the negative double.

$$1\spadesuit - 2\heartsuit$$

This auction deprives opponents of three possible responses, 1NT, 2♣, and 2◊, but it isn't as effective as it might be because there is no unbid major. The nature of scoring is such that bidding is geared to finding either a major suit fit or notrump. If responder had enough to respond two clubs or two diamonds, had you not overcalled, your two heart overcall will not do much to make life difficult for opponents. On the other hand, there are many, many hands where responder can bid one heart or one spade but which are nowhere near worth bidding two hearts or two spades when you intervene.

1♠:

♠ 3
♥ A 3
◊ 10 5 4 2
♣ K Q J 7 6 3

A fairly straightforward two club call.

1♠:

♠ 10 6 5 2
♥ A J 10 9 6 3
◊ K 3
♣ 5

This is the sort of hand on which many people pass, yet it is nearly a mandatory bid at all forms of scoring. Game could be cold opposite a singleton spade and four hearts to the king.

Unlikely? Perhaps. But opposite a doubleton spade and three hearts to the queen, you have a play for three hearts. And no one can say that that's asking too much. If partner raises to three hearts, it would be reasonable to carry on.

How does this hand fulfill the requirements for a good hand and a good suit?

Well, the suit is obviously good enough and the hand qualifies because of the excellent distribution. What is the risk in over-calling? Opposite a bad hand, you would go down but your good heart spots should be a safeguard against such mishaps as a foul trump break.

Will partner be disappointed with your defensive potential if he doubles something? He should not be. This hand rates to take two tricks in defence, which is adequate for an overcall.

1♠:

♠ 8 7 2
♡ A J 10 8 6 3
♢ K 2
♣ 4 3

This hand is the same hand again but with one spade fewer. This has the effect of taking away one potential winner, the fourth spade you hoped to trump in dummy, and replacing it with a club loser. Now a bid is marginal at best, but it *could* lead to further action and therefore *could* work at matchpoints.

1♠:

♠ 3
♡ K 4 2
♢ K Q 9 8 7
♣ K 5 4 2

Pass, double, or two diamonds? This hand is similar to one held earlier:

♠ 8
♡ K 10 7 3
♢ K Q 9 8 2
♣ K 5 4

I suggested two diamonds after a one heart opening bid. This hand is included to emphasise the distinction you have to make when you have four or more cards in opener's suit and when you hold one card. The first hand was clearly worth a bid while this is a grey area. So what's right? I don't know. At match-points, I would feel obliged to do something, but I wouldn't like it. I think I'd double. Perhaps tomorrow I'd try two dia-monds. At IMP's — nothing . No bid. Always.

TWO LEVEL OVERCALLS VULNERABLE

Vulnerable two level overcalls require a bit more in high cards or distribution. In the example hands, everyone is vulnerable.

1♡:

♠ 8
♡ K 10 7 3
◇ K Q 9 8 2
♣ K 5 4

Pass. While this was a two diamond bid not vulnerable, it would be stretching things a bit to call now. If any of those kings were an ace, I would incline the other way. If at matchpoints you wanted to bid, go ahead. It can certainly work. But not at IMP's.

1♠:

♠ 10 7 6 2
♡ A Q 10 9 6 3
◇ K 4
♣ 2

This hand is almost the same as the one in the previous section. The heart queen has been substituted for the jack and now it is an overcall of two hearts, vulnerable or not, IMP's or not. This is a safe overcall with game potential.

1♠:

♠ Q J 3
♡ K J 8 7 2
◇ A 4 3
♣ Q J

This hand is a disaster. It's not worth a bid anywhere at any time. A trap for point counters.

1♠:

♠ 3 2
♡ Q J 9 8 6 2
◇ A K 9 7
♣ 5

At matchpoints, two hearts is clear enough. At IMP's, it is somewhat dangerous. You are a favourite to get six tricks, but it's no certainty. Again, at matchpoints, you bid when you think you can improve on other results by any amount, no matter how small. Add the ten of hearts and it would become a minimum vulnerable IMP overcall.

1♡:

♠ K 2
♡ J 6 3
◇ K Q 8 6 5 4
♣ A J

This is typical of a matchpoint overcall, injudicious at IMP's. It is not safe and game potential is minimal.

1♡:

♠ K 2
♡ 7 3
◇ A Q 10 8 7 2
♣ A K 7

Two diamonds every time. You may have been wondering what the upper limit may be for an overcall. Where does an overcall become a takeout double followed by a new suit? I'll cover that later. In the meantime, this hand does not qualify for anything but an overcall.

1♠:

♠ 8
♡ 10 9 8 6 4 2
◇ A Q 10
♣ A K J

Here is an extension of those bad five card suits which were sometimes worth a one level overcall. We have added one card to the long suit and the rest of the hand is outstanding. Two hearts at matchpoints or IMP's. It's clearly right to bid something and a double would run the serious risk of losing the heart suit.

1♡:

♠ K J 10 6
♡ A 8 3
◇ 3
♣ K Q J 9 7

An interesting hand. If you play a cue bid as showing spades and clubs, (the High-Low cue bid) you might try that. As you've seen in an earlier section, one spade is a possibility, but then you would never be able to show the clubs. The hand is good enough to try two clubs, hoping to show spades later.

1♠:

♠ A 3
♡ 10 9 8 7 4
◇ A K Q 10 7
♣ 8

Well? I don't know either. I think that I would bid two hearts and follow with diamonds. I'll have to have second thoughts about this though if it's at the four spade level before my next turn. If I get doubled, I will run to three diamonds.

One of the requirements of a two level overcall is a good suit. This hand is a clear violation, but I think, reasonably well-judged. Note that the objection of partner getting off to a bad lead does not apply here too strongly. Partner is not likely to be on lead.

If you play a cue bid as showing the two higher ranking unbid suits (High-High) then you would be well placed. You may have noticed that on the previous hand, I mentioned a High-Low cue bid. This was no coincidence. These two hands clearly demonstrate that regardless of the conventions you use, situations will come up requiring decisions. It's obvious that had you had a convention to show one of the hands, you couldn't show the other.

1♡:

♠ 5 2
♡ 8 7 2
◇ A K Q J 10
♣ J 8 7

At matchpoints, this is a good hand for a two diamond overcall. Your expectancy is probably as low as on any hand you may ever have, but you hope that opponents can't cope. This is a valid hope, for many people just don't know how to handle an overcall. It's obvious that you could go for 800 opposite a poor dummy, but the risk is worth it. Note that the only time you might make a bid like this is when you have a solid trump suit. Neither opponent will be too eager to double you. If partner raises you, you may not like it, but since he can't have much in trumps, he will have compensating values. Perhaps you will escape for down one undoubled.

Please don't try this at IMP's.

5

WHEN BOTH OPPONENTS HAVE BID

When you are considering an overcall, or any other action for that matter, the course of the auction is an important factor. Are you acting directly after the opening bidder, or after a response to the opening bid?

For some reason, many players seem to think that they are the same thing and act accordingly. And they get bad results without knowing why.

There are a number of specific cases, each different from the others.

1. RHO bids a new suit at the one level and you overcall at the one level.

2. RHO bids a new suit at the one level and you overcall at the two level.

3. RHO bids 1NT and you overcall at the two level.

4. RHO raises and you overcall at the two or three level.

5. RHO bids a new suit at the two level and you overcall at the two or three level.

As it is easier to understand principles when they are illustrated with examples, we'll look at various cases. This is a very important section in that you will see why a hand may be a clear cut overcall on some auctions and a clear cut pass on others.

There are several things to consider when opponents have had a chance to open and respond.

Firstly, your RHO, or responder has made a bid. His call, whatever it was, has conveyed significant information.

A 1NT response shows about 6-10 points, no support, and no suit higher ranking than opener's. His hand is limited.

A raise shows about 6-10 points and a fit. If the opening bid was 1♣ or 1◊, then responder will probably not have a four card major. His hand is limited.

A new suit at the one level shows 6+ points with length in the suit bid. Note that RHO has not limited his hand. He can have up to 20+ points and still respond at the one level.*

A new suit at the two level shows 10+ points and is also unlimited. RHO can have 20+ points.

Once RHO has made a bid, their auction has established a rapport and it will be more difficult for you to intervene effectively. Remember, if you overcall after an opening bid on your right, opponents must somehow communicate both their suits and their strength. But, when there has been a response, much of that information will have been exchanged.

This does not mean your overcall has no effect on opponents' bidding. If the auction has gone 1♣—pass—1◇, a one spade bid here may make it difficult for them to locate a heart fit.

But if the auction has been 1◇—pass—1♡, a one spade bid by you will have no pre-emptive or obstructive value. You should remember this rule in deciding whether or not to overcall.

RULE: When overcalling, part of the value of your bid lies in hampering opponents' exchange of information. If your bid does not take up space, your hand must be correspondingly better.

ONE LEVEL OVERCALLS AFTER
A ONE/ONE RESPONSE

The first case to cover here is when RHO has responded and you are considering a one level overcall. There are only three auctions where this can occur. These are

LHO	RHO
1♣ — Pass — 1◇	
1♣ — Pass — 1♡	
1◇ — Pass — 1♡	

If RHO has bid 1♠ or higher, you won't be able to bid at the one level. Curiously enough, you will run into one of these

---

*This is a matter of style. Few players in Britain would fail to force with a jump in another suit on a 20 count.

three sequences about once per session. I would have thought the frequency would be higher, but not so. Anyway . . .

There are moderate dangers in overcalling after a one over one response.

1. Partner has passed, suggesting weakness. This is not a guarantee of course, but the possibility is greater than if he has not had a chance to bid.

2. With the opening bid on your left, your high cards will be in greater jeopardy. Opener rates to have most of the outstanding strength so your finesses will be generally unsuccessful. This particular objection holds true whenever LHO has opened the bidding. It's the sort of thing which should become second nature to you when deciding whether or not to take action.

3. There is the danger that you will be doubled. Opener can count on partner for a modicum of strength and if he feels there is a misfit, he might well decide to take a shot at your overcall. For that matter, RHO, too, may want to double you. RHO's one level response, while promising only six points or so, is unlimited. Note that when the auction goes 1♣–pass–1♡, RHO does not deny a spade suit. He may easily have both a good hand and length in the suit or suits higher than the one he has bid.

4. Lastly, if you judge that opener on your left will be declarer, you should be careful in suggesting a lead to partner.

Make it a rule: When there has been an opening bid and response and you are considering a one level overcall, do so if it is *constructive*. Have either a good hand or a good suit. There is danger in bidding on some of the trash on which you would have called over an opening bid on your right.

With no one vulnerable, the auction proceeds:

$$1♣ - Pass - 1◇$$

♠ K Q 10 8 5   A normal one spade call. Clear cut at IMP's
♡ 7 3   too.
◇ A J 9 7
♣ 8 6

1♣ — Pass — 1◇

♠ J 8 7 6 5
♡ 8
◇ K Q 9 6
♣ A 10 8

Again, one spade. Note that even though the suit is bad, you have some expectations of a mild fit with hopes for more. The safety factor suggests a call at IMP's as well. One curiosity here. Your spade bid makes it difficult for them to find their heart fit. Against that, you know that hearts will not break well for them.

1♣ — Pass — 1♡

♠ J 8 7 5 4
♡ K 5 4
◇ A 2
♣ K 9 7

Pass. This is the kind of hand on which you give up. While you might try one spade after an opening bid of one club, you should not bother here. Under no circumstances should you ever contemplate an overcall at IMP's.

1◇ — Pass — 1♡

♠ A Q 10 7
♡ A 6 5 4 2
◇ 3
♣ 10 8 7

One spade. Regardless of the auction, a good four card suit is adequate if the rest of the hand warrants a bid. Such hands usually qualify for an overcall at IMP's as well.

1◇ — Pass — 1♡

♠ A Q 10 7
♡ 8 6 3
◇ 4
♣ A 8 6 5 4

Double. One spade would give up the club suit.

1◇ — Pass — 1♡

♠ A K J 8
♡ 8 7 2
◇ A 5 4
♣ 4 3 2

You can bid one spade here, but you must realise that this is far more dangerous than bidding one spade over an opening one diamond. Once opponents have had an exchange, they will be well placed to double you when you are in trouble. For this reason, you would tend to give up the IMP overcall. As usual, you need either safety or some expectation of game to justify bidding at IMP's.

1♣ — Pass — 1♡

♠ A K 8 2
♡ 8
♢ 9 7 6
♣ A K 4 3 2

One spade here is certainly worthwhile, but it is hardly safe. You have length in a suit bid by an opponent, but it was bid on your left. This suggests that your right hand opponent may be able to overruff dummy if you try to ruff clubs. Also, there is the danger that the defence will start with hearts, forcing you to ruff. Note that, had there been an opening one club bid on your right, you would have bid one spade with some safety. The defence would be expected to lead clubs and your trumps would not be subject to immediate danger. But, after 1♣—Pass—1♡, the picture is completely different. It is very important to understand why.

The reason you might bid one spade at IMP's as well is that you have a very good hand which rates to take some tricks. Here your safety is not predicated on a hoped for fit but, rather, on the high cards you yourself hold.

1♣ — Pass — 1♡

♠ K Q J 8
♡ 10 6 5 2
♢ 3
♣ A Q 9 6

One spade. When you overcall on four card suits, you have to consider how the defence will go. If you expect the defence will be able to negotiate a forcing game where they make you ruff, then you should not rush to call on four card suits. Here, your singleton is in an unbid suit so there is no reason to expect the defence to lead it. Once again, this is an IMP overcall as well.

Vulnerable, you are going to need a better hand, of course, but the considerations are still the same. If you have a four card suit or a bad five card suit, you should still get in there if you feel the hand otherwise meets the requirements.

TWO LEVEL OVERCALLS AFTER A ONE/ONE RESPONSE

These are somewhat similar to overcalls directly over the opening bidder. You will remember that by definition, two level overcalls show good hands and good suits (page 19). The fact that both

opponents have bid should engender caution. This is one of the
more dangerous moments, so you should be on reasonably firm
ground.

The dangers are similar to those described on page 27 when
making a one level overcall after RHO has responded, but they
are more pronounced. I will summarise them briefly.

1. Partner has passed. He could easily have a weak hand.
Remember that RHO, while showing only six points for his
1/1, has not denied a good hand. Compare with a 1NT response
showing 6-10.

2. The opening bidder is over you. Your high cards may be
poorly placed.

3. It is far more likely that you will be doubled in a two-level
overcall than in a one-level overcall. It's amazing how many tops
are acquired by doubling an indiscreet overcall.

Other common considerations:

1. Does your bid deprive opponents of useful bidding space?

> LHO   RHO You
> 1♣   Pass 1♡   2◇

Your 2◇ bid means LHO cannot rebid 1♠, 1NT or 2♣. While
1NT and 2♣ may not be much of a loss, losing the 1♠ bid may
turn out to be serious. The important point is whether or not
there is an unbid major and whether or not your overcall makes
it hard for opponents to locate it.

> 1♡   Pass 1♠   2◇

There is no unbid major so your bid loses much of its obstructive
value.

> 1♣   Pass 1♠   2◇

Here there is an unbid major, but opener, if he was going to bid
it, would have had to do so at the two level. Your 2◇ bid does
not take away as much room as appears at first sight.

This means that after RHO has responded, some of your
overcalls can be more obstructive than others. Bear this in mind.

Here is a simple hand to show you how it feels from the
opener's point of view.

♠ A K 7 3
♡ Q 3
♢ 4 2
♣ K Q 8 7 6

You	LHO	Partner	RHO
1♣	Pass	1♡	2♢

They have got you! Your nice 1♠ rebid is not available and you haven't the values for 2♠. You must pass. Whatever happens next doesn't really matter. What does matter is that your side will have to work harder to get back to par.

2. How has the auction gone? Once again, the auction is all important. If I emphasise that point once, I'll emphasise it a hundred times. It is possible that on a given hand it might be right to overcall after 1♠ on your right but wrong to overcall after 1♣—Pass—1♠.

Let's look at cases.

NO ONE VUL.   1♣ – Pass – 1♡

♠ 4 2
♡ A J 7
♢ A Q J 9 7 6
♣ J 3

This is a reasonable two diamond call at either IMP's or matchpoints. You have a good suit and a good hand as well. Your heart holding is over the bidder. With any luck you could have two heart tricks. This sequence also makes it difficult for opponents to find a spade fit.

Note again. The fact that RHO has responded makes action by you more dangerous than action directly over an opening bid. *But!* When RHO has responded, you have more information on which to evaluate your hand. Marginal decisions become easier. I hate to repeat constantly certain ideas, but their importance just can't be overemphasised.

Which hand is worth more?

LHO		RHO
1♢	– Pass –	1♠

♠ 4 2   ♠ K J 7 6 5
♡ A Q 10 8 7   ♡ A Q 10 8 7
♢ K J 7 6 5   ♢ 4 2
♣ 3   ♣ 3

In my opinion, the second hand is worth from 2½ to 3 tricks more than the first. The K J 7 6 5 of spades are a huge plus. They are well located and with any luck LHO will lead them. The K J 7 6 5 of diamonds however are poorly placed and there is little chance that LHO will break the suit for you.

1♡ — Pass — 1♠

♠ A 8 4	♠ K J 3
♡ K J 3	♡ A 8 4
◇ K Q J 8 7	◇ K Q J 8 7
♣ 5 4	♣ 5 4

These hands are also easy to compare. In hand one, the K J 3 of hearts is a very dangerous holding while on hand two, the K J 3 of spades could easily provide two tricks. I would call 2◇ on the second hand at any vulnerability at matchpoints and even perhaps at IMP's. The first hand might be a non-vulnerable 2◇ call at matchpoints, but surely not at IMP's. While it's not too hard to evaluate a hand on any particular auction, it is necessary to take all available facts into consideration and to know what's important. I've yet to see anyone discuss it in print.

BOTH VUL.   1♣ — Pass — 1♠ — ?

♠ Q 8 4
♡ A K J 7 4
◇ Q 5
♣ K 8 6

At matchpoints, two hearts might work, but I'd be nervous to try it, even not vulnerable. Passing is best. Your black suit holdings are not worth much. On a bad day you could go down 1400. On a good day you could make 140. In spite of 15 so called points, your game potential is virtually non-existent.

BOTH VUL.   1♣ — Pass — 1♡ — ?

♠ K 8 7 6
♡ K 2
◇ A Q J 10 7
♣ 4 2

Double. You don't want to lose the spade suit.

BOTH VUL.   1♣ — Pass — 1♠ — ?

♠ K 10 6 5
♡ A J 10 8 6 5
◇ Q 5
♣ 7

Clear cut 2♡ at matchpoints and reasonable at IMP's. You'd rather the diamond queen were the spade jack, but nothing is perfect. The spade length is an asset.

BOTH VUL.   1♣ — Pass — 1♠ — ?

♠ 7
♡ A J 10 9 7 5
◇ Q 5
♣ K 10 6 5

Two hearts at matchpoints, but pass at IMP's. Even though your hearts are better, your clubs are going to be a liability. The opening lead will probably be a spade and that's unlikely to help.

BOTH VUL.   1♣ — Pass — 1♠ — ?

♠ K 4 2
♡ A Q 10 7 4
◇ K 2
♣ K J 3

Dangerous hand. Your king of spades is the only well placed card you have, but the distribution is vile and the rest of your high cards are of dubious value. When you consider that partner doesn't rate to have much more than three or four points you can see the lack of future for this hand. Overcalls are made of tricks, not points. Two hearts here might be OK not vul at matchpoints, but if you can bring yourself to pass, you will be taking a step in the right direction.

BOTH VUL.   1♡ — Pass — 1♠ — ?

♠ 8 6 2
♡ Q J 3
◇ A K Q 8 7
♣ K 3

This is typical of most well-judged passes. While two diamonds might work at matchpoints, it would be highly injudicious at IMP's. The best you can hope to achieve is a small plus while risking a large minus. Look at all the defects:

1. You have the worst possible spade holding. Three small in the suit bid on your right.

2. Secondary honours in the suit bid on your left.

3. Opponents have bid both majors. Two diamonds by you has little to gain tactically.

Here is a typical layout which you might find if you bid two diamonds:

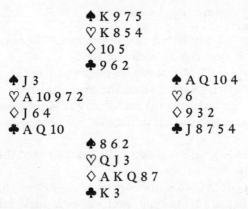

♠ K 9 7 5
♡ K 8 5 4
◇ 10 5
♣ 9 6 2

♠ J 3   ♠ A Q 10 4
♡ A 10 9 7 2   ♡ 6
◇ J 6 4   ◇ 9 3 2
♣ A Q 10   ♣ J 8 7 5 4

♠ 8 6 2
♡ Q J 3
◇ A K Q 8 7
♣ K 3

While you're lucky, sort of, to find dummy with two kings and diamonds dividing three-three, you will go down four tricks against the best defence. They will take three spades, the heart ace and two heart ruffs, two clubs, and then lead a fourth spade allowing West to score his trump jack. —400. If East makes a sporting double, it's —1100. A stiff price considering their maximum is 110 or 120.

NO ONE VUL.   1♣ — Pass — 1♡ — ?

♠ A 2   Two diamonds is right in all forms of the game.
♡ 9   Don't consider doubling with an eye to bidding
◇ A K Q J 7 5   diamonds later. Partner would be entitled to
♣ J 7 6 4   compete in spades and might get too high.
                     Note that two diamonds makes it hard for
opponents to find spades. If you play strong jump overcalls, then three diamonds may suit you and on this hand I would prefer to have that convention available.

VUL. VS. NOT   1♣ — Pass — 1♠ — ?

♠ 8 2   Bid two hearts. The good suit should encour-
♡ K Q J 10 8 7 5   age you to bid. The vulnerability and bad
◇ A 4   distribution should discourage you from
♣ 3 2   bidding too much. If partner can't contribute
                     anything, you should go quietly. This hand
rates to produce a sure part-score but game is most unlikely. On hands where game is out of the question, or unlikely, you need a good suit.

BOTH VUL.   1♣ — Pass — 1♠ — ?

♠ A Q 10 3   I would bid two hearts here. The reasons you
♡ 10 9 7 5 4   try this on such a suit are:
♢ 4   1. Game is possible if you have any kind of
♣ A K 7   fit. Note that on the previous hand four card
                 heart support can't even guarantee a part-score.
    2. You have a good hand, sure tricks, not unsupported kings
and queens.
    3. Your spade length makes a mild heart fit probable and a
good one likely.
    4. Your spade honours are well placed. Better still, LHO
may well lead one. When you overcall with such suits, it is
exceptional and you need outstanding side values to compensate.

BOTH VUL.   1♣ — Pass — 1♠ — ?

♠ 4   Double. I hate takeout doubles when holding
♡ 10 9 7 6 5   a five card major but bidding hearts here is
♢ A Q 10 7   too dangerous. The defence is likely to lead
♣ A K 5   spades and you will be subject to the tap
                 sooner than you wish. When you anticipate a
forcing game by defenders you must have good trumps. In the
previous hand,

                    ♠ A Q 10 3
                    ♡ 10 9 7 5 4
                    ♢ 4
                    ♣ A K 7

the auction did not indicate a diamond lead. The forcing game
was not a serious threat and could be discounted.
    Here is a summary of two level overcalls after a one over one
response:
    1. It is more dangerous than overcalling directly after an
opening bid.
    2. You need a good suit or a good hand with playing tricks.
    3. You should not count unsupported kings and queens at
full value except when they are in the suit bid by RHO.
    4. Length in RHO's suit, four cards or more, is a big plus.
    5. Length in LHO's suit, four cards or more, is only mildly
advantageous.

6. Three small in RHO's suit is awful.

7. Any three cards in LHO's suit not headed by the ace is a poor holding.

8. Your overcall is less likely to be obstructive. Know the exceptions!

TWO LEVEL OVERCALLS AFTER
1 OF A SUIT, PASS, 1NT

For a change, we enter an area of competitive bidding where you should be encouraged to bid, relegating to second place the safety first approach of the previous two sections.

When the bidding goes

$$1\clubsuit - Pass - 1NT$$
$$1\diamondsuit - Pass - 1NT$$
$$1\heartsuit - Pass - 1NT$$
$$1\spadesuit - Pass - 1NT$$

there are some very important facts you should immediately recognise.

Let's assume 1NT is a natural bid. Then we expect that:

1. RHO has 6-10 HCP.

2. RHO does not have a suit higher ranking than opener's.

3. RHO does not have support for his partner. This is certainly true of a 1NT response to a major. It is not necessarily true of a 1NT response to a minor.

What this means to you is that on some auctions you will be able to take certain liberties, because:

1. When RHO responds 1NT, he shows from 6 to 10 HCP, averaging perhaps seven, maybe eight. When RHO responds in a new suit, he is showing an unlimited hand. After a 1NT response therefore, you are entitled to moderate optimism regarding partner's strength. It will probably average out to a queen or so more than when RHO's bid was one of a new suit.

2. This is the real bonus. Licence to steal. When RHO bids 1NT, he is denying a suit higher than the suit opened and this in turn means that it is safer to compete in one of these *higher ranking* suits.

I would say that when RHO bids 1NT, it is incumbent on you to act on almost any excuse. Bid!

A warning. Don't forget that when RHO bids 1NT, he may well be loaded in any or all of the lower ranking suits. This is extremely important, as you will see.

Let's get into specifics.

NO ONE VUL.   1♣ — Pass — 1NT — ?

♠ K Q 8 7 6 5   Two spades. Quite clear cut at any game.
♡ J 8 7   On some auctions it is safe for you to act, and
♢ 3   this is one of them. You have a higher-ranking
♣ A 5 4   suit well worth mentioning and a decent hand
                 besides. Your chances of finding a fit are very
good. RHO's 1NT bid is usually based on four clubs, as he didn't seem to have a suit worth mentioning. This suggests that partner has only one or two clubs and increases the chances of his holding a few spades. You can just about expect three spades, you can hope for four, and if you should find only two, that would be a bit unlucky. One or none is all but impossible.

Once in a while you will run into someone who chooses to open 1♣ with only two. And now and then his partner will decide to bid 1NT with one or both four-card majors. When this happens you may get nailed, but even against such people, it's unlikely. If they bid this way, their defence won't be any better. Don't worry about the occasional fix. These people will repay you with interest by their other mistakes.

One last aside here. Some people play 1♣—Pass—1NT as showing a good hand in the 8-11 point range. If this is the case, you should tighten up a little.

NO ONE VUL.   1♣ — Pass — 1NT — ?

♠ A Q 3   Two hearts at matchpoints. When you are
♡ K 10 9 7 5 4   faced with a "safe" auction, try to get in there
♢ 8 7   whenever possible. Even at IMP's, 2♡ would
♣ 10 5   not be terrible.

NO ONE VUL.   1♣ − Pass − 1NT − ?

♠ Q J 10 8 3   Not vul. at matchpoints, there is a lot to be
♡ 8 7   said for 2♠. You have a good suit and decent
◇ A K 6 5   shape which includes useful side values.
♣ 4 2   Minimum hands which have all their values
                     concentrated to best advantage are usually
better than hands with greater point count but with scattered
honours. If vul., you might try this if you were a passed hand.
Partner would not expect more.

Some people insist on substantial values for overcalls on the
theory that partner will always protect when the auction dies.
This is nice when it works, but I can't believe it's right for
partner to reopen after

                1♣ − Pass − 1NT − Pass
                Pass

when holding something like:

        ♠ 9 7 2   ♠ Q J 10 8 3
        ♡ K 10 4 2   ♡ 8 7
        ◇ Q 3   ◇ A K 6 5
        ♣ K 9 7 5   ♣ 4 2

Yet these two hands will make two or three spades with no
trouble. As against this, we may or may not beat 1NT. I like the
odds. Remember though, that much of the reason you are
acting on some of these marginal hands is that the auction is one
defined as "safe".

One other reason for bidding two spades is that the auction
might very well continue in this fashion:

                1♣ − Pass − 1NT − Pass
                2♣ − Pass − ?

If RHO passes 2♣ then you can reopen with 2♠ which is fine.
But if RHO raises to 3♣, then it will be all over for you. And
believe me, it can go that way.

If you choose to bid 2♠ at your first opportunity, LHO may
not be able to call 3♣ because of insufficient values and RHO
may hesitate to compete with 3♣ fearing that opener may have
only three clubs.

NO ONE VUL.   1♣ – Pass – 1NT – ?

♠ 10 3
♡ J 10 7 5 4 2
♢ 3
♣ A K 8 7

This is an example of how far you can go. Two hearts is quite reasonable and is far safer than might first appear. Note that partner surely has a singleton or doubleton club. He probably has a weakish 4—4—4—1 or perhaps 4—3—4—2. Note that the objection to overcalling on a weak suit doesn't apply here because partner is unlikely to be on lead. For that to happen, LHO would have to end up in clubs, which suits you fine, or he would have to rebid 2♠ or 3♢, which is most unlikely. Even were this to happen, partner's lead doesn't have to be costly.

NO ONE VUL.   1♣ – Pass – 1NT – ?

♠ 4 2
♡ A K Q 10 3
♢ 8 3
♣ 10 6 5 4

Because of the safe auction and the length of clubs implying a fit, I would call 2♡. Note that the opponents *do* have a club fit.

NO ONE VUL.   1♢ – Pass – 1NT – ?

♠ 4 2
♡ A K Q 10 3
♢ 10 6 5 4
♣ 3 2

More dangerous to bid 2♡ here than on the previous hand. While RHO may have some diamonds, he may have a bunch of clubs and no diamond support. This would mean that partner's diamonds are not necessarily as short as you would like them to be.

Remember:

1♣ – Pass – 1NT guarantees a fit.
1♢ – Pass – 1NT suggests a fit.

NO ONE VUL.   1♢ – Pass – 1NT – ?

♠ A Q 10 7 6
♡ 4 2
♢ A 4 3
♣ K 6 5

Reasonable to bid 2♠. RHO doesn't have hearts or spades so it becomes safe to overcall.

Compare with the next hand:

NO ONE VUL.   1◇ − Pass − 1NT − ?

♠ K 6 5   Pass. Very dangerous. When RHO responds
♡ 4 2   1NT, he is denying length in partner's suit and
◇ A 4 3   higher-ranking suits. This perforce means he
♣ A Q 10 7 6   has length in the lower-ranking suit or suits.
                     After 1◇−Pass−1NT, you can be sure that
RHO has clubs. On this sequence, a 2♣ bid must show a *very*
good suit. If you don't have it, you're going down and probably
doubled too in the bargain. This auction is one of the few that
tells you in advance how your prospective trump suit, clubs, will
divide.

BOTH VUL.   1♡ − Pass − 1NT − ?

♠ Q 3   Be careful. Bidding 2◇ is rather risky. After
♡ A 4 2   1♡−Pass−1NT, it is "safe" to bid spades
◇ Q J 9 7 6   which is a suit higher-ranking than opener's.
♣ A J 7   It is true that RHO has a limited hand as far as
                     high cards are concerned. You can hope to
find partner with a few points. But distributionally speaking
you cannot hope for a fit. There is the real danger that partner
won't have any support for diamonds and even if he has, they
may break poorly. RHO rates to have clubs and diamonds since
he doesn't have hearts or spades.

Here's another very important point. RHO's 1NT bid can be
passed by LHO. There is a good chance that you will be able to
defend against 1NT. On hands with more defensive than offensive values you shouldn't be too anxious to get into the auction.
In the example above if partner has a little something you can
set 1NT. If he has nothing, you won't, but you couldn't make
anything either.

When the bidding goes 1♣−Pass−1♠ for example, there is
no chance, barring a psyche by opener, that 1♠ will become the
final contract. The possibility of defending against 1♠ is not a
real consideration as compared with that of defending against
1NT.

NO ONE VUL.   1♣ – Pass – 1NT – ?

♠ Q 10 8 7 6   Get in there with 2♠. The all-important
♡ A 2   distinction between this hand and the previous
◇ A 6 5   one is the safety this sequence offers. Even
♣ Q 8 5   though you may defeat 1NT, you may not,
    yet you can make something. This is because
the "higher-ranking suit" concept suggests you have a fit, which
alone may carry you through. If partner has something as little
as ♠ J 5 2 – ♡ Q 10 6 4 3 – ◇ K 7 4 – ♣ 10 2, you might find
2♠ while opponents could make 1 or even 2NT.

NO ONE VUL.   1◇ – Pass – 1NT – ?

♠ K J 8 7 6   You want to bid something, and the question
♡ A Q 10 6 4   is what? Your choices seem to be 2♠, 2♡,
◇ 3 2   double, and 2◇. Two things you shouldn't do
♣ 7   are 2♡ and double. If two diamonds would
    show the majors, you should do that. Other-
    wise, bid 2 spades.

BOTH VUL.   1◇ – Pass – 1NT – ?

♠ 3   When you have a hand with a good suit, and
♡ Q J 10 8 7 6   other factors are in your favour, you should
◇ A 10 6 5   bid. The auction is "safe" and you can hope
♣ 10 3   for a fit of some sort. It might be minimal, in
    which case you will get no higher, but it
could be spectacular, in which case you might even make a
game.

In practice, I would expect +140 as against –120 or –110.
Some of the time you get a small plus when the opponents go
–50 or –100, so much better than passing.

Another consideration is that if you pass, partner might
reopen with 2♠. Now if you wish to play in hearts, you will
have to do so at the three level.

NO ONE VUL.   1♡ – Pass – 1NT – ?

♠ A 2   Bid 2♣. This is clear enough, but you should
♡ 4 3   not feel too optimistic. You are not likely to
◇ K 7 6   find much of a fit, and even with this hand,
♣ K Q J 8 7 5   you might be doubled and go down a couple

of tricks. In your favour is that you will get a club lead. And on occasion you will be able to compete higher if partner's hand is suitable.

Note that overcalling in a suit lower-ranking than opener's requires that you have a decent hand and a good suit. Bidding is based on solid values rather than on speculation.

Conversely of course, when you are contemplating over-calling in a suit higher-ranking than opener's, you can take liberties.

One more important point to note. After a 1NT response, your overcalls will have no significant obstructive value. There is no sequence where it would make it impossible for opener to show an unbid major.

$$1\spadesuit - \text{Pass} - 1\text{NT} - 2\clubsuit$$

Opener can always show hearts and diamonds if he wants to do so.

$$1\heartsuit - \text{Pass} - 1\text{NT} - 2\diamondsuit$$

Opener can't rebid 2♣, but this is a small loss. If he wants to show spades or rebid his hearts, he can do so.

$$1\heartsuit - \text{Pass} - 1\text{NT} - 2\spadesuit$$

Opener can't show any new suit at the two level, but he has already shown his most important suit. Note that however small the obstructive value of 2♠ may be, it is much more annoying to the opener than 2♡, 2◇, or 2♣, each bid being less embar-rassing than the one before.

NO ONE VUL. $1\heartsuit - \text{Pass} - 1\text{NT} - ?$

♠ K J 4 2   In no circumstances 2♣. *Double.*
♡ 3
◇ A Q 2
♣ Q 6 5 4 2

OVERCALLS WHEN RHO HAS RESPONDED
WITH A 2/1

This one is easy. Don't.

Of all the situations where it is dangerous to bid, this one is the worst. It's scary. Fortunately, it is easy to see why this is so. Four simple reasons:

1. LHO has an opening bid, and may have more.
2. RHO has 10+ HCP and may have more.
3. Their side has 24 HCP and may have more.
4. Your side has 16 HCP, on a good day, and may have less.

This means that if you hear it go 1♠—Pass—2◊ and you elect to get involved, you will be trying for eight or nine tricks on hands where you can't possibly have more than 40% of the high cards. If you overcall and fail to find a fit, or if dummy is broke, you have had it.

Does this mean that you should never bid after 1♠—Pass—2♣?

No, but it does mean that your tactics must lean strongly towards safety. You must have values in your own hand. In no circumstances should you expect to find useful cards in partner's hand. You won't find them. At least, you won't find them often enough to make it worthwhile.

You may, however, hope to find a fit when your hand suggests it may exist. Hoping for a fit and hoping for high cards are not by any means the same.

NO ONE VUL.   1♠—Pass—2◊—?

♠ K 3 2   Pass. *So* important to pass on these hands.
♡ Q 10 7 6 5   Your spades are suspect. You don't want a
◊ K Q 7   heart lead. You will never be able to outbid
♣ A 2   the opponents.

Assume the best that can happen. Give partner three points. This is unlikely because it would give opponents only 23 − (40 − your 14 − partner's 3). But it could happen. Let's give partner the heart king. The best of all worlds. If he happens to have four hearts, nothing much will happen. You won't be doubled. Opponents will get to wherever they were going and get an average. Perhaps declarer will play the hand well, helped by your overcall, and get a top.

If partner has one, two, or three hearts to the king (we're still hoping) you may get doubled or opponents will do whatever else they like. Nothing good can happen as a result of your over-call.

This is what you can expect:

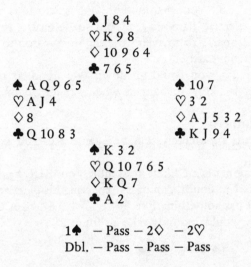

                    ♠ J 8 4
                    ♡ K 9 8
                    ◇ 10 9 6 4
                    ♣ 7 6 5
    ♠ A Q 9 6 5   ♠ 10 7
    ♡ A J 4   ♡ 3 2
    ◇ 8   ◇ A J 5 3 2
    ♣ Q 10 8 3   ♣ K J 9 4
                    ♠ K 3 2
                    ♡ Q 10 7 6 5
                    ◇ K Q 7
                    ♣ A 2

            1♠ — Pass — 2◇ — 2♡
            Dbl. — Pass — Pass — Pass

When this hand came up, a well-judged double by West net-ted 500 out of nothing. And East didn't even have enough for 2◇.* Now if East had a little more, dummy would have had a little less, and declarer would have gone for 700 or 900.

VUL. VS. NOT.   1♡ — Pass — 2♣ — ?

♠ K J 10 7 6 5   Pass again! This hand came up in practice and
♡ A 8 2   was judged to be worth 2♠. It wasn't. Dummy
◇ K J 7   had a scattered four count which turned out
♣ 3   to be worth zero. Minus 1100.

The only time you could consider acting with this hand is not vul. vs. vul. And your object would be less to find a good contract than a save. Note that you have no reason to expect a fit and even not vul. vs. vul. −300 could be bad if they have no game.

*This is not a criticism of 2◇. It depends on your system. Most Americans would bid 1NT. ACOL players bid 2◇. Both are right.

BOTH VUL.   1♠ — Pass — 2◊ — ?

♠ K J 8   Belive it or not, you should pass. Even better
♡ A K Q 8 7   if you do so for the right reasons, which are:
◊ 5 4 2   1. Partner is broke.
♣ A 9   2. Your spades are likely to be worthless.
           3. Your diamond holding is atrocious.

With the expected diamond lead and spade return, this hand could easily fall apart. You haven't the slightest reason to expect heart support from partner.

If you bid 2♡, you could go down two hundred to eight hundred. This is likely to happen whenever an opponent has four hearts.

Consider further:

1. Opponents are unlikely to have a game, so −200 would be a bad result.

2. Both opponents are likely to double you. RHO has a good hand. Opener, if in doubt, can pass, expecting his partner to bid again. If RHO has something like ♠ 3 − ♡ J 9 6 − ◊ A Q 9 7 5 − ♣ K J 8 2 he would certainly take a shot at 2♡.

NO ONE VUL.   1♠ — Pass — 2♣ — ?

♠ 3   Here it is quite right to act. You have a decent
♡ K Q J 4 2   suit and every right to expect a fit. If partner
◊ 3 2   has three hearts and no high cards at all, 2♡
♣ A Q 8 6 5   could succeed. The implied fit is all-important.
           If partner likes hearts, you have a good save or
           even a make.

NO ONE VUL.   1♠ — Pass — 2◊ — ?

♠ 3   Whatever you do, don't bid 2♡. Either double
♡ K Q J 4 2   or bid 2NT (unusual).
◊ 3 2
♣ A Q 8 6 5

VUL. VS. NOT.   1♠ — Pass — 2♡ — ?

♠ 4 2   Pass! Pass! Pass! You are too high and you are
♡ K 2   out-gunned. Dummy has nothing. On a good
◊ A Q J 8 6 5   day, you get seven tricks. Whenever it is
♣ K Q 3   wrong to bid, you will be doubled and go

down. It is never right to bid. PASS. This would be a likely holding for opener:

♠ A Q 9 8 5   After 1♠—Pass—2♡—3◇ opener should double,
♡ 9 6   especially once the 3◇ bidder is vulnerable.
◇ K 10 4
♣ A 10 5

BOTH VUL.   1♠ — Pass — 2♣.

♠ 9   In spite of having only ten HCP, you should
♡ A 8 7   bid 2◇. There are tricks here no matter what
◇ K Q J 10 7 3 partner has. If you are unlucky, you may go
♣ 10 5 4   down 500. On some of the "better" hands
               shown earlier, you would have to be lucky to
               go down *only* 500.

BOTH VUL.   1♠ — Pass — 2♣.

♠ 8 6 5   It's right to bid 2♡, but don't enthuse over it.
♡ A K Q J 8 7 Bid it and feel subdued.
◇ 7 3
♣ 4 2

NO ONE VUL.   1♡ — Pass — 2◇.

♠ J 10 8 7 6 5 I would bid 2♠ expecting to find a fit. If part-
♡ 3   ner has little support, nothing much will
◇ A Q 9 6 3   happen. But if he has good support and can
♣ 5   raise, you could have a good save or even a
               game. It's safe to bid here because you know
               where your tricks are coming from.

NO ONE VUL.   1♡ — Pass — 2♣.

♠ J 10 8 7 6 5 If you want to experiment, you could try
♡ 3   2♠. You have no reason to expect a fit, but
◇ A Q 9 6 3   if partner does have a few spades, you could
♣ 5   do well.

The dangers here, compared with the previous hand, are worth noting.

   1. The chances for a fit are substantially less.

2. You are likely to get a diamond lead on the first hand but not on the second.

3. If opponents play the hand, partner will probably lead a spade and this may work out poorly. Note that this objection doesn't hold true for the first auction, 1♡–Pass–2◇–2♠. If you pass, instead of bidding 2♠, partner if on lead would usually select an unbid suit, i.e. clubs or spades, and you don't care for either. After 1♡–Pass–2♣–?, 2♠ tends to ensure a spade lead and you would prefer a diamond. Had you remained quiet, partner might well have selected one.

The rule to follow after a 2/1 response is simple. You bid when it is safe. POINTS BY THEMSELVES do not constitute safety. They do not take tricks.

It is safe to bid when you have tricks. These usually come from good suits or hands on which the auction has told you to expect a fit. I will have a lot to say about this later, but the concept is worth introducing now.

Partner should not expect too much of you when you do overcall after a 2/1 response. Your side has few high cards so anything you make must be on the basis of a fit with good distribution. There is no way your side can make 3NT. This auction, for example, is impossible:

$$1♠ - Pass - 2♣ - 2♡$$
$$2♠ - 2NT$$

Think about it.

In practice, the only bids the partner of the overcaller can make are to raise or to double. A raise should show a good hand with useful cards. It should not be made on dubious values.

BOTH VUL.   Pass – 1♠ – Pass – 2♣ – 2♡ – ?

♠ Q 10 7 6   You should pass.
♡ 10 6 4 2
◇ Q 10
♣ K 10 7

But,

♠ 10 8 7 6 5   with this hand you should bid three or even
♡ Q 10 6 5   four hearts. Probably four is best. You values
◇ K 4 2   are all working overtime with no wastage.
♣ 3

OVERCALLS AFTER A RAISE

This section is also easy. Bid. If there was ever a sequence where
you should compete, this is it. Everything is in your favour.

1. RHO has a limited hand.

2. Some of RHO's values will be distributional. The high
card strength could be modest.

3. After 1♣–Pass–2♣ or 1◇–Pass–2◇, RHO won't hold a
major suit. After 1♣–Pass–2♣ RHO probably won't have a
diamond suit. After 1♡–Pass–2♡ RHO probably won't have a
spade suit.

A responder holding ♠ Q 10 6 2 – ♡ K 8 3 – ◇ 4 2 – ♣ K
10 8 7 should raise 1♡ to 2♡, in spite of holding Q 10 6 2 of
spades. There are bad bidders, who bid 1♠ but in practice a heart
raise does tend to deny spades.

4. Opener will not be inclined to double an overcall by you.
More likely than not, he will bid again, even when he should
pass or double. Human nature is such that when a fit is found,
most people try to buy the contract.

5. That is why an overcall will often push opponents too
high. This is especially important on hands where your partner
could not reopen had you passed.

NO ONE VUL.   1♣ – Pass – 2♣ – ?

♠ K J 8 7 5   2♠. Clear cut. Above average in values. Note
♡ 3   that RHO does not have four spades or hearts.
◇ K 8 7 2
♣ A 5 3

NO ONE VUL.   1♣ — Pass — 2♣ — ?

♠ 3
♡ K J 8 7 5
◇ Q 8 7 2
♣ A 5 3

2♡. Slightly lower values than on the preceding hand. An additional reason for bidding is that you don't want to hear partner reopen with 2♠.

NO ONE VUL.   1♣ — Pass — 2♣ — ?

♠ 8 7 2
♡ 4 3
◇ K Q 10 9 7
♣ A 8 7

2◇ at matchpoints. Pass at IMP's. At matchpoints, when your suit is good, you don't need much more. At IMP's, you do have to keep an eye for safety.

NO ONE VUL.   1♣ — Pass — 2♣ — ?

♠ Q 10 8 6 4 2
♡ A 7 3
◇ —
♣ 8 7 6 5

2♠. The length in clubs makes this safe enough for IMP's as well.

NO ONE VUL.   1♣ — Pass — 2♣ — ?

♠ A Q 8 6 5
♡ 4 2
◇ K 10 8 7 6
♣ 3

2♠. When RHO raises opener, an interesting situation arises.

1. If you have length in their suit, you can overcall safely because partner rates to have a fit in yours.

2. If you are short in their suit, you should try to overcall because partner may not have the distribution to reopen. After 1♣—Pass—2♣—Pass—Pass—?, partner will not reopen with ♠ Q 7 3 — ♡ A 5 4 — ◇ K 8 7 — ♣ J 9 6 3 or other balanced minimum hands, including length in the enemy suit. Take the pressure off him.

NO ONE VUL.   1♣ — Pass — 2♣ — ?

♠ 4 3
♡ A J 10 8 7 6
◇ Q 8 4 2
♣ 3

2♡ at matchpoints and IMP's. When you have any excuse to bid at the two level, do so. Note the emphasis on the two level. This is because any suit available to you at the

two level is safe since RHO couldn't bid it at the one level.
And it may hamper any further action by opener.

VUL. VS. NOT.   1♣ — Pass — 2♣ — ?

♠ 3   2♡ always. Even vulnerable there would be
♡ A K 8 7 6   something to spare.
◇ A 4 3 2
♣ 8 7 3

VUL. VS. NOT.   1♣ — Pass — 2♣ — ?

♠ 8   2♡ always. When you have a guaranteed fit,
♡ K J 8 6 2   you should compete. Here, partner is likely to
◇ 8 2   reopen, but:
♣ A 8 6 3 2   1. He may reopen with 2♠.
                    2. Opener may bid no trumps and partner
                    will lead a spade.

BOTH VUL.   1♣ — Pass — 2♣ — ?

♠ K Q J 9 3   When you have a good suit which can be bid
♡ ?   at the two level, don't hold back. If the other
◇ ?   eight cards are small ones, you may pass, but
♣ ?   if you can think of any excuse to bid, you
                    probably should.

NO ONE VUL.   1♣ — Pass — 2♣ — ?

♠ ?   A little will go a long way. After this sequence
♡ ?   you can bid any of the remaining suits at the
◇ ?   two level. They are all safe. RHO is limited;
♣ ?   etc. etc. etc. Of all the auctions in the world,
                    here it is imperative that you should bid.
If you can't overcall, perhaps you can make a takeout double.

NO ONE VUL.   1◇ — Pass — 2◇ — ?

♠ 3 2   After 1◇—Pass—2◇, you should feel almost
♡ K J 8 7 6   the same enthusiasm for bidding as you did
◇ 9 2   after 1♣—Pass—2♣. The only difference, of
♣ A K 8 6   course, is that one suit has become more diffi-

cult to bid. But this is a minor, clubs, and both majors are available. You should bid 2♡.

NO ONE VUL.   1◇ — Pass — 2◇ — ?

♠ 3 2
♡ A K J 8 7
◇ 3
♣ J 9 7 6 3

Here, also, 2♡ is right. With such disparity between your clubs and hearts, it would be wrong to try the unusual 2NT. See next hand.

NO ONE VUL.   1◇ — Pass — 2◇ — ?

♠ 3 2
♡ Q 9 7 6 3
◇ 3
♣ A Q J 8 7

If you play 2NT as showing the lower two unbid suits, that would be correct. If not playing this, it would be right to call 2♡. It is far safer to bid 2♡ than 3♣.

1. You are at the two level.
2. RHO does not have hearts.
3. Clubs would require action at the three level.
4. RHO could easily have clubs.

BOTH VUL.   1◇ — Pass — 2◇ — ?

♠ 4 2
♡ K 8 7
◇ Q 9 7
♣ A Q J 8 3

Pass. Three level actions require additional values and are more dangerous. Any time you consider a three level overcall, it is perforce in a lower-ranking suit than opener's and RHO can be strong.

Evaluate these hands:

NO ONE VUL.   1◇ — Pass — 2◇ — ?

♠ K J 8 7 2   ♠ K 9 7
♡ A 6 3   ♡ A 6 3
◇ 4 2   ◇ 4 2
♣ K 9 7   ♣ K J 8 7 2

How do you feel about bidding 2♠ on the first hand?

How would you feel about bidding 2♣ on the second, if it were legal?

My estimate is that hand one will produce 1½ more tricks in

spades than hand two will produce in clubs. When you consider that you must bid *three* clubs, the relative dangers become apparent.

BOTH VUL.   1♦ − Pass − 2♦ − ?

♠ 8 3
♡ Q 7 6
♦ 3 2
♣ A K Q 10 8 7

You could bid 3♣ at matchpoints, and perhaps at IMP's. The important point is that you have a near-solid suit.

VUL. VS. NOT.   1♦ − Pass − 2♦ − ?

♠ A J 8 7 5
♡ K J 9 8 7
♦ 8 2
♣ 3

2♠. Not only do you bid, but if opener tries 3♦, you should bid three hearts, given the chance. There are two traps to avoid:
          1. Passing. You will lose all sorts of partscores and a few games besides.
    2. Doubling. If partner responds 3♣, you are in trouble.
    One other possibility is a cue bid, showing the majors. But this will get you too high when partner has a wishy-washy hand with no liking for either of your suits.
    The only time 2♠ works out poorly in practice is when it is passed out and hearts would have been a better spot. But this is unlucky.

NO ONE VUL.   1♦ − Pass − 2♦ − ?

♠ K 8 7 6 5
♡ A 5 4 3 2
♦ 3
♣ Q 2

This is a minimum hand, but still worth a bid. Try 2♠. A very important point is that your doubleton is in clubs, not diamonds. The worst holding you can have in a suit bid and raised is a doubleton. And of these holdings, the worst of the lot are Q x, J x, and Q J. These will be wasted points of no value to you. They would have been valuable to opponents, and since they lack them, they must have honours elsewhere to compensate − honours which you can no longer hope to find with partner. Your expectations must be reduced accordingly.

NO ONE VUL.   1◇ − Pass − 2◇ − ?

♠ A Q 10 6 5	♠ A Q 10 6 5
♡ 8 6 3	♡ 8 6 3
◇ 4 2	◇ Q 2
♣ A 8 6	♣ A 8 6

Both of these hands are worth a 2♠ bid at matchpoints. You would prefer, though, to have the first hand.

Let's say that opponents have 22 HCP. In the first hand, your partner therefore has eight, and in the second, six. As far as you are concerned, both hands are the same, since the diamond queen is worthless. So you would rather have hand one because you hope to find a better dummy.

Another factor is that values in opponents' suits make your hand better suited to defence.

BOTH VUL.   1◇ − Pass − 2◇ − ?

♠ A Q 8 7
♡ Q 10 6 5 4 2
◇ 3
♣ 9 7

Bid 2♡ and be satisfied. Even though you might feel guilty about losing the spade suit, you can at least get one of your suits into the picture. Passing or doubling would be to court disaster. 2♡ is positive and may lead to a worthwhile result. This is typical of hands where you want to tell all sorts of things but don't have the tools to do it. When this happens, try to describe the single most important feature.

NO ONE VUL.   1◇ -- Pass − 2◇ − ?

♠ Q 8 6 5 2
♡ K J 3
◇ Q 4
♣ Q 10 7

Pass. You want to bid on this sequence, but lack minimum values.

NO ONE VUL.   1◇ − Pass − 2◇ − ?

♠ Q J 8 7 2
♡ 4 2
◇ A K J
♣ 10 7 6

You have values for 2♠, and you should bid it, but it's nothing to write home about. If partner has a singleton or doubleton diamond, it won't have its normal value as you have no diamond losers anyway.

NO ONE VUL.   1◇ — Pass — 2◇ — ?

♠ Q 2   Pass. Another case of wasted values in dia-
♡ J 8 7 6 5   monds and not enough elsewhere.
◇ K Q 10
♣ K 6 3

BOTH VUL.   1◇ — Pass — 2◇ — ?

♠ A K 2   Bid 2♡ happily. When RHO has raised, it is
♡ 10 6 5 4 2   no longer necessary to have a good suit to
◇ A 8 7 3   overcall in a higher-ranking suit. When the suit
♣ 2   is as bad as here, however, you do need a
                      decent hand. Here you have tricks and you
can expect a fit. Bid 2♡, and go to game if partner raises.

NO ONE VUL.   1♡ — Pass — 2♡ — ?

♠ Q 8 7 6 5   Once again, a safe auction plus a fit, though
♡ A 4 3 2   a poorish suit.
◇ A 7 3
♣ 3

VUL. VS. NOT.   1♡ — Pass — 2♡ — ?

♠ K Q 2   At matchpoints, 3♣ would be dangerous. At
♡ K 7 6   IMP's, it would be silly. Hands like this have
◇ Q 5   no future. You have no game, so you are
♣ A Q 10 6 2   competing only for a part-score or a small plus
                      by pushing them too high. If you are wrong,
you could be set two or three tricks and, on occasion you will
be doubled. Competing in suits lower-ranking than the
opponents' lacks the same margin of safety and the level is
higher.

BOTH VUL.   1♡ — Pass — 2♡ — ?

♠ Q 8 7 6 2   Pass. Your heart holding is the worst possible
♡ Q 10   and you have no compensating values.
◇ K 5 4
♣ A 8 7

NO ONE VUL.   1♡ – Pass – 2♡ – ?

♠ J 10 8 7 5   2♠. This hand is far too good to pass. Your
♡ 3   alternative is to double, but that runs the risk
◊ K 4 2   of losing the spade suit.
♣ A K 8 7

NO ONE VUL.   1♡ – Pass – 2♡ – ?

♠ J 8 7 6 5   2♠. Bad suit but good hand.
♡ A K 3
◊ A Q 3
♣ 4 3

NO ONE VUL.   1♡ – Pass – 2♡ – ?

♠ 4 3   A good hand, but no worthwhile action is
♡ A K 3   available. At matchpoints, you might try 3♣
◊ A Q 2   but only to get opponents one trick higher.
♣ J 8 7 6 5   Hope partner doesn't take you seriously. If
   he does, you should apologise.

The reasons you might consider 3♣ on such a bad suit are
that RHO's strength is limited, and your hearts suggest a shortage
in partner's hand and therefore some club support. This is
strictly a matchpoint ploy, inconceivable at IMP's.

NO ONE VUL.   1♡ – Pass – 2♡ – ?

♠ A K 3   Double. 3♣ would be awful. Not only is the
♡ 4 3   hand well suited to a takeout double, but
◊ A Q 2   your doubleton heart no longer suggests a
♣ J 8 7 6 5   club fit.

   This would be a double at IMP's as well,
and at any vulnerability.

NO ONE VUL.   1♡ – Pass – 2♡ – ?

♠ A K 8 7 6   A matchpoint 2♠ call. You would not bid
♡ 4 2   three of a minor on similar values.
◊ Q 8 6
♣ J 9 7

The most difficult decisions are those hands with doubletons in opponents' suit. When you have three or more in their suit, you can bid with the assurance of finding some sort of fit. When you have a singleton, you have at least some distribution. But when you have a hand like the one above, you have no clear-cut directive. Bidding can be right or wrong. How can you tell? You can't, really. But you can be right more often than not by raising your requirements a little, either suit-wise or points-wise. Since a doubleton in their suit is a distinct minus value, you need something to compensate for it. I've been advocating a free-wheeling approach to overcalling when RHO raises and you can compete at the two level. But in this one case, I suggest you pull in your horns a little.

NO ONE VUL.   1♠ − Pass − 2♠ − ?

Whoever owns the spade suit rules, and this auction is typical. Even though it is safe for you to bid on in terms of hoped-for strength in partner's hand, you must bid at the three level to compete, and you are more vulnerable to a double than if your bid was at the two level. Face it, it's hard to fight the spade suit. After 1♠−Pass−2♠ you are under pressure; and while I still recommend bidding on close hands, you need something extra.

Remember that from a distributional point of view, all suits are dangerous. Your RHO, holding any of these hands would raise 1♠ to 2♠.

♠ K 8 7	♠ K 8 7	♠ K 8 7
♡ A 10 8 6 2	♡ 4 2	♡ 4 2
◇ 4 2	◇ A 10 8 6 2	◇ J 3 2
♣ J 3 2	♣ J 3 2	♣ A 10 8 6 2

As has been noted before, RHO can easily have length in any of the suits lower-ranking than that which he is raising.

NO ONE VUL.   1♠ -- Pass − 2♠ − ?

♠ 8 7 2
♡ A Q 8 7 6
◇ K J 3
♣ Q 9

Somewhat sketchy. This is a good aggressive 3♡ bid at matchpoints, but in no other circumstances. If you could bid at the two level, your values would be adequate. Defer to the spade suit.

NO ONE VUL.   1♠ — Pass — 2♠ — ?

♠ 3
♡ A Q 10 6 3
◇ K 5 4
♣ A 6 5 2

Clear to bid something, and I would choose 3♡. Double would lose the heart suit, but it could easily work. Don't pass!

BOTH VUL.   1♠ — Pass — 2♠ — ?

♠ 8 6 2
♡ Q J 10 9 6 3
◇ A Q 3
♣ 2

3♡. You might go down two. You might make a game. Your good suit and three spades look good, and your outside values are excellent. 3♡ at IMP's, too.

BOTH VUL.   1♠ — Pass — 2♠ — ?

♠ Q 2
♡ K J 6 5 4 2
◇ Q 3
♣ K 6 2

Pass. Your spade holding is bad for two reasons:
    1. Q 2 is probably worthless.
    2. The Q 2 lessens the chance that partner will have useful points for you.

The heart suit is good enough for an overcall, but the rest of the hand doesn't justify it.

VUL. VS. NOT.   1♠ — Pass — 2♠.

♠ K 3
♡ J 10 7 6 5 4
◇ A K 4 2
♣ 9

Who knows? If you could be sure that LHO would lead a spade, you would bid 3♡. Perhaps you should bid 3♡ anyway. At match-points, I would go ahead. At IMP's, it's dangerous. The vulnerability is a deterrent.

The K 3 of spades is not as good as it might seem. You hope for a spade lead, but a good defender will not lead one from some such holding as A J x x x, even after a raise from partner.

NO ONE VUL.   1♠ — Pass — 2♠.

♠ 8 6 4 2
♡ J 9 8 6 2
◇ A K 3
♣ A

When the auction screams that you have a fit, you can come in on poor suits or poor hands. Not, please, on both. Your hand here is quite good enough for 3♡ so the quality of the suit can be overlooked.

6

QUIZ ON OVERCALLS

WHAT HAVE YOU LEARNED?

We've now looked at almost every conceivable overcall. There are still a few left, but they can wait. The ideas behind what qualifies for an overcall and what doesn't are complex. Make no mistake about it and it's made more difficult by considerations of vulnerability, auction, strength, distribution, matchpoints, IMP's, etc. This next section will help pull it all together. The format is this: there are three hands. We will look at each of them in the light of different bidding sequences and observe how, each time, the picture changes.

♠ A Q J 8　　　　This is your first hand. No one is vul.
♡ 4 2
♢ A 10 8 6 5
♣ 8 3

	1◇ – ?	1♣ – Pass – 1♠ – ?	
	1♡ – ?	1♡ – Pass – 2♣ – ?	
	1♠ – ?	1♣ – Pass – 2♣ – ?	
1♣ – Pass – 1♡ – ?		1◇ – Pass – 2◇ – ?	
1♣ – Pass – 1NT – ?		1♡ – Pass – 2♡ – ?	
1♡ – Pass – 1NT – ?		1♠ – Pass – 2♠ – ?	
1♡ – Pass – 1♠ – ?			

1◇ – ?

1♠. Good four card suit, implied fit, very obstructive to opponents. Clearcut.

$1\heartsuit - ?$

Not clearcut. Your choices are:

1. Pass. Safe. Maybe you can balance later.

2. $1\spadesuit$. Intending to give up on the diamond suit. If partner can raise, you will be very well placed. Note that there is no presumption of a fit, so it is not particularly safe.

3. $2\diamondsuit$. Also dangerous. Limited future. Even if you have a fit, you are unlikely to be able to outbid opponents.

4. Double is *not* to be considered. The wrong shape.

$1\spadesuit - ?$

Because of the implied fit, $2\diamondsuit$ would be very reasonable at matchpoints and even at IMP's. You are not likely to make more than a part-score, but you are fairly safe.

$1\clubsuit - Pass - 1\heartsuit - ?$

Double. Clear-cut.

$1\clubsuit - Pass - 1NT - ?$

Awkward. I would try $2\diamondsuit$, and if doubled bid $2\spadesuit$. You need a five card suit to bid, so $2\spadesuit$ is not on.

$1\heartsuit - Pass - 1NT - ?$

Again $2\diamondsuit$, but not with as much conviction as on the previous hand. RHO can easily have diamonds which means your safety margin is less. If doubled, it's off to $2\spadesuit$. One danger is that $2\diamondsuit$ won't be doubled and you will be left in an inferior contract when some other suit (spades) would make. At least it's only 50 a trick.

$1\heartsuit - Pass - 1\spadesuit - ?$

With spades on your right, everything is in your favour. Bid $2\diamondsuit$. This doesn't take much bidding room away from opponents, but with the expectation of a fit, you may be able to push them past their limit. $2\diamondsuit$ is clear-cut at IMP's, too.

$$1\clubsuit - Pass - 1\spadesuit - ?$$

The same. Bid 2◇.

$$1\heartsuit - Pass - 2\clubsuit - ?$$

The only reasonable action would be to double, but with opponents showing strength, you should pass. Any overcall would be suicidal.

$$1\clubsuit - Pass - 2\clubsuit - ?$$

Bid something. After this auction, you bid first and look at your hand later. Try 2◇. You would like to mention spades somehow, but it can't be done. At least not now.

$$1◇ - Pass - 2◇ - ?$$

Hard to believe. They're trying to play in your best suit. You hope. But it won't happen. If you pass, LHO will bid NT or LHO will pass and partner will reopen.

If partner reopens, you will reach some decent contract and get a par result.

If LHO bids NT, however, your partner will be on lead and will almost always lead one of your doubletons. My suggestion here is to bid 2♠. Overcalling at the two level on a four card suit is unusual and this hand is the only exception; i.e., a very good four card suit and five cards in the suit raised by RHO, and a good hand as well.

I can't see anything bad happening. Partner has shape, so you are safe in 2♠, and will get higher only when partner raises. And, if they play the hand, partner will get off to a good lead.

$$1\heartsuit - Pass - 2\heartsuit$$

You want to bid something. Passing would be pusilanimous. As to what to bid, I don't know. Here are your choices:

1. 3◇. Dangerous. You're at the three level and you have no expectation of a fit.

2. 2♠. Only a four card suit but it's a "safe" suit and you are at the two level.

3. Double. But if partner bids clubs, as expected, you have

to pass with inadequate support or correct to 3◇. This would also imply four spades, but would suggest a much better hand.

My choice here is 2♠ because my urge to bid is overwhelming rather than because 2♠ is right.

If you choose to pass, I would rate that as very conservative, but it's not inexcusable.

$$1♠ - Pass - 2♠ - ?$$

3◇. You know you have a fit, and this gives you licence to bid. Opponents will frequently compete and get too high. The only real danger is that partner "saves" against an unmakeable contract. But he shouldn't. I'll be covering how partner should handle your overcalls in the next section.

♠ 7 2
♡ K Q 8 6 5
◇ K 6 5
♣ A 4 2

This is your hand in the following sequences. No one is vul.

1♣ — ?	1♠ — Pass — 1NT — ?
1◇ — ?	1◇ — Pass — 2♣ — ?
1♠ — ?	1♠ — Pass — 2◇ — ?
1♣ — Pass — 1◇ — ?	1♣ — Pass — 2♣ — ?
1♣ — Pass — 1♠ — ?	1♠ — Pass — 2♠ — ?
1♣ — Pass — 1NT — ?	

$$1♣ - ?$$

1♡. Easy. Any game, any vulnerability.

$$1◇ - ?$$

Same. 1♡.

$$1♠ - ?$$

A dangerous overcall at matchpoints which could easily be wrong. A clear pass at IMP's.

$$1♣ - Pass - 1◇ - ?$$

1♡. Always.

$$1\clubsuit - Pass - 1\spadesuit - ?$$

I suppose 2♡ at matchpoints. Ugh. Not at IMP's.

$$1\clubsuit - Pass - 1NT - ?$$

2♡. Only at matchpoints. Feel a bit better about this than after 1♣—Pass—1♠.

$$1\spadesuit - Pass - 1NT - ?$$

Do whatever you like. 2♡ is not really as safe as after 1♣—Pass—1NT, but it might work. Passing 1NT is not bad because there is a chance that this will end the auction. You have a good defensive hand and could easily beat 1NT. At matchpoints, one of the reasons for bidding is that opponents frequently misjudge the situation after an overcall. Of course, if it is wrong, it could be very wrong.

$$1\diamondsuit - Pass - 2\clubsuit - ?$$

Pass. No excuse for anything else.

$$1\spadesuit - Pass - 2\diamondsuit - ?$$

Likewise. You are outgunned. Bidding is a no-win proposition.

$$1\clubsuit - Pass - 2\clubsuit - ?$$

2♡. Always.

$$1\spadesuit - Pass - 2\spadesuit - ?$$

At matchpoints, you could bid 3♡. This works more often than not. The auction is semi-safe (bidding after a raise). RHO has not denied hearts, so bidding is not completely safe. Moreover, you are bidding at the three level. Your good results will be small ones. Your bad results will be spectacular. The sort of thing that suits matchpoints.

♠ K 6 2   This is your hand in the following sequences.
♡ J 9 7 6 3   You are not vul. vs. vul.
♢ 4
♣ A K 8 7

$$1\clubsuit - ? \qquad 1\diamondsuit - Pass - 1NT - ?$$
$$1\diamondsuit - ? \qquad 1\spadesuit - Pass - 1NT - ?$$
$$1\spadesuit - ? \qquad 1\spadesuit - Pass - 2\clubsuit - ?$$
$$1\clubsuit - Pass - 1\diamondsuit - ? \qquad 1\diamondsuit - Pass - 2\clubsuit - ?$$
$$1\clubsuit - Pass - 1\spadesuit - ? \qquad 1\clubsuit - Pass - 2\clubsuit - ?$$
$$1\diamondsuit - Pass - 1\spadesuit - ? \qquad 1\diamondsuit - Pass - 2\diamondsuit - ?$$
$$1\clubsuit - Pass - 1NT - ? \qquad 1\spadesuit - Pass - 2\spadesuit - ?$$

$$1\clubsuit - ?$$

$1\heartsuit$. Any vulnerability, IMP's too. The fit factor is overwhelming.

$$1\diamondsuit - ?$$

$1\heartsuit$. It's bad practice to make a takeout double with a five card major. There is not the same expectancy of a fit so $1\heartsuit$ is not as safe as after $1\clubsuit$. Vul. at IMP's, it would be best to pass.

$$1\spadesuit - ?$$

Pass. The only time you can bid at the two level with J 9 7 6 3, barring an exceptional hand, is after a raise.

$$1\clubsuit - Pass - 1\diamondsuit - ?$$

$1\heartsuit$. More than a minimum overcall.

$$1\clubsuit - Pass - 1\spadesuit - ?$$

Pass. The hearts not good enough and the auction is dangerous.

$$1\diamondsuit - Pass - 1\spadesuit - ?$$

Double. Earlier I said that you should avoid doubling when holding a five card major. Here, though, your suit is not good enough to overcall in this sequence. Fortunately, you have the shape and values to make double a reasonable alternative.

$$1\clubsuit - Pass - 1NT - ?$$

$2\heartsuit$ clearly and with no apologies. This passes the three standard tests for safety. RHO is limited in strength, RHO doesn't have hearts, and RHO has clubs, implying a fit. If RHO didn't have clubs, he would have a suit to bid.

$1\diamondsuit$ — Pass — 1NT — ?

$2\heartsuit$ again although with less enthusiasm. You are missing the strong implication of a fit as on the previous hand. I would never do this vul., and I might hesitate to do this at IMP's. But it would not be terrible.

$1\spadesuit$ — Pass — 1NT — ?

Pass. You spade king is of doubtful value and RHO could easily have the heart suit stacked. Bidding is very unwise.

$1\spadesuit$ — Pass — $2\clubsuit$ — ?

Pass fast. The best policy after a two-over-one response.

$1\diamondsuit$ — Pass — $2\clubsuit$ — ?

Likewise.

$1\clubsuit$ — Pass — $2\clubsuit$ — ?

$2\heartsuit$. Compulsory. No possible reason to pass. Any vulnerability, any game.

$1\diamondsuit$ — Pass — $2\diamondsuit$ — ?

Bid $2\heartsuit$. It is about 1½ tricks more dangerous to bid than after $1\clubsuit$—Pass—$2\clubsuit$, but it is still a clearcut bid.

$1\spadesuit$ — Pass — $2\spadesuit$ — ?

Go quietly. You may be reluctant to pass, but discretion is best. In favour of bidding:
1. You expect some sort of fit.
2. RHO is limited.
In favour of passing:
1. Your spade king is an uncertain asset.
2. You are at the three level.
3. Your suit is bad.
4. RHO can have hearts.

It's amazing how many different actions you can contemplate on any given hand. The preceding three hands were rather ordinary but still offered food for thought.

On some auctions it was right to bid. On others it was right
to pass. On some a takeout double was best. Some of the
decisions were clearcut. Some were vague or marginal. In one
sequence it might be 100% right to make a vulnerable two level
overcall whereas in a different sequence, with the same hand, a
non-vulnerable two level bid would be ridiculous.

Learn to recognise the dangerous auctions and the safe ones.
Does your hand and the bidding tell you anything? Can your
partner have any points? Do you expect a fit? These are the
important things. They will help you with overcalls and they
will help you with many other competitive decisions.

THE PECULIAR PROBLEMS
OF THE OVERCALL

So far this whole book has been concerned entirely with the
overcall. A lot of space has been given to this topic. And a lot of
hands to illustrate it.

The decision to overcall is one of the most difficult you'll
ever have to make. This is because it is irrevocable, final. If you
are wrong there may be no escape.

Look at the other decisions open to you. A takeout double?
These are rarely penalised, for the simple reason that a takeout
double offers a number of possible options. An overcall usually
offers only one.

Other decisions, such as raising partner, are safe and easy.
When you're thinking of raising, you have a fit, which is insur-
ance against disaster.

If you are thinking of bidding NT in response to partner's
overcall or takeout double, you are assured of certain values.

But the overcaller himself has no such security. His bid is a
speculative venture attended by a prayer or two.

Now I do not want you to stop overcalling. I want you to
overcall more, but sensibly. This is why so much time has been
devoted to an analysis of each possible auction. When is it safe
to bid? When is it dangerous? What kind of fit can I expect?
What are my cards worth? How will the hand play? The concepts
I have discussed will be new to some. I suspect to quite a few.
As far as I know, they have not seen print before. Which is

surprising because they are so important. They are the basis of what makes good and effective competitive bidding.

An understanding of this section will help you in later situations. In particular, if your partner has overcalled, you will find these guidelines very important in determining whether or not to introduce a new suit. And other competitive decisions, when to raise, when to pass, will be easier to judge. These ideas are flexible and apply in areas other than overcalls. They will improve your judgement whichever side opens the bidding.

Part II
Responding to an Overcall

When partner opens the bidding, you can generally look at your hand and form an opinion as to your potential. Your auction will be guided by the usual questions such as, "Do we have a game? Do we have a slam? Which suit is best? Should we stay in a part-score?"

Once in a while opponents will get into the act and the questions may now include: "Should we double them? Should we let them buy it? Should we save?"

However, note the sort of questions you must answer when the other side has opened and your side has entered the auction. "How high should we compete? Should we save against their game? What suit do I want partner to lead? Do we have a game?"

It is very important to understand the differences in thinking between the side that opens and the side that overcalls. The side that opens the auction, excluding pre-empts, expects a plus score. The opening bidder assumes that the hand belongs to his side. He has positive expectations. When he finds that his opponents own the hand, the opener is disappointed.

The overcaller is in a totally different frame of mind. His expectations are negative. Thoughts of slam are almost non-existent and even hopes of game are rare. For the most part, the overcaller is happy if he can find a part-score or perhaps suffer a small penalty. A good result might be for opponents to miss game or perhaps a slam. An outstanding result might be for opponents to go down in a poor contract when they had a better one.

Given the difference in objectives between an opening bidder and an overcaller, it seems reasonable that the system of responding to opening bids may differ from the system of responding to overcalls. Different objectives, different methods. Yes? No?

Perhaps.

Let's look at some points of difference.

1. If partner overcalls, should a new suit by you be forcing?

2. If partner overcalls, what should a one notrump response show? Should a jump to two notrumps after a one-level overcall be forcing?

3. What is the range of a simple raise? What is the range of a jump raise? i.e. 1♣—1♠—Pass—3♠. Is it forcing?

4. What should a jump shift look like? Should it be forcing? Does it guarantee a game? Does it suggest a slam?

5. What would a cue bid mean?

7

INTRODUCING A NEW SUIT

To my way of thinking, it should be easy to decide whether a new suit should be forcing or not.

If partner opens the bidding, your new suit response is forcing. This is because your side may well have a game or slam. The new suit forcing principle helps to explore. On occasion, you miss a good part-score because of insufficient values, to show your suit. This may occur here:

♠ A J 8 7 3	♠ 8	1♠ — Pass — 1NT — Pass
♡ K 10 8	♡ 9 7 2	Pass — Pass
◇ K J 3	◇ Q 8 2	
♣ 10 3	♣ K J 9 6 5 4	

You go three down when two clubs would have made. There is no way in Standard American, or, for that matter, most other systems, to get to two clubs. Even three clubs is better than one notrump. And it's almost as hard to reach as two clubs.

This bad result comes about because your system is geared to reaching for as many game and slam bonuses as possible, at the expense of the occasional part-score.

When an opponent opens and your side overcalls, you are faced with entirely different goals. Game is no longer an expectation and slam is almost entirely out of the question. Instead, you are looking for a good part-score or a good save. Now and then, you will be trying to escape from partner's suit when he has picked a poor time to overcall.

Usually, you will be looking for your best fit and a game bid and made will come as a pleasant surprise.

It seems to me that if your primary goal is to find a fit, the best way to do that is by bidding your suits. If you treat a new suit as forcing, then you won't be able to do much exploration because you won't have enough high cards often enough to justify bidding.

Here is a typical situation:

```
        LHO   Partner  RHO  You
        1♣    1♡       2♣   ?
               ♠ K 6 4
               ♡ 3
               ◇ K J 10 9 7 4
               ♣ 10 7 6
```

If you could bid two diamonds nonforcing, you would surely do so. Two diamonds looks like a good spot, and if partner likes diamonds, you aren't averse to hearing a raise. Even if partner doesn't like diamonds, you won't mind. What you don't want is to hear partner bid two hearts. If two diamonds is forcing, then you can't bid it because you will end up in two hearts or three diamonds or higher. You want to be in three diamonds only if partner likes them, not because your system forces you to get there.

The following hands should not be difficult unless you need high requirements for introducing new suits, treating them as forcing.

A word of warning: You have to keep an eye out for safety. You can't go around bidding willy nilly just because it's your turn. On the other hand, if you pass everything in sight, you will be robbed on hand after hand. So try to blend a bit of caution with a modicum of optimism. Let's see.

NO ONE VUL.   1♣ − 1♡ − Pass − ?

♠ K 10 8 7 6   1♠. Fairly straightforward. In this case you
♡ 4 2   don't mind if partner bids again. But if he
◇ A K 8 7   passes, it's probably OK. If partner should feel
♣ 10 7   like making a game try, unlikely, you would
                 be happy to accept.

Passing 1♡ would be very poor tactics. If spades are better than hearts, or if you have a game, you will have done the wrong thing and you will have little chance to recover.

Let's say that you pass and you are lucky. LHO rebids 2♣
which is passed around to you. You have a second chance.

$$1♣ - 1♡ - \text{Pass} - \text{Pass}$$
$$2♣ - \text{Pass} - \text{Pass} - ?$$

What will you do? Will you do anything at all?
Do you bid 2♠ and find partner with:

♠ 3   1♠, 1NT, 2◊, or 2♣ by opponents are better
♡ K J 10 8 7   than 2♠ by you.
◊ Q J 4
♣ A 9 6 5

Do you bid 2♡ and find partner with:

♠ Q 5 3   1♠, 2♠, 3♠ or 1NT are better than 2♡. Any-
♡ A K J 10   one for 2♣ doubled?
◊ 3 2
♣ K J 8 4

Do you bid 2◊ and find partner with:

♠ J 5 4   Anything is better than 2◊.
♡ A Q 8 6 3
◊ Q 2
♣ K 5 4

Or do you pass and find partner with:

♠ 9 5 4 2   4♠, possibly with an overtrick, is better than
♡ A K 9 5 2   beating 2♣ a trick.
◊ 10 2
♣ A 3

Whatever action you choose may lead to a bad result. Partner
will have no reason to overrule you, so if you guess wrong, you
lose. If you guess right, you break even.

Failure to bid one spade over one heart gave partner no
chance to contribute.

Failure to act immediately is one of the most common
errors. Some of the time it is merely bad judgement, but some
of the time it is due to the system. Whatever the reason, it

usually leads to guessing games. Sometimes, the auction proceeds in such a way that you don't even get a chance to guess.

NO ONE VUL.   LHO   You
                     1♣ — 1♡ — Pass — Pass
                     1♠ — Pass — 2♣ — ?

♠ 10 7 2   On this auction, it is too dangerous to bid. I
♡ J 3   suppose you could bid three diamonds on the
♢ A Q 9 7 5 4 theory that you can't have much because you
♣ 8 5   already passed. But, if you go down for 300
              or more, partner won't be interested in theory.
Note how much more constructive it would have been to bid
two diamonds earlier. If partner doesn't like two diamonds, he
may or may not do anything, but at least you won't be in three
diamonds. Also, and very important, is the difficulty the
opening bidder will have. If you bid two diamonds, opener will
have to bid two spades, not one spade. But he may pass allowing you to make a plus score on a hand that belonged to him.
     Or possibly the opening bidder will bid two spades or even
three clubs and go down.
     Or perhaps the opening bidder will rebid on insufficient
values, an unsuspecting partner will raise him and again they will
go down.
     Or perhaps two diamonds will be passed out and prove to be
better than one heart.
     Or sometimes, when opponents compete, partner can raise
diamonds.
     Or sometimes your side can make three notrumps based on
your good diamond suit.
     If you pass, none of these desirable things can happen.
You've got to enter the fray and stir it up. The more problems
you create for opponents, the more often will they go wrong.

NO ONE VUL.   LHO
                     1♣ — 1♢ — 1♡ — ?

♠ Q 10 8 7 6 Bid one spade. It is crucial to bid on hands
♡ 4 2   like this. Most of the time, when you consider
♢ 3   introducing a new suit, it will be at the one or
♣ A J 8 6 5   two level. You won't often have the strength

or the good suit required to try for a three level contract, and at the three level, you are too high to experiment.

My rule for competing at the one or two levels is this: When in doubt, bid.

NO ONE VUL.	LHO
	1♣ — 1♡ — 1♠ — ?

♠ 10 6 5
♡ Q 2
◇ K Q 10 9 5
♣ 8 6 3

This is a dangerous moment to bid, but at matchpoints, you could try two diamonds. True, if partner doesn't like diamonds, you will have no place to go and you haven't any reason to think that he will like diamonds.

Other bad features of this hand are the three little cards in both of the suits bid by opponents.

What you do have going for you is that LHO can't rebid 1NT or 2♣. Also, if partner does like diamonds, he can raise, and maybe push opponents to the three level. This is typical of a matchpoint auction where everyone seems to have something to say. At IMP's, a pass is best. You have too little to gain.

NO ONE VUL.	1♣ — 1♡ — 2♣ — ?

♠ 10 6 5
♡ Q 2
◇ K Q 10 9 5
♣ 8 6 3

This is the same hand as above. If, before, you felt uncomfortable about bidding two diamonds, you should not be now. Look at the difference in the two auctions.

1. Your three small clubs are no longer a liability because clubs have been raised. Partner probably has a doubleton and perhaps a singleton. This improves your chance of finding a diamond fit.

2. Your RHO did not bid one spade as before. If partner has any spade honours, they will be more valuable.

3. RHO's two club bid is limited. He has about six high card points with some distribution. In the previous auction, the one spade bid was unlimited. RHO could have had as much as 10 to 12 points which would lessen partner's high cards of their positional value. You should therefore be more cautious when opponents have not found a fit than when they have.

NO ONE VUL.   1♣ − 1♡ − 2♣ − ?

♠ 8 4
♡ Q 8
◇ K Q 10 7 6
♣ 8 6 4 3

The extra club, four instead of three, just about guarantees a diamond fit. On this auction it would be very poor tactics to pass at matchpoints or IMP's.

NO ONE VUL.   1♣ − 1♡ − 2♣ − ?

♠ 3 2
♡ 8
◇ K J 10 9 3
♣ 9 8 6 4 2

Two diamonds. Scary? Why bid at all? You have five clubs. Isn't it better to pass and hope to beat them?

It might be better to set two clubs, but if that should end the auction, you will almost certainly find you could have made a part score in diamonds. Also, against two clubs, partner is not likely to lead a diamond. He is more likely to lead his suit, hearts. With your actual hand, you can see that a heart lead could work out poorly. A diamond lead should be worth at least two additional tricks to your side.

But, all this is academic, because 2♣ is unlikely to be passed out. Someone is going to bid again. Frequently it will be the opening bidder and the auction will go:

1♣ − 1♡ − 2♣ − Pass
2NT − Pass − 3NT

or

1♣ − 1♡ − 2♣ − Pass
3NT

Both times you want a diamond lead.

The danger in bidding 2◇ is that partner may get excited. But if so, his enthusiasm will be based on a fit and with a sensible partner, you should be able to survive.

You will find more opportunities to bring in a new suit in a competitive auction when RHO has raised or passed than when he has introduced a new suit himself.

When RHO bids a new suit, it leaves only one suit unbid. You will not often have that suit plus whatever values you require to bid it.

1♣ – 1◇ – 1♡ – ?   You can bid 1♠.

1♣ – 1♡ – 2◇ – ?   You must bid at the two level.

1♣ – 1♡ – 1♠ – ?   You must bid at the two level.

These auctions do not imply that you will find a fit if you elect to bid the fourth or unbid suit. Therefore, bearing in mind that RHO is unlimited, you should exercise caution.

NO ONE VUL.   1♣ – 1◇ – 1♡ – ?

♠ J 10 8 7 6   You can try one spade. Only in the unlikely
♡ 8 7 2   event that it will be passed out and that
◇ K 3   partner has a singleton will you regret it.
♣ A Q 3   Should partner raise, you will not mind. If
                  he shows game interest, you will be pleased
to cooperate. This is a clear action at IMP's as well. The poor
quality of your suit should not bother you.

NO ONE VUL.   1♣ – 1◇ – 1♡ – ?

♠ 9 7 6 4 2   Even this hand is not an unreasonable 1♠ call.
♡ 10 8 4 3   In practice, this bid seldom comes to any
◇ K 2   harm. If partner can raise spades, you will
♣ A 10   have a sound basis for competing at the two
                  or even at the three level.

    Note also that you may be on lead. If you are unlikely to be on lead, you might give up on close hands so as to avoid getting partner off to a bad start. Here, your values are sufficient to bid one spade.

    This hand might even warrant another voluntary bid. Typical matchpoint auctions might be as follows:

        1♣ – 1◇ – 1♡ – 1♠
        Pass – Pass – 2♣ – 2◇

            or

        1♣ – 1◇ – 1♡ – 1♠
        2♣ – Pass – Pass – 2◇

These are good matchpoint sequences. So bid on, bearing in mind that either 2◇ or 2♠ should provide a satisfactory resting

spot. You would be very unlucky to find partner with one
spade and only a four card diamond suit. I would expect him to
have two or three spades or five or six diamonds about 98% of
the time.

Let's see what partner might have.

♠ 9 7 6 4 2	♠ K 10 3	You can make
♡ 10 8 4 3	♡ J 2	one or two
◇ K 2	◇ A J 10 6 3	spades.
♣ A 10	♣ Q 9 5	

♠ A 3	You can make
♡ Q J 4	two diamonds.
◇ Q J 10 9 7	
♣ K 6 4	

♠ 10 5	Even this dummy
♡ A 9 7	provides seven
◇ A Q J 8	or eight tricks
♣ 9 8 6 2	at spades.

Note that the reason you were able to make two bids on this
wretched collection was that the few cards you had were known
to be useful. If your hand were

♠ 9 6 5 4 2		♠ 9 7 6 4 2
♡ 10 8 6 3	instead of	♡ 10 8 4 3
◇ A 2		◇ K 2
♣ K 4		♣ A 10

you might still bid one spade,

$$1♣ - 1◇ - 1♡ - 1♠,$$

but perhaps you should refrain later from competing with 2◇.

Very rarely, you might introduce 1♠ on a four card suit.
But you should not go out of the way to do so.

NO ONE VUL.   1♣ − 1◇ − 1♡ − ?

♠ K Q 10 7	Tough, but too good to pass. One spade or
♡ 4 2	perhaps two diamonds.
◇ Q 9	
♣ A 6 5 4 2	

♠ K Q 10 7
♡ 5 4 2
◇ Q 6 3
♣ K 8 7

Two diamonds. No need to bid a four card suit when a reasonable alternative is available.

♠ K Q 10 7
♡ Q 10 8 3
◇ J 2
♣ Q 9 7

One notrump. Again, the most descriptive bid.

When RHO passes, you have more room to respond to partner's overcall and it's safer. In practice, this won't happen too often because RHO will be in there whenever he can.

NO ONE VUL.   1♣ — 1♡ — Pass — ?

♠ K 10 6 4 2
♡ 5 2
◇ 8 2
♣ A J 9 7

One spade. Straightforward.

♠ Q J 8 6 4 2
♡ 3
◇ A 10 8 2
♣ K 4

Again one spade. Would like to hear partner bid again. A spade raise would be super.

♠ 8 7 6 5 4
♡ 2
◇ A Q 10 7
♣ K 4

One spade. Not running from one heart. This is mildly encouraging.

♠ 10 8 6 5 4
♡ —
◇ K 6 5 4
♣ J 10 6 3

Pass. Responding 1♠, while hardly promising a good hand, should show something useful. If one heart is doubled, you may decide to run. But not right away.

♠ J 9 7 6 4
♡ K 6 3
◇ K 8 2
♣ 10 3

Raise to two hearts. One spade would be unwise. A new suit response should deny three card support for partner's major suit overcall. If his overcall had been one diamond,

1♣ — 1♢ — Pass — ?

then one heart or one spade could be reasonable on hands with three card diamond support.

1♣ — 1♢ — Pass — ?

♠ K Q 9 7 6   One spade.
♡ 4 2
♢ K 6 3
♣ Q 5 4

♠ 4 2   One heart.
♡ Q J 10 8 4
♢ A 10 7
♣ K 6 5

In all other auctions where you would like to bid the fourth suit, you will have to do so at the two level.

1♣ — 1♡ — 1♠ — 2♢
1♡ — 1♠ — 2♣ — 2♢
1♢ — 1♡ — 2♣ — 2♠
1♢ — 1♡ — 1♠ — 2♣
etc.

One consideration is of paramount importance. Was RHO's bid at the one level or the two level? For example —

1♣ — 1♡ — 1♠ — ?
or
1♡ — 1♠ — 2♣ — ?

In both cases, diamonds is the unbid suit, and it might appear equally safe to bid it both times. It isn't so. The distinction between the two is vital.

LHO
1♣ — 1 ♡ — 1♠

The one spade bid shows a minimum of six or seven points. It does not necessarily show a good hand. But —

LHO
1♡ — 1♠ — 2♣ — ?

This time, the response is at the two level, showing usually 10 or 11 points, if not more. What this means is that partner's overcall is probably the minimum and you should not bid in the hope that he may have an extra ace or king lurking around.

Opponents' sequence shows a minimum of 23 high card points, leaving fewer for partner. The auction 1♣—1♡—1♠—? by opponents shows only 19 or 20, leaving more for partner.

Let's see how these different sequences affect your decision to bid, i.e. introduce the fourth suit.

NO ONE VUL.   1♣ — 1♡ — 1♠ — ?

♠ 10 6 5   This hand is from the first part of this chapter.
♡ Q 2   I recommended two diamonds.
◇ K Q 10 9 5
♣ 8 6 3

NO ONE VUL.   1♡ — 1♠ — 2♣ — ?

♠ Q 2   Far, far more dangerous to bid two diamonds
♡ 8 6 5   now. If opponents have their values, partner is
◇ K Q 10 9 5   surely minimum. Bidding two diamonds can't
♣ 8 6 3   possibly gain much because your side is
                  known to have insufficient values for com-
peting. Your lack of distribution merely confirms what you already know. If opponents want to bid on, they can and will. If they want to double you, they can and will.

Bidding two diamonds is basically offering opponents a choice — to double or proceed otherwise, as they see fit. Only in very rare situations will your side be able to bid on effectively. This will be when partner has a *super* fit.

When your side is known to have very limited high cards, you have to be careful. When you have found a fit, you can bid strongly on minimum high card values. Otherwise it is best to go quietly.

One last point in defence of bidding two diamonds. The suit is decent and you may induce the best lead. If you think that you may be on lead, this doesn't apply.

In practice, when you introduce a new suit at the two level, it will be after a raise or a pass by RHO.

These are typical auctions:

$$1\clubsuit - 1\spadesuit - 2\clubsuit - \ ?$$
$$1\diamondsuit - 1\heartsuit - 2\diamondsuit - \ ?$$
$$1\clubsuit - 1\spadesuit - \text{Pass} - \ ?$$
$$1\heartsuit - 2\clubsuit - 2\heartsuit - \ ?$$

In sequences where RHO has shown limited strength by a pass or simple raise, you should have no qualms in introducing your suit.

NO ONE VUL. $1\clubsuit - 1\heartsuit - 2\clubsuit - ?$

♠ 3 2
♡ 8
♢ K J 10 9 3
♣ 9 8 6 4 2

As you've seen, this is a two diamond bid. You can be pretty certain of a fit. This hand is shown again to emphasise the lengths you should go to to get into the auction. To my mind, this is not even an extreme case. There will be those who disagree, but their objections will be based on the fear that partner, expecting you to have more, will get too high.

VUL. VS. VUL. $1\diamondsuit - 1\spadesuit - 2\diamondsuit - ?$

♠ 9
♡ A J 8 6 5 4
♢ 8 7 6 2
♣ J 3

Even vulnerable, this is worth two hearts. Your four card diamond holding strongly suggests a shortage in partner's hand and therefore a heart fit of sorts. Partner might well have something like:

♠ K Q 8 7 6
♡ Q 8 5
♢ 2
♣ A 10 5 4

Three hearts would be odds on and on a good day you might make four.

♠ A K 10 7 2
♡ K 10 2
♢ 9 3
♣ A 9 5

Here, four hearts is a spread and yet you have only twenty high card points.

BOTH VUL.   1◊ – 1♠ – 2◊ – ?

♠ J 2   Two hearts. Note the expected fit.
♡ 10 9 8 7 5 2
◊ A 6 5
♣ Q 3

VUL. VS. NOT.   1♣ – 1♠ – 2♣ – ?

♠ 4   This hand is surely a two heart call at any
♡ Q 9 6 5 4   form of the game. Note that if you had the
◊ K 9 4   diamond ace and club king, a pass would be
♣ A 8 6 5   best. Your minimum high cards would not be
                   working as fully as in the actual hand.

I have to admit that at matchpoints, I would feel very much
like bidding two hearts even if they were changed to 10 9 8 7 6 2.
The expectation of a fit counts for so much in these situations.

BOTH VUL.   1◊ – 1♡ – 2◊ – ?

♠ K J 9 7   Who knows? It might be right to play in spades
♡ 3   or clubs. Certainly the hand is good enough
◊ 10 6 5   to do something. But what? Eventually,
♣ A J 9 8 3   we will come to a convention known as the
                   Responsive Double. For the time being,
hands like this are just a guess. If you feel very much as though
you want to do something and aren't sure what, your thinking
is on the right lines.

NO ONE VUL.   1♣ – 1♡ – 2♣ – ?

♠ K 9 7 6 4 2   This is a curious hand. It doesn't look like it,
♡ J 2   but bidding two spades is rather dangerous.
◊ A 10 6 2   Throughout this section and, for that matter,
♣ 9   throughout the book, I've focused attention
                   on the prospects of a fit in partner's hand.
Here, your singleton club is a clear warning. There is no reason
at all for partner to have a spade fit. I would guess his average
holding at about 1¼ spades. Should you pass two clubs? No.
Not really, but you should not be too optimistic about your
chances. What is important is that you understand why two
spades is not as clearcut as it may seem and why it could easily

lead to a minus score.

A few more hands here to underline important points:

VUL. VS. NOT.   1♣ — 1◇ — 1♠ — ?

♠ 8 7 5   Bid two hearts, but don't expect too much.
♡ K Q 10 9 6 3   When there is no reason to expect a fit, you
◇ K 9   need a good suit or compensating high cards.
♣ 10 4   Here your hearts will play adequately even
                       opposite a singleton.

VUL. VS. NOT.   1♣ — 1◇ — 1♠ — ?

♠ 9 7 5   Bid two diamonds. The heart suit is not good
♡ Q 10 8 7 5   enough.
◇ K Q 5
♣ Q 9

BOTH VUL.   1♣ — 1♡ — 2◇ — ?

♠ K J 8 7 3   Pass!!!! This is a death trap. You can make
♡ 4   nothing. Already, opponents have announced
◇ Q 10 8 3   about 23 high card points, leaving partner
♣ Q 9 8   about nine. At this vulnerability, he must have
                       a decent five or six card suit. There is no
reason on earth for you to think that he has a spade fit. On the
other side of the coin, opponents can't make anything either
and if it suits you, you can double them should they get too
high. If you don't want to double, that's OK too. Meanwhile
pass.

NO ONE VUL.   1♣ — 1♡ — 2◇ — ?

♠ K J 9 7   Pass. This is not the time to experiment with
♡ 3   two spades. And don't double two diamonds.
◇ Q 10 8 7 2   It's forcing and opponents will have to bid on.
♣ K 8 4   Perhaps you can double three diamonds. Note
                       again that opponents are conducting a strong
auction. From this you can draw the inference that partner's
overcall is minimum.

BOTH VUL.   1♡ − 1♠ − Pass − ?

♠ 9 2   Two clubs. Routine. You have a good suit, a
♡ A 5 4   moderate hand, and no fit for partner.
◊ J 2
♣ K Q 10 8 7 3

NO ONE VUL.   1♣ − 1◊ − Pass − ?

♠ 8 6 5 4 2   One spade. This is not a weakness bid and
♡ 3 2   partner will continue if his hand warrants it.
◊ A 8
♣ K Q 10 7

NO ONE VUL.   1♣ − 1♡ − Pass − ?

♠ A 8   Here it is better to bid one notrump. While on
♡ 3 2   the preceding hand, one spade was best, there
◊ 8 6 5 4 2   is not the same urgency to look for minor
♣ K Q 10 7   suit fits. Two diamonds would be poor.

BOTH VUL.   1♣ − 1♡ − Pass − ?

♠ K Q 10 9 8 7   This hand is so good that you ought to con-
♡ K 2   sider game. Four spades is a likely candidate
◊ A 10 7   and four hearts or three notrumps are
♣ 5 4   possibles. Now if one spade is correct on

              ♠ 8 6 5 4 2
              ♡ 3 2
              ◊ A 8
              ♣ K Q 10 7

then one spade is probably incorrect on this hand. If this
presented you with a problem, full marks for thinking ahead.
We will come to the solution in due course.

NOT VUL.
VS. VUL.   1♣ − 1♡ − 2◊ − ?

♠ K J 10 9 8 6   This is another case where you must visualise
♡ A 3   partner's strength and distribution. The auc-
◊ 8 6 2   tion has told you that partner's overcall is
♣ 5 4   minimum. He won't have many high cards and

there is nothing to suggest any sort of spade fit. I don't expect anyone not to bid two spades, but it is an aggressive and dangerous action. If, when you bid two spades, you were aware of the dangers, you were on the right track.

Much space has been devoted to commonplace auctions, but these situations are the essence of competitive bidding. An understanding of when to get into and when to get out of an auction is crucial. More points, IMP's, or money are lost in these low level skirmishes than in mightier battles. Unfortunately, many of these losses go unnoticed because no one stops to work out that his side could have made three diamonds on a hand where opponents were allowed to make two spades.

VUL. VS. NOT. $1\diamondsuit - 1\heartsuit - 2\diamondsuit - ?$

♠ J 10 8 6 4 3   At matchpoints, this is a typical aggressive
♡ 3   2♠ bid. All your eggs are in one basket so to
♢ A 8 6   speak, and if you're wrong, you're very wrong.
♣ Q 9 7   An important matchpoint consideration is
                    that opponents are in a minor. If they make
two diamonds, they score 90. If you go one down in two spades, you lose 100. When vulnerable, you must give thought to these things. Similarly, if opponents stop in one notrump, you might decide to let them play there rather than risk going down 100.

Admittedly, you can't often judge the exact number of tricks either side can make, let alone both sides, but in close decisions, the vulnerability and opponents' contract — 1NT or 2♣ or 2♢ — may sway you in one direction or another.

IMP's is much easier. Those 10 point swings don't count. Another case of a matchpoint top being worthless at IMP's.

On the actual hand, opponents will frequently save you by going on to three diamonds when they could have defeated two spades. The irony of it all is when they make three diamonds anyway so that all your hard work was for naught.

THREE LEVEL NEW SUIT RESPONSES
TO AN OVERCALL

This section is going to be shorter and simpler than the long chapter heading may suggest.

Once in a while, partner will make an overcall and the auction will proceed so as to force you to bid your suit at the three level, i.e.

1◇–1♠–2♡	You must bid three clubs.
1♠–2◇–2♡	You must bid three clubs.
1♡–1♠–2♡	You must bid three clubs or three diamonds.
1♠–2♡–2♣	You must bid three clubs or three diamonds.

Once again, you have two situations. RHO has responded in a new suit, or RHO has raised the opener.

The first case is easily dealt with. Opponents have shown that they hold substantial values, an opening bid facing a two over one response, so it will be dangerous to start looking for a fit. You are outgunned.

In the previous section you saw that it was dangerous to bid a new suit at the two level after opponents had shown strength. Bidding at the three level is correspondingly more dangerous. In practice, you will rarely have cause to do anything except raise partner or pass.

NO ONE VUL.   1♡ – 1♠ – 2◇ – ?

♠ J 3
♡ 8 6
◇ J 7 5 2
♣ A Q 8 6 3

Pass. Far too dangerous to act. Your best hope of a plus is to set opponents in their final contract. You can see that partner's overcall is some sort of minimum. Opponents have 23 or 24 high card points and you have eight. Partner has eight or nine. Looking at it this way shows the futility of bidding. If you tried three clubs, you could easily go down a couple, and maybe more, and it will definitely be doubled. As opponents don't even have a clearcut game, 300 can be too expensive.

NOT VUL.
VS. VUL.   1♣ − 1♠ − 2♡ − ?

♠ 4 2   This is a typical three diamond bid. Not much
♡ 9 6 5   in high cards, but a good suit. You should be
◇ K Q 10 9 8 6 3 able to get six diamond tricks most of the
♣ 7   time, and you are sure of five. If you should
                 run into a double, it could cost three or even
five hundred, but if so, it won't necessarily be bad. Opponents
are likely to have a game and you have no particular reason to
think you can beat it. If partner feels like saving, you have the
right hand for it.

VUL. VS. VUL.   1◇ − 1♠ − 2♡ − ?

♠ 5   You can try three clubs without too much
♡ 8 6 5 3   risk. If partner decides to save, your hand is
◇ 2   suitable, and once again, your suit is good.
♣ A J 10 9 8 6 3 You would prefer partner to lead a club unless
                 his spades are so outstanding that he would
lead them in any case.

Partner should be aware of the kind of hand three clubs
shows. He is not expected or encouraged to rebid his suit. More
especially, he should not try three notrumps. If he does bid
three notrumps, you should trust him and pass. His hand should
look something like:

♠ J 10 8 7 6 2
♡ A 9
◇ A 5
♣ K 5 4

You could make a rather remarkable game on only seventeen
high card points.

The crux of it is that partner's three notrumps is bid on the
assumption that you have a good suit. Partner should expect no
more because that is about the only thing you have. In the same
way that you can sometimes tell how many points partner has
for his overcall, partner can sometimes tell what you have for
your response.

Once again, opponents show around 23 for their auction.
If partner has

♠ J 10 8 7 6 2
♡ A 9
♢ A 5
♣ K 5 4

he will add his twelve points to their 23 and realise how little is
left for you. If you have your bid, it must be a long strong suit
and nothing else. Partner's three notrumps bid must be based on
a club fit and he expects to run the suit. He should not bid three
notrumps on a hand such as

♠ A Q 8 7 6
♡ K 6 4
♢ K 9 3
♣ 7 4

There aren't nine tricks on view. Neither are there eight, nor
seven, nor six?

NO ONE VUL.   1♣ — 1♠ — 2♡ — ?

♠ 8 3   Pass. The suit must be playable opposite a
♡ Q 6 5   singleton. Your high cards are of little value
♢ K J 9 7 6 4   and your suit is inadequate.
♣ Q 9

NOT VUL.
VS. VUL.   1♣ — 1♠ — 2♡ — ?

♠ 3   Pass is probably best. You might miss a good
♡ 8 7   save, but if you bid three diamonds, you run
♢ J 9 8 7 6 4 2   a number of risks. Partner may get off to a
♣ A Q 3   bad lead. Or you may take a bad save. You
                      have good defence against four hearts should
opponents try it. Your spade singleton and your club ace suggest
defence. Three diamonds could work out, but is is against the
odds.

If partner were to bid three notrumps over three diamonds,
you should remove to four diamonds. Partner's hand can't be
good enough to stop opponents' suits and to run diamonds. He
is expecting a better suit. Note that partner needs something in
diamonds for his bid, so you are guaranteed support.

BIDDING AFTER A RAISE BY RHO

When RHO raises, you have more reason to be hopeful and can afford to be a bit aggressive.

NO ONE VUL.   1♠ – 2♣ – 2♠ – ?

♠ 3 2
♡ K J 8 6 5 4
♢ Q J 6 3
♣ 2

Pass. Even though partner's overcall guarantees more than a one level overcall would, you should quit. You need a super hand, a super suit, *or* reason to expect a fit. You have none. That extra trick, three level as opposed to two level, requires extra values to make up for the greater risk.

NO ONE VUL.   1♠ – 2♡ – 2♠ – ?

♠ 8 7 6
♡ Q 2
♢ 4 2
♣ K Q J 10 7 6

3♣ is clear: good suit and a probable fit. Not only that, but your heart queen is a considerable plus.

NO ONE VUL.   1♠ – 2♢ – 2♠ – ?

♠ 8 7 6
♡ K Q 9 6 4 2
♢ 4 2
♣ Q 9

This is a matchpoint-oriented 3♡ bid. Your suit is reasonable and you have hopes of a fit. The trouble is that if you're wrong, there's no escape.

NO ONE VUL.   1♠ – 2♢ – 2♠ – ?

♠ 8 7
♡ K Q 9 6 4 2
♢ 4 2
♣ Q 9 3

Pass. The salient feature of this hand is the doubleton spade, the worst possible holding in a suit bid and raised by opponents. It says nothing about partner's fit for you which would be the case if you had three or four spades. With the rest of the hand being marginal, you should pass.

VUL. VS. NOT.   1♠ – 2♢ – 2♡ – ?

♠ Q 8 2
♡ 8 4
♢ 7
♣ K J 9 7 6 5 4

This auction is one of those defined as dangerous and if you always passed without looking at your hand, you would be well off in the long run. This advice certainly holds true here. There is nothing to recommend bidding.

1. You have the spade queen, probably worthless.
2. You have a doubleton heart, hopeless.
3. You have a singleton in partner's suit.
4. You have no reason to expect a fit.

Pass.

Finally there is an auction which is theoretically possible, but in practice, non-existent. It goes something like this:

> *You*
> 1♣ — Pass — 1♠ — 2♦
> Pass — 2♡
>
> 1♡ — Pass — 2♣ — 2♠
> Pass — 3♦
>
> 1♣ — Pass — 2♣ — 2♡
> Pass — 2♠
>
> 1♦ — Pass — 2♦ — 2♡
> 3♦ — 3♠

In all these auctions, the opening bid was on your right. You passed, and then when LHO responded and your partner over-called, you decided to introduce a new suit of your own. Most unusual.

If you were so eager to show this suit, why didn't you do so after the opening bid? Why wait and have second thoughts?

There could be two possible reasons.

1. You didn't have enough strength to bid the first time.
2. You have a fit for partner.

It's easy to dispose of the first possibility. Just because partner overcalls, he does not guarantee enough strength to warrant your bidding on hands which are not worth an initial overcall.

NO ONE VUL.   1♣ — Pass — 1♠ — 2♦
                Pass — ?

♠ 8 7 2   If you passed over 1♣, you might wish to
♡ K Q 10 8 7   bid 2♡, but you should have overcalled in the
♦ K 2   firxt place.
♣ J 4 2

NO ONE VUL.   1◇ — Pass — 1♠ — 2♡
                  2♠ — ?

♠ 4 2
♡ J 7 3
◇ 8 7 2
♣ A K J 8 7

You have the values to raise to 3♡, but you might consider bidding 3♣ instead. If you and partner wished to define this auction and the one before, you could reasonably say that a new suit guarantees a fit for partner's.

NO ONE VUL.   1♣ — Pass — 1♡ — 1♠
                  2♡ — ?

♠ 3
♡ J 8 7
◇ K Q 10 9 7 3
♣ 8 4 2

This hand shouldn't exist either. It's a weak jump overcall or nothing.

NO ONE VUL.   1♣ — Pass — 1♠ — 2♡
                  2♠ — ?

♠ 10 6 5 2
♡ 3
◇ K Q 10 8 7 5
♣ Q 4

You could try 3◇ on the theory that a fit exists. But you can't do that if partner expects you to have heart support. This situation is exceptional in that you might pass and then wish to bid. The reason you didn't make a weak jump overcall was your holding in spades.

Under no circumstances should you confuse these sequences with the ones earlier. Only when RHO opens, you pass, LHO responds, and partner overcalls, can a new suit by you imply a fit for partner. Be sure you discuss it. And don't wait for it to happen first.

NEW SUIT RESPONSES
PARTNER OVERCALLS
AND YOU HAVE A GOOD HAND

So far, the only hands we've looked at are those of marginal value where you wished to compete for the part-score. Game was usually out of the question unless partner could make some forward move.

Once in a while, though, you will have a hand with near game-going values. When this happens, you will want to make a stronger bid than a simple change of suit.

There are two stronger bids available. You can cue bid or you can jump in your suit. In practice, a good workable approach is to jump on invitational hands and to reserve the cue bid for game-forcing hands. More on this shortly.

These are the sequences in which a jump response could be of advantage:

Partner overcalls, and RHO

1. Passes
2. Makes a 1/1 response
3. Bids 1NT
4. Raises
5. Makes a 2/1 response

Let us examine each situation in turn:

1. RHO passes.

The possibility exists that you can have game-going values. A jump to show it is a reasonable treatment.

2. RHO makes a 1/1 response.

There is still the possibility that you have enough to explore game prospects. Again a jump is reasonable.

3. RHO bids 1NT.

While it's barely possible for you to have enough for an invitational jump, there is the more practical alternative of doubling 1NT. Note that the 1NT bidder has seven to ten HCP, while the 1/1 responder may be bidding on distribution and can have as few as four or five HCP. This means that you are less likely to have the strength to jump after 1NT. I suggest using a jump as pre-emptive rather than strong.

4. RHO raises.

Quite possible for you to have a good hand. Moreover, when they have a fit, you do too. Use the jump as invitational.

5. RHO bids 2/1.

There is no way you can have a good hand. LHO has an opener, partner an overcall, and RHO values for a two-level bid. There is little left for you. Since you can't have enough to jump in a new suit invitationally, you should find another meaning for the bid. Again I suggest the pre-emptive jump.

NO ONE VUL.   1♣ — 1♡ — Pass — ?

♠ A Q 10 8 7 6   A normal 2♠ bid. This is not forcing. Partner
♡ K 2   may pass on a minimum. Your bid shows
◇ K J 7   something in the range of a good thirteen to a
♣ 4 2   poorish fifteen with a very good five card or
    longer suit. If partner passes 2♠ you'll be in a
good spot. If partner has any kind of fit, he will raise and you
will continue accordingly.

NO ONE VUL.   1♣ — 1◇ — Pass — ?

♠ 4 2   2♡. Too many losers for a direct jump to 4♡.
♡ K Q 9 7 6 5 2   This is a good hand for systemic understand-
◇ Q   ings. You'll get to game when it's right and
♣ K Q 4   you'll stay in a part-score when that's right.

VUL. VS. NOT.   1◇ — 1♠ — Pass — ?

♠ 8 7   3♣. Hoping that partner can bid 3NT. If he
♡ K 5   passes, you should be in a good spot.
◇ 8 7 6
♣ A K Q J 8 7

BOTH VUL.   1♡ — 1♠ — Pass — ?

♠ Q 2   3♣. The jump does not guarantee a solid suit.
♡ 8 7
◇ A K 5
♣ K J 10 9 7 4

NO ONE VUL.   1♣ — 1♡ — Pass — ?

♠ K Q J 8 7   2♠. Good five card suit with game interest.
♡ Q 2
◇ 4 2
♣ A J 6 5

NO ONE VUL.   1♣ — 1♠ — Pass — ?

♠ J 2   Who knows? Some people will point to hands
♡ A Q 8 6 5   like this one and tell you that 2♡ should be
◇ A 10 6 5 4   forcing. Here it would be useful. But you
♣ 3   would have problems on many part-score

hands. I would bid 2♡ and hope to hear somebody bid again. I would object to 3♡, but not too strongly.

NO ONE VUL.   1♣ — 1◇ — Pass — ?

♠ Q 9 7 6 5   1♠. If partner can't raise, you won't be miss-
♡ A Q 4 2   ing much.
◇ A 5
♣ 8 7

VUL. VS. NOT.   1♣ — 1♡ — Pass — ?

♠ J 7 6 5 2   I would lean towards 2NT. Spades might be
♡ Q 2   your best spot, but there's no number of
◇ A K 8   spades you can bid without misleading partner.
♣ K 10 7

NO ONE VUL.   1♣ — 1♠ — Pass — ?

♠ Q 6 5 2   4♠. With a major suit fit, you don't need to
♡ K Q J 10 7   look around.
◇ 3
♣ K Q 7

BOTH VUL.   1♣ — 1◇ — Pass — ?

♠ A J 2   1♡. Partner will raise on most hands con-
♡ K 10 7 6 5   taining three card support unless he has a sub-
◇ K J 3   standard overcall.
♣ J 3

NO ONE VUL.   1♠ — 2♣ — Pass — ?

♠ 4 2   3◇. You want to hear 3NT, but you don't
♡ 9 3 2   want to force the issue. 3◇ does it nicely.
◇ A K Q 10 8 7 6   Whatever you do, don't bid 2◇.
♣ 3

NOT VUL.
VS. VUL.   1♡ − 2♣ − Pass − ?

♠ J 10 9 7 4 2   **3♠.** This suit is pretty poor for a jump, but
♡ A K J 7   your values are adequate. Without well-
♢ 2   defined methods for situations such as this
♣ Q 3   you will be reduced to guessing games.

NO ONE VUL.   1♠ − 2♣ − Pass − ?

♠ 8 2   **3♡.** Because a two level overcall promises
♡ K Q 10 9 7 6   more than a one level overcall, your jump can
♢ A Q 5   be based on a little less. When you jump to
♣ 10 2   the three level, however, you do need a good
                   suit.

BOTH VUL.   1♠ − 2♡ − Pass − ?

♠ Q 2   The only good bid is 3♢ forcing. But it's not
♡ 10 2   forcing, so you have to select from:
♢ A K J 10 8 7   1. 2 or 3NT; insufficient spade stopper
♣ K 5 4   2. 3 or 4♡; insufficient trumps
                     3. 3♢; grossly conservative
    4. 2♠; my choice, but awkward
    5. 4♢; gets past 3NT
More on this hand later.

When RHO makes a 1/1 response after your partner's overcall, your jump will be about the same as if RHO had passed.
There are a few minor differences that you have to contend
with.

1. RHO's bid will usually force you to jump to the three level.

                1♣ − 1♢ − Pass − 2♡
                1♣ − 1♢ − 1♠ − 3♡

That 1♠ forced you to change your bid.

2. You have more distributional information to help you
with your decision.

NO ONE VUL. ♣ — 1♡ — 1♠ — ?

♠ K 8 7
♡ Q 2
♢ A Q J 9 8 3
♣ 8 7

3♢. Don't fall into the trap of bidding 2♢ and thinking that's sufficient because it's a free bid. You should bid 2♢ without either the spade king or the heart queen.

NO ONE VUL. 1♣ — 1♢ — 1♡ — ?

♠ Q J 8 7 6 2
♡ K 10 4 2
♢ A J
♣ 3

2♠. This is the only auction where RHO bids and you can still jump to the two level. One advantage of jump responses to show a good hand is that they remain the same for all forms of Bridge; IMP's, matchpoints, etc.

BOTH VUL. 1♣ — 1♢ — 1♠ — ?

♠ K J 3
♡ Q 6 5 4 2
♢ K 2
♣ A 10 3

Where are they all finding their bids? Someone is stretching. Hope it's not partner.

I would try 2NT but feel unhappy about losing the heart suit. On the other hand, 2♡ is an underbid while 3♡ shows a much better suit.

There is a convention to handle this hand called the responsive double. More on this later.

Of paramount importance is good partnership understanding. The methods I am recommending have proved their worth. They work most of the time and make it easier as a rule to bid the good hands. On poor ones you have to ask yourself first: 'Shall I bid at all?' and if the answer is 'Yes', comes the second question: 'What shall I bid?' On good hands only the second question calls for an answer.

When RHO raises after partner's overcalls, you will hold a fair number of hands worth an invitational jump. More hands, in fact, than after a 1/1 by RHO. This is because

1. After a raise, there are two unbid suits for you to bid.

2. They have a fit which suggests that you also have one. When good fits exist, it has the effect of increasing the points around the table, so that everyone has more than his usual quota. More points, more bidding.

One problem you will encounter is that a raise by RHO is

perforce at the two level, so a jump by you must be to the three level or higher. Even though you may have the values to jump, the level of the auction may make life difficult.

NO ONE VUL.   1♣ — 1♡ — 2♣ — ?

♠ K Q 10 8 7 6 2   3♠. If partner has a singleton spade and a
♡ 3   weak hand, you will be high enough. 4♠
♢ A 2   would be an overbid and 2♠ could result in
♣ J 5 4   missing game opposite a minimum overcall.

NO ONE VUL.   1♡ — 2♣ — 2♡ — ?

♠ A J 2   This is a difficult hand. I would bid 3♢.
♡ 4 2   Anything else would be misleading and this
♢ K Q 10 8 7 6   way, at least, I would be sure of a plus score.
♣ Q 2

NO ONE VUL.   1♢ — 2♣ — 2♢ — ?

♠ K 10 9 6 5   You have the strength to bid and you have
♡ A Q J 8 7   high hopes of a game if partner can fit either
♢ 3   major. The solution is the responsive double,
♣ Q 4   to be discussed later.

BOTH VUL.   1♠ — 2♣ — 2♠ — ?

♠ 8 2   Very awkward. You want to bid hearts, raise
♡ K Q 10 7 6 5   clubs, and show a good hand all at once.
♢ A 10   Unfortunately, you have no assurance of a
♣ K 6 5   heart fit. That doubleton spade tells you
                   nothing about partner's distribution and
is a distinct liability. Best to bid a conservative 3♡.

BOTH VUL.   1♠ — 2♣ — 2♠ — ?

♠ 10 6 5 2   Once again the known fit strikes. 3♡ would be
♡ K J 10 9 8 3   an underbid. Bid game. You should have a
♢ 3   good chance.
♣ A Q

BOTH VUL.   1♡ – 1♠ – 2♡ – ?

♠ 8 2   Bid 3♣. You would like partner to bid 3NT,
♡ 4 2   but that is unlikely. Sadly, you have no strong
♢ 7 2   bid available which is both safe and sensible.
♣ A K Q 10 7 6 5 Even if 3♣ were forcing, it wouldn't neces-
                sarily work. You really wish RHO had passed
so that your 3♣ bid would have been a jump. But it didn't go
that way.

So once again you have to take the path of least resistance.
3♣ won't get you to many games, but it will result in a good
safe contract. Some of the time you'll get the only available
plus.

WHEN GAME IS UNLIKELY

When RHO bids 1NT after partner's overcall, the chances of
game by your side are virtually non-existent. Opponents have at
least half the high cards and RHO has values in partner's suit. In
practice, the best you can achieve is a part-score.

If you are not likely to have the values for a jump in this
situation, another meaning for the jump shift should be found.
One possibility is to play it as pre-emptive.

Let's see if it works.

NO ONE VUL.   1♡ – 1♠ – 1NT – ?

♠ 7 2   If you play 3♣ as a pre-empt, then this hand is
♡ 9 7 3   just about right. You aren't likely to make it,
♢ 8   but you won't go down many, either, and
♣ K Q J 10 9 7 3 with the suit as good as it is, nobody will be
                rushing to double.

As with most pre-empts, you take up a fair amount of room.
LHO can't rebid 2♡ or 2♢, and for that matter, neither can
RHO. You won't have many of these pre-emptive jumps, but
when they occur, you'll do well. There are a couple of things to
look out for, though.

1. RHO has made a descriptive bid and LHO will be able to
double you when it's right.

2. If opponents have no game, then −200 or −300 will

be bad results. To minimise the risk you need a fairly good suit.

NO ONE VUL.   1♣ – 1◇ – 1NT – ?

♠ 4 2
♡ Q 10 8 6 5 4 2
◇ Q 3
♣ A 4

2♡ is fine and quite enough. Your suit is too poor to jump.

BOTH VUL.   1◇ – 1♠ – 1NT – ?

♠ 10 3
♡ Q J 10 9 8 6 3
◇ –
♣ K 10 8 7

On this vulnerability, you need a pretty good hand, so 3♡ is about right.

NOT VUL.
VS. VUL.   1♡ – 1♠ – 1NT – ?

♠ 3
♡ 2
◇ K Q J 10 8 7
♣ J 6 5 4 2

I would try 3◇. Good suit, weakish hand. Clubs might be right, but with such suit disparity, I'd rather bid the maximum the hand can stand. Let them guess.

VUL. VS. NOT.   1♣ – 1♠ – 1NT – ?

♠ J 2
♡ K Q 10 8 7 5
◇ A Q 4
♣ 9 7

Very unlikely that you will ever have so good a hand on this sequence. If it does happen, though, you have to forego the invitational 3♡ bid. On this auction it would be weak. Your choices are a conservative 2♡ or a penalty double. I would choose the double, expecting someone to run, after which I would introduce the hearts.

In the sequence below, RHO makes a 2/1 response after partner's overcall. Everyone has a good hand. Except us.

So, if we don't have much to fight with, maybe we can put up a fight with what we have. This isn't easy, though, because bidding is very dangerous in this situation.

As your side does not have many high cards, your tricks will have to come as the result of a good fit, or a long, strong suit.

NOT VUL.
VS. VUL.   1♣ — 1♠ — 2◊ — ?

♠ 8 6 2   Opposite a spade overcall, this hand should
♡ Q J 10 8 7 6 5   produce six tricks easily. If doubled, this
◊ 3   would be −500, perhaps less. This would not
♣ 9 5   be good unless opponents have a game. Here
                     it seems likely that they do. Try 3♡.

When the auction begins with a 2/1 by responder, the chances of their making game are very real, so your saves have a much wider range of success. If opponents can do no better than a part-score, −200, −300, or −500 will be disastrous regardless of vulnerability. But against a game, these minuses will turn into rewarding plusses.

NO ONE VUL.   1♣ — 1♠ — 2◊ — ?

♠ 3   Far too dangerous to bid 3♡. Your suit is bad.
♡ K J 7 6 4 3 2   You have no reason to hope for a fit. You
◊ Q 8 7   have some defence. If you must do something,
♣ J 2   2♡ is enough. But it's not as safe as it looks.
                     It is useful to consider what games op-
ponents have available. They are NT, clubs, and diamonds, and you have some values in defence against all these.

BOTH VUL.   1♡ — 1♠ — 2♣ — ?

♠ Q 2   Just 2◊. When you don't wish partner to
♡ 8 3   sacrifice, you should be content to indicate
◊ K J 10 8 7 6 5   the best lead.
♣ 4 2

NOT VUL.
VS. VUL.   1♡ — 2♣ — 2◊ — ?

♠ J 10 7 6 5 4 2   With this defensive wonder it would not be
♡ 7 3   surprising to see opponents score a grand
◊ 2   slam, let alone various games. 3♠ is a good
♣ K 8 7   practical way to make life hard for them while
                     showing your best suit. This vulnerability is
so much in your favour that you can get away with almost

anything, at least when:

1. Opponents have a game.
2. You have a fit or a good suit.

Here, both conditions hold. If they have no game, they'll never have one. And you have a fit. If not in spades, then in clubs. Note that you won't be in more than 3♠ unless partner raises.

VUL. VS. NOT.   1◊ — 1♠ — 2♥ — ?

♠ —

♥ Q 10 3

◊ Q 4 2

♣ K J 8 7 6 5 4

Pass. You are about to get a good score. But you won't get it by bidding. You have no suit, no fit, no tricks. Just defence. And the vulnerability is unfavourable. Occasionally partner will overcall and you will have enough to guarantee a game. Some of the time you can raise to game or maybe bid 3NT. But on some hands, the best game contract is in doubt. It could be in partner's suit, in one of your suits, or in NT. Perhaps you need partner to stop opener's suit or to provide half a stopper. Perhaps you need to know if partner has a six card suit. All sorts of questions arise. Usually, when you have values for game and no certain way of getting there, the correct action is a cue bid.

It would be logical to discuss cue bids at this point, but there is another use for them which also requires attention. More powerful hands will come under the spotlight in a later chapter.

8

RAISING PARTNER'S OVERCALL

When partner overcalls, you will often want to raise his suit. Depending on the auction there are several ways of doing it. Let us examine each one in turn.

1. simple raises
2. invitational raises — on balanced hands
3. invitational raises — on distributional hands
4. game forcing raises

CASE 1

PARTNER OVERCALLS AT THE ONE LEVEL; RHO PASSES.

The Single Raise — This is pretty much the same as the raise of an opening bid. The only difference is that your range extends slightly. Where you raise an opening bid on from six to some ten counts, you raise an overcall on some fives to some elevens. This range may seem too wide, but in practice it's not so bad. The main objection is that it makes game bidding difficult, but when you are bidding defensively, game considerations are not as important. What is important is setting a firm foundation, i.e. the trump suit, so your side can compete effectively.

NO ONE VUL.   1♣ — 1♡ — Pass — ?

♠ Q J 8 6 2   When you have good trump support and a
♡ K 8 7   major suit fit, you should raise. Both 1♠ and
♢ J 7 6   pass would be poor.
♣ 4 2

NO ONE VUL.   1♣ — 1♠ — Pass — ?

♠ K J 8 7
♥ 3 2
♦ 10 8 6 5 2
♣ 8 7

Good trumps. Bid 2♠. Even with a minimum, it is a clearcut raise.

NO ONE VUL.   1♣ — 1♥ — Pass — ?

♠ 7 6 2
♥ K Q 8 2
♦ 8 7 3
♣ 9 6 2

This is close, but the distribution suggests a pass. Add the jack in spades or diamonds and you would have a minimum raise.

NO ONE VUL.   1♣ — 1♠ — Pass — ?

♠ 8 6 2
♥ A Q 6 4 2
♦ 8 6 3 2
♣ 4

A clearcut raise. Don't worry about partner having only four spades. Your hand will be very useful. 2♥ would be wrong.

VUL. VS. NOT.   1♣ — 1♥ — Pass — ?

♠ Q 10 2
♥ 8 6 2
♦ K J 8 3
♣ Q 5 4

Are your opponents playing negative doubles? If so, it is reasonable to pass. There is the danger that RHO has good hearts and is waiting for opener to double. Three small trumps suffice for a raise if supported by outside values. Here they are not.

VUL. VS. NOT.   1♣ — 1♠ — Pass — ?

♠ Q 10 2
♥ 8 6 2
♦ K J 8 3
♣ Q 5 4

This is the same hand as the previous one, but this time partner's overcall is 1♠. Raise to two. Good trump support makes up for the lack of other values.

It is a common error to pass on this and other minimum hands. You lose much of the benefit of partner's overcall. Opener can now rebid at a low level and nothing will have been gained.

NO ONE VUL.   1♣ — 1♠ — Pass — ?

♠ Q 8 3   Raise to 2♠. This is about a maximum, and
♡ A Q 8 7   yet, opposite most overcalls, two spades
◇ Q J 2   could well be the limit.
♣ 5 4 2

BOTH VUL.   1♣ — 1♠ — Pass — ?

♠ 9 8 7   You would not be wrong to bid only 2♠ with
♡ K J 3   this hand, either. In spite of eleven HCP, the
◇ K Q 8 3   values must be scaled down in the light of
♣ Q 4 2   poor trump support and bad distribution.

NO ONE VUL.   1♣ — 1♠ — Pass — ?

♠ K Q J 4   Again 2♠. It is important to give partner a
♡ Q 8 7   little leeway. These hands with odds and
◇ J 8 2   ends are not nearly as good as they look.
♣ Q 4 2   There are two areas where people frequently
               err. They jump to three on hands like this
one and fail to raise to two on some of the minimum holdings
shown earlier. Both errors can be expensive.

THE DOUBLE RAISE VS. THE CUE BID

There will be some hands where you hope to make a game and
the time-honoured way to invite it is by means of a jump raise.
This works well enough when partner can continue to game, but
now and then he passes and proceeds to go down. Usually when
this happens, your jump raise was on some balanced hand or
just three trumps, as here:

♠ Q 4 2
♡ A 8 6 5
◇ K J 8 7
♣ Q 10

LHO opened 1♡, partner bid 1♠, and you raised to three.
Partner passed and didn't make it.

I would like to make a suggestion. It smacks of science, but
it does work well. Here goes.

When you have an invitational raise of partner's overcall, you jump raise with distributional values which include four or more trumps and you cue bid when you are balanced or have three trumps. You will always be able to do this when partner overcalls at the one level and often when partner overcalls at the two level. You may be wondering why I'm recommending a cue bid to show a good raise when I've already recommended a cue bid to show a game force with a new suit. Because you can do both. This section will include a number of examples showing the difference between a cue bid raise and a jump raise. In a subsequent section I'll discuss partner's responses.

Now for the usual examples.

NO ONE VUL.	1♣ — 1♠ — Pass — ?

♠ J 8 7 6
♡ 3
◇ K Q 4
♣ A 10 9 7 4

3♠. If partner has anything approaching a maximum, you'll have a game. Partner will know he is facing four trumps and a useful distribution so his decision will be well reasoned.

NO ONE VUL.	1♣ — 1♡ — Pass — ?

♠ K 8 6
♡ Q J 7 6
◇ K J 7
♣ Q J 7

With a balanced distribution, you are anxious not to get too high. Try **2♣.** If partner is underweight, you can stop in two hearts.

The reason you don't cue bid with both types of hand is that when you are distributional, opponents may have good distribution, too. If so, your jump will make it harder for the opener to get back into the auction. Also, by offering two forms of an invitational raise, partner will be better able to judge if he should continue.

BOTH VUL.	1♣ — 1♠ — Pass — ?

♠ Q 10 7
♡ 8
◇ A K J 7 6
♣ J 9 7 4

Bid **2♣.** You have only three trumps, a serious flaw. A jump promises four trumps whenever the alternative of a cue bid exists.

NO ONE VUL.   1♢ — 1♡ — Pass — ?

♠ K J
♡ Q J 7 6 5
♢ K 8 5
♣ Q J 7

2♢. This time you have poor distribution, notwithstanding your five card trump support.

Note that without the cue bid you would have no choice but to jump raise on all these hands.

NO ONE VUL.   1♣ — 1♢ — Pass — ?

♠ K 3
♡ K 6 2
♢ A Q 8 6
♣ 8 6 5 4

I would treat this as distributional and jump to 3♢ to erect a barrier. There are two major suits missing and opponents might well get together in one of them.

GAME FORCES

When you have game values, you can either bid game in a major with four trumps or you can cue bid, looking for 3NT.

NO ONE VUL.   1♣ — 1♡ — Pass — ?

♠ A 4 2
♡ K J 7 6
♢ A Q 8 3
♣ 4 2

Just bid 4♡. No reason to cue bid.

NO ONE VUL.   1♣ — 1♡ — Pass — ?

♠ A J 3
♡ Q 6 5
♢ K Q J 7 3
♣ J 8

2♣. You have game values, but 3NT could be your contract. The cue bid will help you to find out.

NO ONE VUL.   1♣ — 1♠ — Pass — ?

♠ K Q 10 7
♡ A K 8 7 6 5
♢ 4
♣ Q 3

You know you have a game, but a slam is possible opposite two black aces. Or opposite two aces and a singleton club. Or two aces and the king of clubs. I don't know how the auction will progress, but 2♣ is the way to start.

CASE 2

PARTNER OVERCALLS AT THE ONE LEVEL. RHO BIDS ONE OF A NEW SUIT.

This situation is treated in exactly the same way as if RHO had passed. You have slightly more information to go on, but the inferences are the same.

CASE 3

PARTNER OVERCALLS AT THE ONE LEVEL. RHO BIDS 1NT.

THE SINGLE RAISE

This sequence demands caution. RHO has shown moderate values, and, of more importance, he has a trump trick. Or more. This means you should not raise on some minimum hands, especially those with three small trumps.

NO ONE VUL.   1♣ − 1♠ − 1NT − ?

♠ 8 7 2
♡ K 8 6 5 4
♢ K J 3
♣ 4 2

Best to pass. Minimum values and poor trumps. While it is true that 2♠ could work out, it is tempting fate. When you overcall aggressively, you give opponents problems. Here, RHO seems to have solved the problem, so there is no point in exerting further pressure. After RHO bids 1NT, you should raise when you *expect* to have a play for the contract, not when you *hope* to have a play for it. When RHO bids 1NT, a raise by you will be doubled whenever you are too high. It is one of the easiest auctions for opponents to judge.

NO ONE VUL.   1♢ − 1♡ − 1NT − ?

♠ 8 7
♡ 10 6 5 4
♢ A 8 7
♣ Q 6 5 4

2♡. You have a moderate playing hand with a fourth trump. Partner knows the trump honours are offside and will take that into consideration.

VUL. VS. NOT.   1♡ – 1♠ – 1NT – ?

♠ K J 8 7   2♠. Good trumps plus good distribution
♡ 8   means anything goes. RHO probably has
◊ 7 6 4 2   something like Q 10 3 in spades and will be
♣ 9 6 3 2   disappointed to take no trump tricks.

NOT VUL.
VS. VUL.   1♣ – 1♠ – 1NT – ?

♠ Q 8 6 5 4   In spite of your good hand a raise to 2♠ is
♡ K Q 3   sufficient. Game prospects are dim. One alter-
◊ A 7 6   native is to double, but a general rule in bridge
♣ 10 6   is to take the path of least resistance. You
                     have a safe part-score and a speculative double.
Perhaps some people wouldn't overcall with your partner's
hand. If so, you will be in the auction on hands where others
do not compete. Game in this sequence will need a lot of
distribution and your pattern is somewhat pedestrian.

NO ONE VUL.   1♣ – 1♠ – 1NT – ?

♠ 9 6 3   A raise with three small trumps should be
♡ A K 4 3 2   avoided on this auction. The rest of this hand,
◊ 7 6 5 3   though, is so good that you can raise to 2♠.
♣ 4   Everything is working overtime. Even the
                     opening lead will be in your favour. RHO
will lead a club which is exactly what you would have had him
do had the choice been yours.

THE DOUBLE RAISE VS. THE CUE BID

1♣–1♠–1NT: Game is almost out of the question except as
the result of exceptional distribution. On balanced hands,
content yourself with a raise or a double. I can't remember
making a cue bid on this auction. I can, however, remember
making a jump raise. This calls for distribution with good
trumps.

NO ONE VUL.   1♣ — 1♡ — 1NT — ?

♠ A 8 7 6 5 4
♡ K J 4 3
◇ 3
♣ 4 2

3♡ is just about right. Good trumps, good shape, useful high cards.

BOTH VUL.   1♣ — 1♠ — 1NT — ?

♠ Q 10 6 5 4
♡ A J 4
◇ 7
♣ 8 5 4 3

3♠ again. Even four could be right. This is the sort of hand where four spades could depend on a spade finesse for the king. But the auction suggests that it won't work.

VUL. VS. NOT.   1♡ — 1♠ — 1NT — ?

♠ K J 8 7
♡ A 4 2
◇ K J 8 7
♣ Q 3

This hand does not exist. Someone is spoofing, probably LHO. No way everyone can have his bid. I would double 1NT and jump to game if someone runs, as will probably happen. Who knows, though, maybe the double will be left in. Note that there is no need to cue bid.

GAME FORCES

After 1♣—1♠—1NT, any leap to game by you will depend entirely on shape and trumps. Your hand will be along the lines of:

♠ 8 6 5 4 2   ♠ Q 10 6 5
♡ A 10 6 5 4 3   ♡ A J 8 6 5 4
◇ 7   ◇ —
♣ 6   ♣ 6 5 4

♠ K J 6 5 4   ♠ J 7 5 4
♡ K 2   ♡ 3
◇ 8 6 5 4 3 2   ◇ A 10 6 5 4 3 2
♣ —   ♣ 9

A very unlikely auction.

CASE 4

PARTNER OVERCALLS AT THE ONE LEVEL. RHO RAISES.

This is treated the same as if RHO had passed. Raises are made freely as this is a safe auction. When fits exist for both sides, there are a lot of tricks lying around. You have to fight for your share.

Jump raises remain distributional in nature and the cue bid is still a good flattish hand or one with only three trumps.

NO ONE VUL.   1♡ − 1♠ − 2♡ − ?

♠ 8 6 2   2♠. If RHO had bid 1NT, it would be dan-
♡ 8 6 2   gerous. But after a raise, it is OK. These
◇ K Q J 7 3   auctions have a way of going on. The danger
♣ J 2   in bidding is that partner will lead a spade or
                 will bid again and go down. Both are possible,
but not very likely. On the other hand, selling out to 2♡ is
pusilanimous.

VUL. VS. NOT.   1♣ − 1♡ − 2♣ − ?

♠ J 6 5 4 3 2   2♡. Every time. Good trumps plus a singleton.
♡ K 8 7
◇ 2
♣ 7 6 5

BOTH VUL.   1◇ − 1♠ − 2◇ − ?

♠ Q J 3   Had RHO passed, you might have tried 2◇
♡ K J 7 6 5   as an invitational cue bid. After 2◇ by RHO,
◇ Q 2   you might just bid 2♠. The reason is that the
♣ K 9 7   cue bid would force you a trick higher and
                 you need something more to make up for the
                 higher level.

A balanced hand suggests defence. This means that opponents can't make much. You do not want to go down in 3♠ when they can do no better than make only one or two diamonds.

THE JUMP RAISE VS. THE CUE BID

NO ONE VUL.   1♡ – 1♠ – 2♡ – ?

♠ K 7 6 5   3♠. Four trumps, shape, and useful values.
♡ 8 6 4 2
◇ A J 3 2
♣ 7

NO ONE VUL.   1♡ – 1♠ – 2♡ – ?

♠ K J 8 7 2   3♠. But less clearcut than the previous hand.
♡ 4 2   The extra trump is not particularly valuable.
◇ A 10 8 7
♣ 4 2

BOTH VUL.   1◇ – 1♠ – 2◇ – ?

♠ K J 3   3◇. Very close to game. Partner will know
♡ A Q 10 7 5   pretty well what he's facing and can make an
◇ 8 6 3   accurate decision. If partner's overcalls are
♣ Q 2   very sound, I would go ahead to game. Oppo-
                site an aggressive partner, an invitation is best.

NO ONE VUL.   1♣ – 1♠ – 2♣ – ?

♠ Q J 8 7 2   3♣. Spades are good enough to jump. Even
♡ K Q 9   though the shape is poor, 3♠ should also be
◇ K 10 8   okay.
♣ J 2

NO ONE VUL.   1♣ – 1◇ – 2♣ – ?

♠ A Q 2   3♣. The best chance you have to get to 3NT.
♡ J 4 2   Note that RHO raised. This denies a major
◇ A J 6 5 4   suit, so you no longer fear that they will
♣ 10 3   find a new fit. On this hand, that doesn't
                matter, but when RHO raises clubs it can
be useful to know that he won't have hearts or spades.

GAME FORCES

When RHO raises and you have a game-going hand, you should usually go ahead and bid it. After a major suit overcall by partner you can jump to game. There is a very important concept here. When opponents raise each other, there is much less chance that partner has length in their suit. You will remember that when you overcall on a four card suit, you usually have length in the suit opened. It follows that if partner doesn't have length in opponents' suit, his overcall will be on a five card suit. Therefore, you can raise to game on suitable hands holding only three trumps.

CASE 5

PARTNER OVERCALLS AT THE ONE LEVEL. RHO BIDS A NEW SUIT AT THE TWO OR THREE LEVEL.

This is easy in one sense and difficult in others. The easy part is that your side will never have game-going values, so games bid and made will be outstanding fits which will tend to be obvious. This means there will never be a hand worth a cue bid. Your decisions will all be whether or not to raise, and how far to raise. I suggest you do this. Inasmuch as you will never have a good hand, give up the invitational meaning of a jump and play it as pre-emptive. It will be similar to the situation where RHO bid 1NT over partner's overcall.

NO ONE VUL.   1♣ – 1♠ – 2♡ – ?

♠ K 8 7 6   Bid 2♠. When this auction occurs, it is not
♡ 4 2   your hand. Therefore you should not raise
◇ J 7 6 3   on hands with scattered points and no playing
♣ 9 6 3   tricks. Your bid will never end the auction.
                        The only time your raise can contribute to
your side's future is when partner can bid again or when it helps
him to get off to a good lead.

NO ONE VUL.   1♡ − 1♠ − 2♣ − ?

♠ 8 7 6 2   Pass. It's right in theory and probably in
♡ K J 3   practice. You have no tangible assets and a lot
♢ Q J 3   of minuses.
♣ Q 4 2

NOT VUL.
VS. VUL.   1♡ − 1♠ − 2♢ − ?

♠ K 8 7 6   A case can be made for two, three, or four
♡ 8 7 6 2   spades. I would opt for three. It cramps
♢ 9 4 3 2   their exchange of information and doesn't
♣ 9   overdo things. Your four hearts suggest that
                 they may not have a game there and your
spades suggest that they can't make 3NT. Maybe they can make
5♣, but if not, 4♠ could be expensive. It is a good idea to consider their available games when deciding how high to jump.

NOT VUL.
VS. VUL.   1♡ − 1♠ − 2♣ − ?

♠ 8 7 6 5   2♠. What you have will be worthwhile if
♡ 4 2   partner bids again. If he leads a spade, you
♢ A J 7 5   may not be happy, but you can't have every-
♣ 9 7 6   thing.

BOTH VUL.   1♢ − 1♠ − 2♣ − ?

♠ K Q 3   2♠. These are good trumps.
♡ 9 7 6 5 4
♢ 8 7 6
♣ 4 2

NO ONE VUL.   1♡ − 1♠ − 2♢ − ?

♠ Q 8 6 5 4   3♠. Partner will save if it's right.
♡ 8 2
♢ 8 4 2
♣ J 5 4

NOT VUL.
VS. VUL.   1◇ – 1♠ – 3♣ – ?

♠ K 6 5 4   Bid 4♠. The stronger the opponents' bidding,
♡ 8   the less you are likely to have. In this situa-
◇ 9 7 6 3 2   tion, your jumps are weak. This is a standard
♣ 8 6 5   defensive bidding concept which we have
                     already seen and will meet again.

NO ONE VUL.   1♡ – 1♠ – 2♣ – ?

♠ 8 7 6 5 4   Bid 3♠. 4♠ is acceptable but slightly danger-
♡ 9 7 5   ous. The important point is the meaning of
◇ K 10 5 4   of the jump.
♣ 3

NOT VUL.
VS. VUL.   1♡ – 1♠ – 3◇ – ?

♠ K 6 5   3♠. The vulnerability is in your favour and
♡ 4 3 2   you want to be sure partner leads a spade.
◇ 9 7 6 5
♣ 8 6 2

CASE 6

PARTNER OVERCALLS AT THE ONE LEVEL.
RHO MAKES A NEGATIVE DOUBLE.

This situation is different from others because RHO has an
undefined hand. He probably has four cards in the unbid major
or majors, but it is not a certainty. His values, too, are not clear.
The negative double is a worthwhile convention, but you can
take advantage of its imperfections.

There are several things you can try after the negative double,
but in the absence of detailed discussion, I would suggest something along these lines.

THE RAISE

NO ONE VUL.   1♣ — 1♠ — Dbl. — ?

♠ K 8 7
♡ 8 7 4
◇ K 6 5 4
♣ 8 4 2

2♠. The raise is straightforward. The only concession you should make is to skip raising on three small with bad hands. In this sequence LHO will often be declarer. Also, this auction could be dangerous and calls for caution on doubtful holdings.

NO ONE VUL.   1♣ — 1♡ — Dbl. — ?

♠ K 8 6 5 4
♡ J 6 2
◇ Q 2
♣ Q 6 2

Make your normal raise. If you have anything to say, say it.

VUL. VS. NOT.   1◇ — 1♠ — Dbl. — ?

♠ K J 2
♡ K 10 7 5 4
◇ 8 2
♣ Q 6 3

About as much as you can have for a raise.

THE REDOUBLE

Once in a while you will hold a good hand with interest in penalising opponents. A redouble would show values but clearly denies a fit.

NO ONE VUL.   1♣ — 1♠ — Dbl. — ?

♠ 4 2
♡ K Q 8 7
◇ A J 6
♣ J 10 7 5

This would be a minimum redouble. With anything less you would try 1NT or pass. Note that there is no danger of 1♠ redoubled being the final contract. Partner doesn't have to pass if he doesn't like it. You've denied trump support, promising outside strength. If he's nervous he can run to 1NT. I've never seen this happen, but I suppose there could be a first time.

THE JUMP RAISE

Opponents have established a shaky rapport, but you can do something to impede their further exchanges. Playing a jump as pre-emptive, just as if RHO had bid a 2/1, will create problems for them.

NOT VUL.
VS. VUL.   1♣ – 1♠ – Dbl. – ?

♠ K 8 7 5   A lot to be said for 3♠. You have good
♡ 3 2   trumps and shape, so you should be fairly
◇ J 6 5 4 2   safe.
♣ 9 7

THE CUE BID

We come to good hands with support for partner. You have the cue bid. In fact you can add an extra twist here by using two cue bids. On balanced hands you can make a simple cue bid and on distributional hands you can use a jump cue bid.

You won't lose much if you decide to use the simple cue bid to show all your supporting hands, but the jump cue bid is available, and there is a useful distinction to be made.

NO ONE VUL.   1♣ – 1♠ – Dbl. – ?

♠ K J 7   2♣. Too good for a raise. You intend, how-
♡ Q 2   ever, to stop in 2♠ if partner expresses no
◇ A Q 10 6   interest.
♣ 9 7 4 2

BOTH VUL.   1♣ – 1♡ – Dbl. – ?

♠ Q 2   2♣. If partner shows no interest you can prod
♡ A Q 8 7   him again by carrying on to 3♡. It would be
◇ K Q 7 6   overambitious to go directly to game. Don't
♣ 9 5 4   punish partner for being aggressive.

BOTH VUL. 1♣ – 1♡ – Dbl. – ?

♠ A 6 5 4 2   2♣. You have good shape but you do want
♡ K J 2   another trump. Treat three card trump
◇ 3   holdings as balanced.
♣ Q J 3 2

VUL. VS. NOT. 1♣ – 1♠ – Dbl. – ?

♠ Q J 7 3   Bid 3♣. This shows a distributional raise. It is
♡ A Q 8 6 5   coincidence that you have a singleton club.
◇ Q 10 6   The bid shows values, four trumps, distribu-
♣ 3   tion, and is not a game force.

NO ONE VUL. 1♣ – 1♡ – Dbl. – ?

♠ 7 2   3♣. Invitational with good trump support
♡ K Q 8 6 5   and some shape.
◇ A Q 6 2
♣ 3 2

NO ONE VUL. 1◇ – 1♠ – Dbl. – ?

♠ K Q 6 5   3◇. A good minimum for the jump cue bid.
♡ 2
◇ 8 7 6 5
♣ A 6 5 4

If you don't wish to make any distinction between balanced
and shaped hands, you would make the minimum cue bid each
time. It won't make all that difference. The one situation where
you may lose is when you make the minimum cue bid and
opener is able to compete. Perhaps the distributional jump cue
would have raised the level too high for him.

CASE 7

PARTNER OVERCALLS AT THE TWO LEVEL.
RHO PASSES.

When partner overcalls at the two level, you have less room to
explore. You can make a single raise or a game raise, whereas

after a one level overcall you can raise to the two, three, or game levels. Even with the inclusion of the cue bid, you still have fewer options. This means that you have to give something up. In practice, a structure like the following works well.

A raise is mildly encouraging and a cue bid is highly encouraging. But whereas after a one level overcall, the cue bid shows a good balanced raise, after a two-level overcall it shows a good raise with no distributional requirements. It can be balanced *or* distributional.

NO ONE VUL.   1♠ — 2♡ — Pass — ?

♠ Q 2   Just about right for three hearts. You discount
♡ A 4 3   the spade queen as being of dubious value.
♢ K J 4 2   You would raise without it.
♣ 8 7 5 4

NO ONE VUL.   1♠ — 2♡ — Pass — ?

♠ 9 7 6 5 4   Three hearts again. After a two level overcall,
♡ 10 7 6   three small is not as inadequate, however, as
♢ A Q 4 2   after a one level overcall.
♣ 7

VUL. VS. NOT.   1♠ — 2♢ — Pass — ?

♠ 7 2   Two spades. This is much too good for a
♡ A 4 3 2   simple raise.
♢ K Q 7
♣ Q 5 4 2

VUL. VS. NOT.   1♠ — 2♡ — Pass — ?

♠ 8 6 5 4   This is too good for a simple raise to three.
♡ A 6 5 2   I would either cue bid two spades or go
♢ Q 10 7 6   straight to game.
♣ 5

VUL. VS. NOT.   1◇ — 2♣ — Pass — ?

♠ Q 6 5 4 2
♡ 8 6
◇ A 7 3
♣ K 5 4

Three clubs. It would clearly be an error to introduce spades.

NO ONE VUL.   1◇ — 2♣ — Pass — ?

♠ 8
♡ A 8 4 2
◇ 10 6 5 4
♣ K 10 7 3

Three clubs. You would like to bid a little more. But if you cue bid, and partner veers into notrumps, your hand will be a disappointment. If, after three clubs, partner tries three notrumps, you can be content.

BOTH VUL.   1♠ — 2♡ — Pass — ?

♠ A 3
♡ J 7 5
◇ A 8 6 5 4 2
♣ 7 6

This is a good hand. Anything less than a direct four hearts would be poor. Three diamonds runs the risk of a pass from partner, and three diamonds down one, instead of four hearts making, would be the likely result.

You have the values for a cue bid, but there is no reason to clutter up the auction when you know what the final contract should be.

CASE 8

PARTNER OVERCALLS AT THE TWO LEVEL. RHO RAISES.

This is easy, sort of. The decisions themselves aren't easy, but that raise by RHO has taken away so much room that you don't have many options. Look at a typical auction.

1♠ — 2♡ — 2♠ — ?

You can raise to three or four hearts. You can also cue bid, but if you do, you can't stop short of game, so the net result is the same. One treatment is for a double to show some sort of raise. But then you forego the *Responsive Double*, which is far more important. That, however, deserves a chapter on its own.

In practice, when partner overcalls and RHO competes, the cue bid will be a rarity. You won't be strong enough. If you are, the responsive double will work better.

NO ONE VUL.   1♠ − 2♡ − 2♠ − ?

♠ J 4 2
♡ K 4 2
◇ Q 10 3 2
♣ 7 6 5

When you have the ace or king of partner's suit plus adequate length, you should raise on any excuse. This hand just makes it. If RHO had passed, you would not have raised.

NOT VUL.
VS. VUL.   1♠ − 2♡ − 2♠ − ?

♠ Q 10 7 6
♡ 8 6 4
◇ K 5 4
♣ Q 10 7

You could try three hearts, but at matchpoints only. You're hoping that opponents will continue to three spades. In fact, at matchpoints, three hearts will get you three spades about seventy percent of the time. And as often as not, opponents will be wrong.

But you can't afford to get too carried away with bids like these. Even though LHO will make many bad decisions, there are serious dangers.

1. You may be doubled. LHO is allowed to be right some of the time.

2. You may go down undoubled, but find that they could make nothing.

3. Your partner may take you seriously and bid again himself. Even when you succeed in getting opponents one trick higher, partner may give it back. Note that partner may be bidding quite reasonably. It's just that your values were poorly placed.

Had RHO passed, you would have had no excuse for bidding. It is curious that in competitive auctions, a free bid is the reverse of the usual concept. On hands where you would normally pass, you take action only when RHO takes action. He passes, you pass. He raises, you raise.

NO ONE VUL.   1♠ − 2♡ − 2♠ − ?

♠ 8 7 6   Had RHO passed, you would have cue bid two
♡ K J 7   spades intending to show a strong raise. But
◇ A Q 6 2   when RHO raised, your options were reduced
♣ 7 3 2   to choosing between three and four hearts.
                 In situations like this it is good practice and
good tactics to take the bull by the horns and leap to game. This
is a bit of an overbid, but three hearts would be more of an
underbid. Note that when you step out a little, your values are
proven. You have nothing wasted in spades. You have good
trumps. Your diamonds are potentially useful. Even when four
hearts doesn't make, opponents may fail to double, or they
may even save. This will happen often enough, especially if you
bid a cheery confident four hearts.

VUL. VS. NOT.   1◇ − 2♣ − 2◇ − ?

♠ A Q 3   Three diamonds. When partner overcalls in
♡ 9 7 3 2   a minor suit and RHO raises, if you happen to
◇ 8 7 3   have game strength, you may wish to explore
♣ A Q 2   three notrumps as well as five of a minor.
                 In any case, your cue bid will show some sort
of fit except when you have a game force with a suit of your
own.

NO ONE VUL.   1♡ − 2◇ − 2♡ − ?

♠ A 8 7   Again, the cue bid. Either three notrumps, or
♡ 4 2   else four or five diamonds could be right.
◇ Q 10 7   The cue bid is the only action that both
♣ A J 6 4 2   expresses the strength of the hand and leaves
                 all options open. Raising to only three dia-
monds would probably end the auction. You have at least an
ace more than that.

CASE 9

PARTNER OVERCALLS AT THE TWO LEVEL. RHO BIDS A NEW SUIT.

As usual, when RHO has the values to bid a new suit, the hand does not belong to your side. The only reason for raising is to get partner off to a good lead or to suggest a save. This means good trumps (an honour) or distribution. As when partner overcalled at the one level and RHO bid a new suit at the two level, you can play a jump as pre-emptive.

NO ONE VUL.   1♠ – 2♣ – 2♡ – ?

♠ 8 6 5 4   Three clubs. When opponents show strength, a
♡ 8 6 2   raise by you is not particularly encouraging. It
◇ Q 5 4   is just a little squeak. A squeak with a purpose,
♣ K J 7   but a squeak nonetheless.

NOT VUL.
VS. VUL.   1♠ – 2◇ – 2♡ – ?

♠ 7 2   You could bid four diamonds if it were agreed
♡ J 8 4 2   as pre-emptive. Note the good things that can
◇ K Q 6 2   come of it.
♣ 9 7 3   1. LHO can't rebid three hearts or three
                 spades.

2. If he chooses to bid four hearts or four spades, it will be ambiguous. Is he strong making a slight underbid? Or has he been pushed into an overbid?

You can be sure that opponents will misjudge their values frequently on such auctions. Sometimes they will misjudge their fits as well. LHO might have six spades and three hearts and decide to raise hearts. Maybe spades was the right spot. When you bid four diamonds, you create guessing games. When opponents do the right thing, you get about average. When they do the wrong thing, you get a top. Not bad odds.

At the actual vulnerability, you could even try five diamonds. This strikes me as excessive but there is much to be said for it. Note that this is the only vulnerability where three down will still be worthwhile. And then, only if they have a game.

Bidding four diamonds has the advantage of letting partner contribute something to the final decision. He will know more about your hand than you know about his.

| NO ONE VUL. | 1♠ — 2♣ — 2◇ — ? |

♠ 8 2
♡ J 7 6 5 4 2
◇ 3
♣ Q J 7 2

A good four club bid. If opponents were vulnerable, a jump to five would be reasonable.

| VUL. VS. NOT. | 1♠ — 2◇ — 3♣ — ? |

♠ 3
♡ K 6 5 4 2
◇ K 7 5 3 2
♣ 8 3

This vulnerability should deter you from anything rash. Five diamonds would be right any other time. Vul. vs. not however dictates second thoughts. Partner will realise that you have a good playing hand and will bid accordingly.

When partner overcalls at the one and two level and RHO bids a new suit at the two level or higher, it is very important to accept that the hand belongs to opponents. It follows that there won't be room for constructive bidding by your side. But you can still participate in some of the auctions. By changing the meaning of various bids from strong or invitational to preemptive you can harass opponents on some of your distributional hands when you have a good suit or a good fit. All that is required is an awareness of what various auctions mean.

When opponents have good hands, you haven't, so you change the definition of your bids accordingly. This is an extremely important concept. Successes won't be frequent, but they will be big ones. But only if you make the required systemic adjustments.

CASE 10

PARTNER OVERCALLS AT THE TWO LEVEL. RHO BIDS 2NT.

Don't bother. It's so dangerous that if you're wondering whether you should bid, you clearly shouldn't. Only when you are sure that you have a bid is it likely to be right. The one thing that is clear is that you will never be bidding from strength. You will be bidding on shape and fits. Nothing you bid can be encouraging.

NO ONE VUL.   1♠ − 2♡ − 2NT − ?

♠ 8 6 5 4 2   Three hearts. Not because you expect to make
♡ J 6 5 4   it, but because it might cause LHO slight
◇ 2   embarrassment. LHO can't rebid 3♣ or 3◇.
♣ K 9 7

NOT VUL.
VS. VUL.   1♠ − 2♣ − 2NT − ?

♠ 8 6 5 2   Pass. Three clubs takes away no room from
♡ 8 6 4 2   LHO and it warns opponents. RHO with
◇ 3   Q 8 2 of clubs thought that he had a stopper.
♣ K 6 4 3   Why disillusion him?

NO ONE VUL.   1♠ − 2◇ − 2NT − ?

♠ Q 8 2   Pass. Opponents don't have game values. Two
♡ 4 2   notrumps is likely to end the auction. Three
◇ 3   clubs would offer them 300 or more on a
♣ K Q 10 9 7 6 5   hand on which you might score a plus.

CASE 11

PARTNER OVERCALLS AT THE TWO LEVEL. RHO MAKES A NEGATIVE DOUBLE.

This is treated much as a one level overcall and negative double. With a minimum raise, you raise. With a maximum raise, you cue bid. On good hands with no fit, redouble. But be sure that your cards will be useful if your redouble is passed out. Jumps are pre-emptive.

NO ONE VUL.   1♠ — 2◇ — Dbl. — ?

♠ 8 6   Three diamonds. So important to speak when
♡ K 8 6 2   you have something to say. And when that
◇ K J 4   something is a raise of partner's overcall . . .
♣ 10 7 6 5   passing with the intention of bidding later just
                  isn't bridge. Why let opponents have an un-
obstructed discussion? Perhaps partner will be able to compete further after your help. It's bad to hide your head in the sand. You get your head kicked and you don't even see it coming.

NOT VUL.
VS. VUL.   1♡ — 2♣ — Dbl. — ?

♠ A 8 7 6   Cue bid two hearts. In spite of RHO's double,
♡ 8 6 5   game is not out of the question. Probably
◇ K 5 4   not in clubs, but perhaps in three notrumps.
♣ K J 7

NO ONE VUL.   1♠ — 2♣ — Dbl. — ?

♠ 8 5 4 2   A jump to four clubs is reasonable. Partner
♡ 10 6 3   should visualise this type of holding. If op-
◇ 9   ponents were vulnerable, you could consider
♣ K 10 6 5 4   jumping to five clubs.

BOTH VUL.   1♠ — 2♡ — Dbl. — ?

♠ A 8 7 6 5   Jump to four hearts. In this one specific
♡ K J 8   sequence, your jump is not necessarily pre-
◇ Q J 4 2   emptive, although it could be. You intend to
♣ 3   bid four hearts anyway, leaving opponents
                  no room for discussion.

NO ONE VUL.   1♠ — 2♡ — Dbl. — ?

♠ A 8 6 2   Redouble. Hope partner can do something
♡ 4 2   expecting me to have a good hand but with no
◇ K J 8 7   fit.
♣ Q 5 4

NO ONE VUL.   1♠ — 2◇ — Dbl. — ?

♠ A J 8 7 3   Pass. The danger in redoubling is that it might
♡ K J 5 4   be passed out. When you pass, LHO will
◇ —   always bid and you can start doubling. If you
♣ J 10 7 3   redouble, partner will expect a balanced hand
                   of some sort.

9

NO TRUMP RESPONSES
TO AN OVERCALL

These are fairly easy. Hands on which it is right to respond in notrumps are usually self-evident. They call for a rational point range with appropriate stoppers or near stoppers. The difficult hands are those on which you have values for something, but nothing seems clearcut.

NO ONE VUL.   1♣ − 1♡ − Pass − ?

♠ K J 7 2
♡ 8 3
♢ Q 10 8 2
♣ Q J 3

A clearcut one notrump. Your range is about seven to eleven so this hand is average. As your values approach the top of your range, your stopper may become suspect. With a minimum, however, you must have a full-blooded stopper.

NO ONE VUL.   1♡ − 1♠ − Pass − ?

♠ J 2
♡ 9 7 5
♢ K Q 5 4
♣ A 10 6 3

One notrump. Without a stopper, you should have at least three cards in the suit.

VUL. VS. NOT.   1♢ − 1♡ − Pass − ?

♠ K Q 6 2
♡ 8 3
♢ Q 5 4
♣ 8 6 5 4

With a minimum, no spots, a marginal stopper, and vulnerable besides, I would pass. One notrump would not be terrible, but isn't very good either.

NO ONE VUL.   1♣ – 1♡ – 1♠ – ?

♠ Q 10 8 7
♡ 8 3
♢ K Q 10 7
♣ Q 5 4

One notrump. When RHO bids a suit, you should not bid on seven or eight point hands. Also, while your stopper in opener's suit may be questionable, your stopper in RHO's suit must be real.

NO ONE VUL.

You

Pass – 1♣ – Pass – 1♡ –
1♠ – Pass – ?

♠ 8
♡ Q 10 8 3
♢ K Q 3 2
♣ K Q J 7

Normally, you would jump to two notrumps showing an invitational hand of twelve to fourteen points. Here though partner is a passed hand. This plus your singleton spade suggests a conservative one notrump. Perhaps one of your opponents will try again and your underbid will reap a reward. If you had a second spade, you could jump to two notrumps in spite of partner's original pass.

NO ONE VUL.   1♣ – 1♡ – 2♣ – ?

♠ K 8 7
♡ Q 2
♢ J 9 6 5
♣ A 10 9 3

You won't have a two notrumps bid very often if RHO raises. It requires ten to twelve points with a sure stopper. You also need a mild fit for partner or you would have no source of tricks. Many hands which look like two notrump bids will be better described by bidding another suit or by the responsive double.

BOTH VUL.   1♡ – 1♠ – 2♣ – ?

There is no hand worth notrumps on this auction. Only when you are so good that you *know* someone has psyched could you bid notrumps. On this auction you will have at most six points about 98% of the time.

NO ONE VUL.   1♠ — 2♣ — 2♡ — ?

As above. If you miss the one hand in 100 where you should have bid two notrumps, you will save a fortune on the other 99.

NO ONE VUL.   1♠ — 2♣ — Pass — ?

♠ Q 10 7
♡ Q 8 2
◇ A J 9 7 5
♣ Q 3

Two notrumps. This sequence does guarantee a stopper. It shows ten to twelve points allowing for good spots and some fit for partner's suit.

NO ONE VUL.   1♠ — 2♡ — Pass — ?

♠ Q 8 6 5 2
♡ —
◇ K Q 8 2
♣ K Q J 2

Even with this full thirteen, two notrumps is sufficient. Your spade spots are weak and you have no quick tricks to cash. Your heart void is so grave a liability that a pass could be best.

BOTH VUL.   1♠ — 2♣ — 2♠ — ?

♠ J 10 8 3
♡ A 8 6 5
◇ A 4 2
♣ Q 9

Three notrumps. This is the perfect hand. A fit for partner's suit. A stopper. And sure tricks on the side. Two notrumps would be too conservative.

10

THE RESPONSIVE DOUBLE

No area of bidding is free of conventions. One of these, the negative double, is used only by the side that opens the bidding. Nothing has been said about using it, only about defending against it.

Other conventions are used by the defending side and we'll be looking at them in more depth. For the most part, however, the discussion will be on how to use these conventions in general rather than on how to use any one in particular. One convention stands out, and I will go much further in describing it than any other. If you get the impression that I am recommending it, I am. It is the responsive double.

The responsive double takes many forms, but two of them account for over ninety percent of its usage.

1. LHO opens Partner overcalls RHO raises You double
2. LHO opens Partner doubles RHO raises You double

THE RESPONSIVE DOUBLE AFTER PARTNER OVERCALLS

Usually the auction looks like this.

$$1\clubsuit - 1\spadesuit - 2\clubsuit - \text{Dbl.}$$
$$1\diamondsuit - 1\heartsuit - 3\diamondsuit - \text{Dbl.}$$
$$1\heartsuit - 2\clubsuit - 2\heartsuit - \text{Dbl.}$$
$$1\heartsuit - 2\clubsuit - 3\heartsuit - \text{Dbl.}$$
$$1\diamondsuit - 1\heartsuit - 4\diamondsuit - \text{Dbl.}$$

Note that partner's overcall is not a jump overcall. After a jump overcall, your double is for business. Note also that RHO's bid is a raise. The following auctions are not responsive:

1♣—2♠—3♣—Dbl.   Partner's bid was a jump.
1♣—1♠—2◇—Dbl.   RHO did not raise.

It would not be unreasonable to include these auctions as responsive as well if opponents are using the weak two bid:

$$2♡^* - 2♠ - 3♡ - \text{Dbl.}$$
$$2♠^* - 3♣ - 3♠ - \text{Dbl.}$$
$$2◇^* - 2♡ - 3◇ - \text{Dbl.}$$

*Six card suit, 6-12 HCP.

What is the responsive double?

Basically, the responsive double is a takeout double which announces sufficient strength to enter the auction and length in the unbid suits.

NO ONE VUL.   1♣ — 1♠ — 2♣ — ?

♠ 8
♡ K J 8 7 2
◇ A 10 5 4 2
♣ 8 3

This is the usual example quoted to show the responsive double. You have values to compete, but no idea which suit is best. The double shows interest in both hearts and diamonds. Should partner persist with spades, he will probably have six or seven of them. If he has only five spades, he should have at least three in one of the red suits. Only if he is 5—2—2—4 will you be in trouble. A small price to pay for the ability to compete successfully the rest of the time.

How important is the responsive double?

Extremely! The important feature of the convention is that it is used when opponents have a fit. When they have one, you have one. If partner's overcall fails to locate a fit, then a fit will exist elsewhere. Some of the time you will have a suit to bid, but frequently you will have a hand similar to the example hand. You know a fit exists and you must find it.

How safe is the responsive double?

Very safe. As long as no one forgets the bid or loses all sense of proportion, you will have average to good results. Only when you suffer the occasional fix will you get a poor result. Everything is in your favour. Remember! When RHO raises, it creates the safest of all auctions.

What do you lose by using the responsive double?

You lose the penalty double. In theory. In practice, I believe that this is no loss at all. In fact, it is more likely to be a blessing. The one thing that you are not likely to have is a penalty double when partner overcalls and RHO raises. Even on those rare occasions where you do have a sound penalty double, partner sometimes removes the double, or more likely, declarer, warned by your double, plays the hand very well.

You don't have a sound trump holding often enough to want to use the double for penalties when there is a much better alternative.

Another gain incidentally is that you will not be tempted to make bad penalty doubles and conceding −670 or −180 when you should be scoring a plus. You will also find that the responsive double comes up ten to twenty times as often as a penalty double. Your side will play more hands, which is easier than defending them.

Does this mean that you can never double for penalties?

Not at all. In fact the contrary is true. Some of the time partner will pass your responsive double. When this happens, his trump holding will be well-located, over the bidder.

And, some of the time when you would make a penalty double, you pass instead and partner may be able to reopen with a takeout double. You can then pass for penalties.

How does the responsive double differ from other defensive bids such as the takeout double, the unusual notrump or Michaels cue bid?

The major difference is that you can expect some values from partner. He has overcalled, or doubled, guaranteeing a foundation to build on. When they open and you make a takeout double or an overcall, you are faced with the possibility that partner is broke. You haven't a clue as to his shape or values. But when partner has made a contribution and RHO raises, everything is different. The auction is now safe, you know that partner has some values, and that you have a fit. You are well placed to estimate your side's potential. Optimism is the password.

NO ONE VUL.   1◇ − 1♡ − 2◇ − ?

♠ K J 10 3
♡ 8
◇ 8 6 5
♣ A 5 4 3 2

Double. You do not promise five cards in each unbid suit. Even if partner bids a three card spade suit, as he should on some hands, support will be fine.

NO ONE VUL.   1♣ − 1◇ − 2♣ − ?

♣ Q 8 6 5 4
♡ K 10 6 5 2
◇ 3
♣ 6 5

Double. You have two five card suits and partner can bid either at the two level. Hands like these are made for the responsive double. What would you do without it? You'd guess between two spades, two hearts, and pass.

NO ONE VUL.   1♡ − 1♠ − 2♡ − ?

♠ 8
♡ 3 2
◇ Q 9 7 6 5
♣ K 8 6 5 4

At matchpoints only and non-vulnerable only, this is a minimum responsive double.

VUL. VS. NOT.   1◇ − 2♣ − 2◇ − ?

♠ A J 6 5
♡ Q J 10 3
◇ 8 6 5 4
♣ 3

In spite of only four card support for the unbid suits, your hand is otherwise good enough. Opposite a vulnerable overcall, you have plenty to compete.

NOT VUL.
VS. VUL.   1♣ − 1◇ − 2♣ − ?

♠ 8 6 5 4
♡ J 6 4 2
◇ 3
♣ A J 6 5

No need to go to extremes. Your values are adequate, but your suits aren't. There is a chance that if partner has a singleton club, he will re-open.

NO ONE VUL.   1♡ − 1♠ − 2♡ − ?

♠ 8 2
♡ 8 7 5
◇ K J 4
♣ K 10 6 5 4

Pass. You need at least four card support for each unbid suit. Remember that partner may innocently bid a three card suit expecting support. Don't disappoint him.

NO ONE VUL.   1♣ — 1♡ — 2♣ — ?

♠ Q 10 8 7   Two hearts. Don't overlook the raise. As a
♡ Q 5 4   general rule, a responsive double denies sup-
◇ A 7 6 5 2   port. The purpose of the bid is to find a fit.
♣ 2   When one exists, and a major suit fit at that,
                  there is no reason to look elsewhere. If you
double and partner bids two spades, you may be past your op-
timum spot, i.e., two hearts. Or, if you double and LHO bids
three clubs, passed back to you, you won't be happy bidding
three hearts and you'll be reluctant to pass.

VUL. VS. NOT.   1◇ — 1♡ — 2◇ — ?

♠ A Q 10 8 7   You expect a game contract, but there's no
♡ Q 2   clear route to it. Until now, the only forcing
◇ 3   bid available would have been the cue bid.
♣ A Q J 8 3   But here is a case where the responsive double
                  can help with strong hands as well. A double,
showing clubs and spades, will help you to get your suits into
the game and you can catch up on your strength later. Note the
difficulties if you cue bid. Now try to get your suits in and still
stop in three notrumps if that is the best spot. Not easy.

NO ONE VUL.   1♣ — 1♡ — 2♣ — ?

♠ A Q J 7 5   With such suit disparity and the expectation
♡ 3   of a fit, try two spades.
◇ 10 7 6 5
♣ J 5 4

NO ONE VUL.   1♣ — 1◇ — 2♣ — ?

♠ J 10 7 5   This is the matchpoint responsive double.
♡ J 9 5 4   Hardly ideal suits, but good enough to pass
◇ 3 2   muster. I've seen penalty doubles on hands
♣ A K 3   like these which is a good reason to take that
                  bid away. After the responsive double, a
typical result would be two hearts or two spades making 110 or
−50. Or else one of your opponents might go on to three clubs.
I wouldn't care to double that either, which shows you what I
think of a penalty double of two clubs. Don't hang partner.

BOTH VUL.   1♣ — 1♠ — 3♣ — ?

♠ Q 2
♡ J 10 8 7 5
◇ A Q 6 4 2
♣ 3

You are unlikely to hold this hand if three clubs is a game force. But many use three clubs as either weak or merely invitational. If so, you might well hold this hand and the responsive double is the perfect answer. The fact that partner must bid at the three level calls for a reasonable hand. Otherwise, it's the same as if RHO had bid two clubs.

VUL. VS. NOT.   1♡ — 1♠ — 3♡ — ?

♠ 3
♡ J
◇ A J 10 7 6
♣ K 10 9 6 5 4

Double is still responsive. Here you are vulnerable and partner must bid at the four level, so you need a useful hand. This one is not much over a minimum. Without the responsive double, anything would be a guess. Does partner have:

♠ A Q 6 5 4		♠ A Q 6 5 4
♡ 8 6 2		♡ 8 6 2
◇ K 8 5 4	or	◇ 3
♣ 3		♣ A 7 3 2

The first hand offers a play for five diamonds, and the second could make six clubs. Happy guessing.

NO ONE VUL.   1◇ — 1♠ — 4◇ — ?

♠ Q 3
♡ A 10 7 3
◇ 8 6 2
♣ K J 9 3

Double. When RHO makes a mighty leap like this, your double is no longer responsive by definition. But, inasmuch as you are unlikely to have good trumps, your double will tend to show something like this hand, i.e. balanced with scattered values and no particular interest in partner's suit.

When the auction begins with a weak two and RHO raises after an overcall, there is some merit in responsive doubles, but some snags, too. By and large, there's not much in it. Flip a coin and choose. If you do decide on responsive doubles, you should be aware of the level of the auction and will need values to match.

2♠–3♣–3♠ is much more difficult to contend with than 2♢–2♡–3♢ so you will require a better hand. Errors to avoid are doubling for takeout when you should be supporting partner, and forgetting that your double is for takeout. One last admonition. Don't let the fact that they are using weak two bids cause you to bid for the sake of bidding. RHO can easily have a good hand for his raise.

THE RESPONSIVE DOUBLE AFTER PARTNER'S TAKEOUT DOUBLE

These doubles are *always* responsive:

1♣ – Dbl. – 2♣ – Dbl.	1♣ – Dbl. – 3♣ – Dbl.
1♢ – Dbl. – 2♢ – Dbl.	1♢ – Dbl. – 3♢ – Dbl.
1♡ – Dbl. – 2♡ – Dbl.	1♡ – Dbl. – 3♡ – Dbl.
1♠ – Dbl. – 2♠ – Dbl.	1♠ – Dbl. – 3♠ – Dbl.

These doubles *should* be responsive:

2♢* – Dbl. – 3♢ – Dbl.   *Weak two bid.
2♡* – Dbl. – 3♡ – Dbl.
2♠* – Dbl. – 3♠ – Dbl.

These doubles *tend* to be responsive:

1♣ – Dbl. – 4♣ – Dbl.   *Weak two bid.
1♢ – Dbl. – 4♢ – Dbl.
2♢* – Dbl. – 4♢ – Dbl.
3♣ – Dbl. – 4♣ – Dbl.
3♢ – Dbl. – 4♢ – Dbl.

These doubles are primarily *penalty*:

1♡ – Dbl. – 4♡ – Dbl.   *Weak two bid.
1♠ – Dbl. – 4♠ – Dbl.
2♡* – Dbl. – 4♡ – Dbl.
2♠* – Dbl. – 4♠ – Dbl.
3♡ – Dbl. – 4♡ – Dbl.
3♠ – Dbl. – 4♠ – Dbl.

This can all be summarised fairly simply. After partner's takeout double, your double of any raise to the three level is responsive. If you wish, you can include the double of a raise to four clubs or diamonds as well. Initially, I would suggest limiting your range to the three level until you feel comfortable with the convention. Whatever you decide, you will run into the law of diminishing returns. Four level decisions aren't frequent, so the convention doesn't help much. In fact, you could limit the area to doubles of three diamonds or lower. But this would be trimming it unduly. For the purposes of examples, I will assume the responsive double is being used up to four diamonds.

To give you a cross section of opinions, there are some who play the responsive double as high as seven hearts. This is too much of a good thing. I do not recommend responsive doubles on all auctions, but I strongly recommend them on some auctions. Very few partnerships have tried and rejected them.

NO ONE VUL.   1♣ — Dbl. — 2♣ — ?

♠ J 8 7 5
♡ Q 8 6 5
♢ K 6 5 4
♣ 3

Double. This hand is clearly worth a competitive effort. But which suit should it be? Whatever partner bids will please.

NO ONE VUL.   1♣ — Dbl. — 2♣ — ?

♠ K 8 7 6
♡ A 10 5 4
♢ 4 2
♣ 7 5 3

Again double. You hope partner will bid hearts or spades. If he bids diamonds, you will bid hearts telling him you were interested in hearts and spades, not diamonds. If you had hearts only, you would bid them.

BOTH VUL.   1♣ — Dbl. — 2♣ — ?

♠ Q J 3 2
♡ 4 2
♢ K 10 6 5 3
♣ 8 6

Bid two diamonds or two spades. Whichever takes your fancy. Double would imply hearts and spades for sure, and maybe diamonds. Here you are missing a prime suit. Note that the responsive double helps a lot, but not every time.

VUL. VS. NOT.   1♣ — Dbl. — 2♣ — ?

♠ K Q 8 7   Double. The responsive double is not a weak
♡ K J 10 7   bid. Here you will raise either major to three.
♢ Q 5 4   Game is a strong possibility.
♣ 3 2

BOTH VUL.   1♣ — Dbl. — 2♣ — ?

♠ K 8 7 6 5   Probably better to bid two spades. You will
♡ Q J 5 4 2   follow with three hearts if the auction permits.
♢ 3
♣ 8 7

BOTH VUL.   1♣ — Dbl. — 2♣ — ?

♠ K Q 7   Double. Whatever partner bids will be fine.
♡ K J 9   You may end up in a four-three fit, but your
♢ 8 7 5 4   high cards will make that a better proposition
♣ 9 7 4   than defending against two clubs. If you had
                   better diamonds, you could bid them instead.

NO ONE VUL.   1♣ — Dbl. — 2♣ — ?

♠ Q 2   Two diamonds. Even with bad diamonds it is
♡ K Q 9   right to bid them. Your values are adequate
♢ J 6 5 4   but your doubleton spade precludes a respon-
♣ 8 6 4 2   sive double.

NO ONE VUL.   1♢ — Dbl. — 2♢ — ?

♠ Q 9 7   Double. Something to say but no suit stands
♡ K J 3   out. Typically, the responsive double can be
♢ 5 4 2   used when you just wish to compete at the
♣ Q 5 4 3   two level. You may have no interest in doing
                   more than pushing opponents. You know you
have some sort of fit and it only remains to find it. Without the
responsive double, any sort of action is dangerous. Consider how
you would feel about bidding two hearts, two spades, three
clubs, and passing. All four would make me feel nervous.

NO ONE VUL.   1◇ – Dbl. – 2◇ – ?

♠ K Q 8 7   Just two spades. A fair suit, but a minimum
♡ 8 6 5   hand.
◇ 4 3 2
♣ J 7 6

NO ONE VUL.   1♡ – Dbl. – 2♡ – ?

♠ K 8   When opponents bid and raise a major, that
◇ 8 7 5   leaves only one major for you. You would
◇ Q 5 4 2   bid it if you could. Therefore, a responsive
♣ A J 3 2   double should emphasise the minors. Partner
                 may well bid spades here and you could easily
have three. With a doubleton you will remove to three clubs.

BOTH VUL.   1♡ – Dbl. – 2♡ – ?

♠ Q 8 7 5   Two spades. It's nearly always right to bid the
♡ 3 2   missing major when opponents bid the other.
◇ Q 8 7
♣ A 10 5 4

NO ONE VUL.   1♡ – Dbl. – 2♡ – ?

♠ J 8 7   Double again, but pass if partner bids two
♡ 4 2   spades. While you could be better off in clubs
◇ K 6 5 2   or diamonds, you would be a trick higher.
♣ K J 8 3   Two spades will be playable if it is the final
                 contract. The responsive double makes non-
descript hands like this easy to deal with. I feel like saying it
after each example. With much difficulty I will try to restrain
myself and will ask you instead to imagine each time what you
would do without the responsive double. If you decided to pass
because you didn't know what to do, you would probably lose a
lot of part-score battles that you should be winning. If you
select a suit, you might select the wrong one.

NO ONE VUL.   1♡ — Dbl. — 2♡ — ?

♠ 4 2
♡ 8 6 5 3
◇ A J 10 7
♣ Q 10 2

Bid three diamonds. This does not promise five. Passing would be wrong at any game or vulnerability and double would be misleading.

BOTH VUL.   1♡ — Dbl. — 2♡ — ?

♠ J 3
♡ K J 7 5
◇ J 10 2
♣ A 10 6 3

Whatever you do, you can't double. This hand is typical of the bad doubles which you can no longer make. Either two notrumps or three clubs is acceptable.

NOT VUL.
VS. VUL.   1♡ — Dbl. — 2♡ — ?

♠ 3
♡ Q J 10 8 2
◇ A 5 4
♣ Q 10 5 4

This is the good penalty double you have to give up. If you pass, partner may be able to double again. If not, two hearts down two may be a good result anyway. And for the really greedy, you can try three clubs. You'd be surprised how often someone will compete. Now you *can* double three hearts!

NO ONE VUL.   1♡ — Dbl. — 2♡ — ?

♠ 8 6 5 4
♡ 2
◇ Q 10 6 5
♣ K 9 6 3

Double. Normally you don't have four spades for this bid. Partner, however, might not have four, in which case a minor suit would be best. If you double, anything partner bids will be fine and you will be assured of a four-four fit.

When you hold spades and elect to make a responsive double, you have very bad spades.

NO ONE VUL.   1♠ — Dbl. — 2♠ — ?

As usual, the spade suit is difficult to overcome. The responsive double will help you, but you need a little extra since partner will be bidding at the three level.

NO ONE VUL.   1♠ – Dbl. – 2♠ – ?

♠ 8 2
♡ K Q 7
◊ J 9 8 4
♣ K 10 5 2

A normal responsive double. Partner will tend to respond in a minor expecting you to bid hearts if you had them. Compare these two auctions:

1♡ – Dbl. – 2♡ – Dbl.
Pass – 2♠ – Pass – ?

Responder can bid three clubs or diamonds.

1♠ – Dbl. – 2♠ – Dbl.
Pass – 3♡ – Pass – ?

That three hearts got in the way. If responder doesn't care for hearts, it is hard to escape. This means that on the second auction, partner should be careful about bidding hearts.

You can in fact make a very fine distinction here if you wish to take the trouble. You can play that

1♠ – Dbl. – 2♠ – 3♡
shows a decent hand, and
1♠ – Dbl. – 2♠ – Dbl.
Pass – 3♣ – Pass – 3♡
shows a weak competitive hand.

This is quite reasonable and only lack of frequency is against it.

BOTH VUL.   1♠ – Dbl. – 2♠ – ?

♠ 4 2
♡ 4 2
◊ A K 8 2
♣ 8 6 5 4 2

Double. Either minor could be right. Let partner choose.

NO ONE VUL.   1♠ – Dbl. – 2♠ – ?

♠ 8 6 5 4
♡ K 2
◊ Q J 8
♣ J 10 8 5

You haven't much in high cards, but the few you have are excellent. Either minor partner bids will be okay. You'd like another diamond, but at least the three you have are good. Double.

NO ONE VUL. 1♠ — Dbl. — 2♠ — ?

♠ 8 6 5 2
♡ K 2
◇ 5 4 3
♣ A Q 6 3

With a good suit and values, three clubs is better than double.

NO ONE VUL. 1♠ — Dbl. — 2♠ — ?

♠ 4 2
♡ K J 8 2
◇ Q 3 2
♣ K 10 5 4

Three hearts. If you double, partner will respond in a minor. Your hand is quite good enough for three hearts if this shows a decent hand, but . . .

NO ONE VUL. 1♠ — Dbl. — 2♠ — ?

♠ 8 7 2
♡ Q 10 8 4
◇ K J 7
♣ 10 6 5

This is barely good enough to compete with three hearts. If you play the responsive double followed by three hearts to be a weakish hand, this qualifies (see above hand). If not, then this is a very minimum three heart call. Both your ten spots are working, however.

NOT VUL.
VS. VUL. 1♠ — Dbl. — 2♠ — ?

♠ 7 6 5 4
♡ 2
◇ Q 10 8 6
♣ K J 4 2

Your shape tells you that there is a very good fit somewhere. Double. This, by the way, is an alert in tournament bridge. On this particular sequence, partner should tell the opponents that your double is for the minors.

VUL. VS. VUL. 1♠ — Dbl. — 2♠ — ?

♠ 3
♡ 2
◇ A Q 8 7 6
♣ K 10 8 5 4 2

It is usually best to show your suits and subsequently catch up on your values. Double first and then make your slam try. Do not cue bid first. Partner might cling too long to the heart suit.

NO ONE VUL.   1♣ — Dbl. — 3♣ — ?

♠ J 8 7 4   A minimum responsive double. If you want to
♡ K Q 6 3   pass, that's conservative but reasonable. I
◇ 4 2   guess I'd bid at matchpoints and pass at IMP's.
♣ 9 7 3   The important point is the resolve to get into
                        the auction whenever possible. Note again
that without the double you would have to pass as either major
could be right or wrong. Only the double will get you to the
right suit all the time.

NO ONE VUL.   1♣ — Dbl. — 3♣ — ?

♠ 8 2   Three hearts. With two major suits unbid you
♡ Q 10 7 6   can't make a responsive double unless you are
◇ A J 4 3   prepared for both.
♣ 9 7 3

BOTH VUL.   1♣ — Dbl. — 3♣ — ?

♠ K J 9 7   Still double. There is no reason to prefer
♡ 8 6 5 4 2   hearts to spades.
◇ Q 5
♣ 4 2

NO ONE VUL.   1♣ — Dbl. — 3♣ — ?

♠ K 8 7   Sigh. Who knows? You're too good to pass
♡ A Q 3   and the diamonds are wretched. I'd double
◇ 10 7 5 4   and hope for the best. The main objection is
♣ J 6 3   that partner will bid a major and maybe we'd
                        miss a diamond fit. However, if partner has a
five card major or only three diamonds, the double could be
best.

NOT VUL.
VS. VUL.   1♣ — Dbl. — 3♣ — ?

♠ J 5 4   Three diamonds. When the case for a double
♡ K 5 4   isn't clear, look for an alternative. Here you
◇ J 10 8 7 4   have a good one.
♣ K 3

NO ONE VUL.   1♢ – Dbl. – 3♢ – ?

♠ J 7
♡ Q 4 2
♢ 4 3 2
♣ K 10 7 5 3

The only difference between this auction and the one before, is that if you wish to bid clubs, it must be at the four level. This hand is worth three clubs, but that's all.

NO ONE VUL.   1♡ – Dbl. – 3♡ – ?

♠ Q 5 4
♡ 3
♢ K J 7 5
♣ Q J 5 4 2

We are getting pretty high and getting there pretty fast. The solution depends on whether you use a responsive double and on your definitions. If, according to your treatment,

1♡ – Dbl. – 2♡ – Dbl.

denies spades, then this applies here, too. The only question is whether this hand is good enough to compete at the four level and the answer's easy. Yes. Double to show the minors. If partner bids three spades, he probably has four and is offering a four-three fit if you have three of them. With five spades, he would probably overcall rather than double.

BOTH VUL.   1♡ – Dbl. – 3♡ – ?

♠ K 10 7 5
♡ 3
♢ Q 5 4 2
♣ J 9 6 3

Three spades. Double would deny spades.

NO ONE VUL.   1♡ – Dbl. – 3♡ – ?

♠ 3
♡ 8 2
♢ K 10 8 7 6 4
♣ A 8 7 5

Four diamonds. With such disparity, give up clubs. Note that two small hearts is a very poor holding, suggesting two fast losers. You would much prefer to have more hearts or fewer.

VUL. VS. NOT.   1♡ – Dbl. – 3♡ – ?

♠ Q 2
♡ 8 3
♢ Q J 8
♣ Q 10 6 5 4 2

Very tough. If not vul., I'd bid four clubs. Perhaps at matchpoints it would be okay anyway, but those two small hearts are a big, big minus. I'd rather have a third heart and no jack of diamonds. Whatever you decide, this is not a double.

1♠ – Dbl. – 3♠ – ?

And the auction gets higher yet. Once again, a double should be for the minors but with the extra values needed to justify four level action.

NO ONE VUL.   1♠ – Dbl. – 3♠ – ?

♠ 8 4 2
♡ K J 7 3
♢ A J 3 2
♣ 7 6

Four hearts. Double would deny them so you can't do that. Your spade length is good and your strength is adequate.

NO ONE VUL.   1♠ – Dbl. – 3♠ – ?

♠ 8 6 2
♡ K J 6 5 2
♢ J 10 3 2
♣ 7

Four hearts. You can't distinguish between good hands with hearts and bad hands with hearts as you were able to do after 1♠–Dbl.– 2♠. The reason is that when you compete with three hearts, partner might easily continue to game, so it is useful for him to know if you have a little or a lot. But after 1♠–Dbl.–3♠–4♡, this problem no longer arises.

NOT VUL.
VS. VUL.   1♠ – Dbl. – 3♠ – ?

♠ K Q J 10 9
♡ 3 2
♢ A Q 2
♣ K 7 6

Well? The biggest penalty in history and you can't get it. Double is for take-out! What you do is bid three notrumps getting a decent but unspectacular result that way, or you can pass. If the hand is passed out, you will beat them a lot. Maybe someone has psyched. In any case, if they go down five or more, you will get a reasonable score. If you have a slam, you have been fixed.

NO ONE VUL.   1♣ — Dbl. — 4♣ — Dbl.
                     1◊ — Dbl. — 4◊ — Dbl.

These two auctions can both be treated as responsive or penalty. If you play the double as responsive, it should show a hand with both majors and ten points or so.

NO ONE VUL.   1♣ — Dbl. — 4♣ — ?

♠ K 10 7 5   Double. Partner will bid a major if he has one.
♡ J 7 6 4 2   If not, unlikely but possible, he'll bid four
◊ A 3 2   diamonds which you will correct to four
♣ 3   hearts.

NO ONE VUL.   1♣ — Dbl. — 4♣ — ?

♠ K J 7   Double again. You may end up in a four-
♡ A 5 4 2   three spade fit, but it should be adequate.
◊ Q J 7 3   Here, if partner bids four diamonds, you
♣ 9 7   should pass. Note that partner may decide
                    to pass your double for penalty if he has a
defensive hand. This would also lead to a good result.

NO ONE VUL.   1♣ — Dbl. — 4♣ — ?

♠ K 4 2   Four hearts. No reason to double. You know
♡ J 9 6 4 2   hearts are right and you have adequate values.
◊ K 10 7 6
♣ 3

BOTH VUL.   1◊ — Dbl. — 4◊ — ?

♠ K J 3   Double. Even though you have only three
♡ A 5 4   card support for both majors, there is a
◊ 7 3   chance that:
♣ Q 5 4 3 2   1. Your high cards will permit you to make
                    game.
    2. Partner has a five card major. He could be 4—5—1—3 for instance.

3. Partner may pass for penalty.

4. They may save.

NO ONE VUL.   1♢ − Dbl. − 4♢ − ?

♠ K 2
♡ A Q 4
♢ 8 5 3
♣ J 6 5 4 2

Awful. You can bid four hearts in fear and trepidation. You can bid five clubs and go down. You can double and wonder what to do when partner bids four spades. Or you can pass. And you have to do it in tempo or everyone calls for the cops and complains about your incredible huddle. No one said bridge was easy. And if you're wondering, I don't know what to do either.

When opponents start with a weak two or three bid and RHO raises after partner's double, you should act as you would after an opening one bid. You treat

2♡ − Dbl. − 3♡   as if it were   1♡ − Dbl. − 3♡
3♣ − Dbl. − 4♣   1♣ − Dbl. − 4♣
2♢ − Dbl. − 4♢   1♢ − Dbl. − 4♢

You can test this by reversing the process and looking back at the auctions which started

1♡ − Dbl. − 3♡   or
1♢ − Dbl. − 4♢

Pretend the auction was really

2♡ − Dbl. − 3♡   or
2♢ − Dbl. − 4♢

The same comments will apply almost exactly both times. The difference is that after 2♠−Dbl.−3♠−4♡, LHO will usually pass. After 1♠−Dbl.−3♠−4♡, LHO may well continue. But in any case, bidding requires certain values which will be similar.

Of course, you can decide to give all this up and play responsive doubles only after a one level opening. I think that would be a loss but not too serious.

However high you decide to play responsive doubles you should be consistent regardless of how the auction has gone. The bulk of your decisions will come at the two and three levels.

Something like

> 60% two level
> 30% three level
> 10% four level

Whatever you choose, make sure that partner knows it.

THE RESPONSIVE DOUBLE EXTENDED

If you wish, you can add refinements to the responsive double. These are popular:

1. When partner overcalls and RHO bids a new suit, you can raise partner on hands with an honour in his suit and double to show a raise with no honour.

$$1\clubsuit - 1\heartsuit - 1\spadesuit - ?$$

♠ 8 2
♡ K 10 7
♢ A 9 5 4
♣ 8 6 4 2

Two hearts. You have the heart king.

$$1\clubsuit - 1\heartsuit - 1\spadesuit - ?$$

♠ 8 2
♡ 10 6 5
♢ K J 5 4
♣ A 10 7 3

Double. A raise with no ace, king, or queen in hearts.

Note that this is not the same as when you double a raise. Here you are doubling a new suit. Note also that this treatment could apply to two level new suits as well.

$$1\heartsuit - 1\spadesuit - 2\clubsuit - \text{Dbl.} \quad \text{or}$$
$$1\spadesuit - 2\clubsuit - 2\heartsuit - \text{Dbl.}$$

Make sure that if you add this weapon to your armoury, you know when to use it. For instance, you do not want to play the convention after

$$1\spadesuit - 2\heartsuit - 3\diamondsuit - ?$$

I suggest you play it after new suits by RHO at the two level or lower.

2. The second variation of the responsive double is used on the same sequences as before. Now, when you double responder's new suit, you show a fair holding in the fourth suit and also a tolerance for partner's suit.

1♣ – 1♡ – 1♠ – ?

♠ 8 7 3 2   You could double to show a good diamond
♡ Q 2   suit and a tolerance for hearts.
♢ A Q 10 8 7
♣ J 2

1♢ – 1♠ – 2♡ – ?

♠ J 2   On this sequence, as we've seen, there is not
♡ 8 7 5   much chance that you'll have a club suit
♢ 10 9 5   worth the three level. When you double,
♣ A Q 10 4 2 you're involved in the auction and you better
             have some safe escape. Let's say you double
two hearts. If partner doesn't like clubs, you'll be stuck in two spades and I would not like that to be doubled. On this sequence you are offering partner a choice between two spades or three clubs. All this when you know partner has a minimum overcall. When the bidding has gone 1♣–1♢–1♠–Dbl., you offer partner the choice of two diamonds or *two* hearts. And there is no reason to believe that partner has the worst hand possible. He may well have something extra.

I favour the following treatment. Doubles at the one level as showing the fourth suit plus half a fit. Doubles at the two level as showing a raise with no honour and the raise itself as a good trump raise. And I would forget about three level doubles. The risk outweighs the gain. Personally, I think the one level double to show the fourth suit plus a semi-fit is reasonable. The rest is not worth the effort unless you are a serious and practiced partnership. I don't use any of these extensions unless pressed and I certainly don't miss them. But some excellent players swear by them. It's up to you.

Here are some hands highlighting the responsive double.

West			East
♠ K J 8 7 6			♠ 3 2
♡ K 10 5			♡ A J 8 2
◇ K 6			◇ Q J 4 3 2
♣ Q 4 2			♣ 9 7

South	West	North	East
1♣	1♠	2♣	Dbl.
Pass	2♡	Pass	Pass
Pass			

In no circumstances should either player find another bid if opponents compete further.

West			East
♠ K 2			♠ 8 7 3
♡ A Q J 7 6			♡ 4
◇ A 2			◇ K J 10 8 7
♣ 7 6 5 4			♣ A Q 9 3

South	West	North	East
1♠	2♡	2♠	Dbl.
Pass	3♣	Pass	Pass
Pass			

West			East
♠ A J 7 4			♠ Q 10 8 2
♡ K J 9 7			♡ A 8 5 4
◇ K 8 7			◇ Q J 6
♣ 4 2			♣ 10 6

South	West	North	East
1♣	Dbl.	2♣	Dbl.
Pass	2♡	Pass	Pass
Pass			

West			East
♠ K Q 8 7			♠ J 10 6 4
♡ A 7 6 5			♡ K Q 4 2
◇ Q J 3			◇ A 10 4
♣ K 3			♣ Q 6

South	West	North	East
1♣	Dbl.	2♣	Dbl.
Pass	2♡	Pass	3♡
Pass	4♡	Pass	Pass
Pass			

Note that a free bid by East would probably result in missing game as West should pass. A jump by East would risk missing the correct suit, and a cue bid would leave East with a guess after West had picked a suit.

West	East
♠ K 10 7	♠ Q 6 5
♡ 8 2	♡ Q 4
◇ A 6 5 4 3	◇ J 10 8 2
♣ A Q 2	♣ K 10 7 4

South	West	North	East
1♡	Dbl.	2♡	Dbl.
Pass	3◇	Pass	Pass
Pass			

West	East
♠ Q J 10 7	♠ A 2
♡ 3 2	♡ 10 5
◇ A J 8 5	◇ K Q 9 2
♣ A Q 9	♣ J 8 6 5 4

South	West	North	East
2♡	Dbl.	3♡	Dbl.
Pass	3♠	Pass	4♣
Pass	4◇	Pass	Pass
Pass			

West	East
♠ K Q 9 7	♠ J 8 4 2
♡ A Q 8 6	♡ K J 7 3
◇ 3	◇ 4 2
♣ A 10 6 5	♣ K Q 9

South	West	North	East
1◇	Dbl.	3◇	Dbl.
Pass	4◇	Pass	4♡
Pass	Pass	Pass	

West
♠ J 8 7 5
♡ A Q 4 2
◇ 3
♣ K J 7 2

East
♠ Q 9 6 4
♡ K 9 5 3
◇ 8 6 5
♣ A 3

South	West	North	East
1◇	Dbl.	3◇	Dbl.
Pass	3♡	Pass	Pass
Pass			

West
♠ 8 2
♡ K J 8 7
◇ Q 5 4
♣ A Q 10 7

East
♠ 9 3
♡ Q 2
◇ K 10 9 6 2
♣ K 9 6 4

South	West	North	East
1♠	Dbl.	2♠	Dbl.
Pass	3♣	Pass	Pass
Pass			

West
♠ Q 8 7 5
♡ K J 9
◇ K 2
♣ A 6 3 2

East
♠ K 10 3 2
♡ Q 10 5 3
◇ J 4
♣ J 9 7

South	West	North	East
1◇	Dbl.	2◇	Dbl.
Pass	2♠	3◇	Pass
Pass	Pass		

East should not make the error of raising to three spades. That would be too encouraging. If West has something extra, he can bid again. Note that the responsive double has helped you to find your best suit. There is no need to push further unless you have something to spare.

West			East
♠ A 10 8			♠ K 9 3
♡ K 10 4 2			♡ Q J 6
◇ A Q 3 2			◇ K 7 6 4
♣ 4 2			♣ 9 8 5

South	West	North	East
1♣	Dbl.	2♣	Dbl.
Pass	2♡	Pass	Pass
3♣	3◇	Pass	Pass
Pass			

This is a good sequence. East-West would have been content to play in two hearts but when pushed found a better fit. East has no reason to make any bid after his original double.

West			East
♠ Q 8 7 6			♠ K J 10 3
♡ A J 9 5			♡ K 7 6 4 3
◇ K Q 4			◇ 8 6 2
♣ 3 2			♣ 7

South	West	North	East
1♣	Dbl.	2♣	Dbl.
Pass	2♠	Pass	Pass
3♣	Pass	Pass	3♠
Pass	Pass	Pass	

This is an unusual situation where East may compete to the three level though he wasn't worth a raise earlier. Sequences like these invite penalty doubles, so they call for good trumps, as here:

West			East
♠ A K J 8 7			♠ Q 2
♡ 10 5 4			♡ A K J 7
◇ Q 6 5 4			◇ K J 10 3
♣ 3			♣ 8 6 2

South	West	North	East
1♣	1♠	2♣	Dbl.
Pass	2◊	Pass	3♣
Pass	3◊	Pass	3♠
Pass	4♠	Pass	Pass
Pass			

Either four spades or five diamonds should be a good result. Five diamonds is cast iron, but four spades will be okay, too. Note that East first doubles to show his approximate shape, followed by a cue bid to catch up on his strength. East could pass three diamonds with different values, but with such a good hand he continued with three spades. This implied two card support, or he would have approached the hand differently, and allowed West to make the final decision. West chose spades because he had a fine suit. Had he overcalled on K 10 8 6 4, he would have returned to diamonds.

West	East
♠ Q 8 7 6 5	♠ K 2
♡ A 2	♡ K 8 7 5 4
◊ K 8 7 6	◊ Q 10 9 5
♣ K 2	♣ 7 3

South	West	North	East
1♣	1♠	2♣	Dbl.
3♣	3◊	Pass	Pass
Pass			

When partner makes a responsive double, you should compete very strongly if you have a fit in either of his suits. When both sides have fits, you have to fight for what's yours. Don't give up quietly.

West	East
♠ A K 8 7 6 5	♠ 3
♡ 3	♡ Q 5 4
◊ J 10 8 7	◊ K 9 6 5
♣ Q 2	♣ A 9 8 5 4

South	West	North	East
1♡	1♠	2♡	Dbl.
Pass	3◊	Pass	Pass
Pass			

With good support for one of partner's suits, it would be a mistake to rebid spades. Note that if either opponent continues to three hearts, you can then bid three spades. Partner with a doubleton can pass or return to diamonds, as he wishes.

West			East
♠ A 7 6 5 4			♠ J 2
♡ K 6			♡ 3
♢ K Q 7 5			♢ J 10 8 6 4
♣ 3 2			♣ A Q 7 5 4

South	West	North	East
1♡	1♠	2♡	Dbl.
Pass	3♢	3♡	Pass
Pass	4♢	Pass	Pass
Pass			

West should not sell out. On a heart lead, four diamonds will make, possibly with an overtrick. The key is that West has a good fit and is willing to compete further, but:

West			East
♠ K J 9 5 2			♠ 10 3
♡ 9			♡ K 10 8 6 5
♢ K 7 6 5			♢ A J 8 3
♣ K 10 7			♣ 4 2

South	West	North	East
1♣	1♠	2♣	Dbl.
3♣	3♢	4♣	Pass
Pass			

Too much defence, too many losers. While the fit entitles you to compete at the three level, once they've continued to four clubs, you've won the war. You need more to contest further.

West			East
♠ K J 7 6 5			♠ 9
♡ K 5 4			♡ A 7 6 4
♢ 3 2			♢ K Q 10 8 7 5
♣ K 7 6			♣ 5 3

South	West	North	East
1♣	1♠	2♣	Dbl.
Pass	2♡	Pass	3◇
Pass	Pass	Pass	

There are various interpretations you can assign to that three diamond call. I think it should be non-forcing showing four hearts and six diamonds and a decent hand. West should not correct to hearts as his hand is adequate for diamonds.

West		East	
♠ A J 3		♠ K Q 7 6	
♡ 2		♡ Q 10 9 8 7 4	
◇ A 10 9 7 6 3		◇ K 2	
♣ Q 5 4		♣ 8	

South	West	North	East
1♣	1◇	2♣	Dbl.
3♣	Pass	Pass	3♡
Pass	3♠	Pass	Pass
Pass			

Each player has to make decisions. East chose to double because the spades were so good and the hearts somewhat attenuated. But he wasn't willing to sell out to three clubs. Hence the three heart bid. West knew that East had four or five spades to go with longer hearts and decided to play what might be a four-three fit. Note that East wasn't even close to raising three spades to four. If West had a good enough hand for game, he would bid over three clubs. This is a difficult hand, reasonably bid.

West		East	
♠ A 10 8 7 6		♠ J 2	
♡ 8 7		♡ 9 2	
◇ K 5 4		◇ A Q 8 7	
♣ K 5 4		♣ A J 9 7 6	

South	West	North	East
1♡	1♠	2♡	Dbl.
Pass	3♣	Pass	Pass
3♡	Pass	Pass	Dbl.
Pass	Pass	Pass	

This is not a penalty double in the sense that East has a vicious trump holding. Rather, East is announcing shape consistent with a responsive double and good defence. Note that East can't be too short in hearts or he would have enough spades to raise West's spades or enough shape to raise his clubs.

	West		East
♠	Q J 9 7 6	♠	4 2
♡	4 2	♡	A 3
◇	A 8 7	◇	K J 9 4
♣	Q J 5	♣	A 9 6 4 3

South	West	North	East
1♡	1♠	2♡	Dbl.
3♡	Pass	Pass	Dbl.
Pass	Pass	Pass	

This might make, but at matchpoints at least, the risk should be taken. Note also that East can count on a better hand from West at IMP's. West will leave in the double of three hearts only if he expects to beat it, or else if he has no reasonable escape suit. In the first case, they will go down. In the second, since partner has no suit long enough to bid, he is unlikely to have a singleton heart.

	West		East
♠	A 10 8 7 5	♠	9 2
♡	Q 6 2	♡	K J 8 7
◇	4	◇	Q 10 2
♣	K 10 8 7	♣	A Q 9 3

South	West	North	East
1◇	1♠	2◇	Dbl.
Pass	3♣	Pass	Pass
3◇	Pass	Pass	Dbl.
Pass	3♡	Pass	4♣ or Pass

East knows that West has exactly 5—3—1—4 and a weak hand. With good or longer hearts than clubs, he would bid them before clubs, and with a good hand he would have bid over three diamonds.

	West		East
♠ K Q J 10 7 6			♠ 8 2
♡ 8 7			♡ J 9 4
◇ K 5 4			◇ A Q 10 6
♣ 4 2			♣ K Q J 9

South	West	North	East
1♡	1♠	2♡	Dbl.
3♡	Pass	Pass	Dbl.
Pass	3♠	Pass	Pass
Pass			

West has no points and a balanced hand. East's auction usually shows around eleven to thirteen. Inasmuch as West's overcall is based on playing strength with little defence, he should rebid his spades. He couldn't do this earlier, over three hearts, as that would show a much better hand.

West			East
♠ K J 8 7			♠ Q 10 6 2
♡ K 10 6			♡ A J 8 2
◇ A 5 4 2			◇ K J 3
♣ 9 3			♣ 10 7

South	West	North	East
1♣	Dbl.	2♣	Dbl.
3♣	Pass	Pass	Dbl.
Pass	Pass	Pass	

East's second double is the action he would have taken had West overcalled, rather than doubled.

West			East
♠ Q J 6 2			♠ K 10 5 3
♡ K 5 4			♡ A J 6 5
◇ A 10 8 7 5			◇ Q 6
♣ 3			♣ Q 10 4

South	West	North	East
1♣	Dbl.	2♣	Dbl.
3♣	Pass	Pass	Dbl.
Pass	3◇	Pass	3♡
Pass	3♠	Pass	Pass
Pass			

East showed restraint by passing three spades. But the important point is that West didn't sit for the double. East's double shows points with defence and some clubs, but not necessarily good clubs. East corrected three diamonds to three hearts, showing four hearts — with five, he would have bid them earlier — and West in turn corrected to three spades, expecting East to have four spades. East would hardly make a responsive double with three spades and four hearts.

West	East
♠ Q 10 3	♠ K J 6 5
♡ A J 8 7 6	♡ Q 9
♢ K 2	♢ Q J 10 9 8
♣ 10 6 3	♣ 4 2

South	West	North	East
1♣	1♡	2♣	Dbl.
Pass	2♠	Pass	Pass
3♣	Pass	Pass	3♢
Pass	Pass	Pass	

As in earlier hands where East made a responsive double and later bid a new suit, he is showing four spades and a willingness to play in three diamonds. Six cards probably, or a good five. The reason East didn't call three diamonds the round before was that it would have been too encouraging. On this sequence, East hopes to play in three diamonds or three spades and is not seeking to get any higher. Note that three diamonds does not preclude a three spade contract but offers an alternative.

11

THE MANY FACES
OF THE CUE BID

We've had several examples of cue bids by the overcaller's partner. There have been cue bids to show a game force in a new suit and cue bids to show a raise of partner's suit. And now there is the cue bid to show good hands where you have no idea what to do.

You've probably noted also that partner won't know which cue bid you are making and his first response will somehow have to cater for all possibilities. First let's look at the "I have a good hand and don't know what to do cue bid" and then we'll see what partner should do.

NO ONE VUL.   1♣ — 1♠ — 2♣ — ?

♠ K 2   Who knows? The usual criteria. Good hand.
♡ A Q 3   Game is possible. But where? Three clubs
◇ K Q J 9 2   starts the dialogue.
♣ 10 6 3

NO ONE VUL.   1♣ — 1♠ — Pass — ?

♠ Q 2   Two clubs. You could have game in anything
♡ A K J 7   except clubs. Often, when you have a good
◇ K J 10 4   hand with no clearcut bid, it will include two
♣ 8 6 2   or three cards in the opener's suit with no
                stopper. With a singleton or void you would
probably have a fit or a suit of your own. With a stopper, you might have been able to bid notrumps.

NO ONE VUL.   1♠ — 2♣ — Pass — ?

♠ J 8 7
♡ K Q 4
♢ A 10 9 6 5
♣ Q 3

Two spades. Game is possible but not guaranteed. If partner shows no interest, you can stop in a part-score.

VUL. VS.
NOT VUL.   1♠ — 2♣ — 2♢ — ?

♠ 8 6 2
♡ A Q 3
♢ K 9 7
♣ K J 4 2

Well? The only explanation for all this bidding is that someone has psyched. Probably the opener. If it's partner, you should get a new one, and if it's RHO, it would be unusual.

Psyching a two over one is an infrequent strategy at best. Identifying the problem though doesn't provide the answer. Should you jump to five clubs? Should you try two or three notrumps? Should you cue bid, and if so, which suit should it be?

Two bids can be eliminated easily. Two notrumps because it's a gross underbid. And five clubs because

1. Three notrumps could be the right game.

2. You could be missing a slam. Partner will expect a highly distributional hand rather than a balanced one. It's unlikely that he could continue.

Three notrumps is not such a bad bid as it may seem. LHO, who has psyched, may well not lead a spade or partner might have a stopper, or the suit might be only four cards long. But it will end the auction and five or six clubs could be best.

This leaves two spades and three diamonds as your strong exploratory bids. Either can lead to complications. Partner should be able to read a psyche and cooperate in untangling the web, but it will be awkward. Here are some questions for which I have no answers.

1. Should you cue bid your stopper?, i.e. your diamond king as opposed to three small spades.

2. Should you automatically make the cheapest cue bid, i.e. two spades.

3. If you cue bid two spades should partner bid notrumps with a spade stop or does he need a diamond stopper as well?

I would try two spades, but I have no idea what will happen.

The questions are valid however and you might find them worthwhile discussing with your partner.

NO ONE VUL.   1♣ − 1♡ − 1♠ − ?

♠ 9 8 2   Here is a more realistic problem with many
♡ Q 3   elements of the last one. This hand came up
◇ A K Q 10 3   and everyone had his bid. Each one had mini-
♣ K 6 5   mum values, but they were real. Once again
                 you have a number of potential games ranging
from three notrumps to four hearts and five diamonds. On the other hand, your limit could be two diamonds or even one diamond. Partner could have something like

                    ♠ K 7 3
                    ♡ A J 10 6 4
                    ◇ J 2
                    ♣ 10 6 3

in which case the defence may take three spades and three clubs. Unlucky, but possible. With good luck though, you might be able to make as many as eleven tricks. So, not bidding a game or at least trying for one is pusillanimous.

To cover all possible cue bidding sequences would require an encyclopedia, rather than a chapter. So in the interest of space, let us look at a few typical examples and the basic factors involved.

NO ONE VUL.   *You*
                 1♣ − 1♠ − Pass − 2♣
                 Pass − ?

♠ K Q 10 7 5   When partner cue bids, there are three likely
♡ A J 4   hands he may have. A game force in another
◇ 3 2   suit, some sort of raise for yours, or a good
♣ 9 7 5   hand with no clear bid available. Your rebid
                 should cater for all these possibilities.

RULE: When partner cue bids, you should assume that he has the weakest hand possible, i.e. a raise of your overcall. If partner has a better hand than that, he will bid again. With the hand here, I would not wish to be higher than two spades if partner has a minimum. He is allowed to pass after this auction:

1♣ − 1♠ − Pass − 2♣
Pass − 2♠ − Pass − ?

If partner raises to three spades I would pass, my three little clubs being the deciding factor. But it is a close decision and continuing to game could be right. Note that three spades is not forcing.

If partner bids three hearts, it is a new suit and a game force. Raise to four hearts.

If partner bids three diamonds it is a game force and I would rebid three hearts. This can't be a suit or it would have been shown earlier. If partner goes back to three spades, I would go on to four spades. If he rebids diamonds, I would consider passing. There is a lot to be said for defining game forcing cue bids as being forcing to three notrumps or four of a suit. This would allow you to stop in four of a minor if other games were not viable.

And finally, partner may pass two spades if he has a minimum cue bid with a spade raise of eleven or twelve points.

NO ONE VUL.   1♣ − 1♠ − Pass − 2♣
                Pass − ?

♠ A 10 8 7 5   Two diamonds. Partner's cue bid is forcing to
♡ 4 2   two spades, so you can afford to make a des-
◇ K 10 9 4 3   criptive bid. Two diamonds does not imply
♣ 9   extra values. If partner returns to two spades,
                it shows a strong but passable raise. I would
pass. If partner bids three spades, continue to four. If partner bids two hearts, game forcing, rebid two spades. I would want a bit more to try three diamonds. If partner bids two notrumps, rebid three diamonds. It's not clear why partner bothered to cue bid and then bid two notrumps, as opposed to jumping directly to two notrumps. Perhaps it shows a little extra. Both auctions are invitational only.

NO ONE VUL.   1♣ − 1♡ − Pass − 2♣
                Pass − ?

♠ 8 7   Two hearts. This does not guarantee a five
♡ A Q 10 8   card suit. It simply says you have a minimum
◇ 3 2   hand with no other bid available, as on the
♣ A 10 9 4 3   preceding hand. This hand is good enough to

go on to game if partner raises to three hearts. If, instead, he bids two spades or three diamonds, you should bid notrumps at the lowest level. You do this in spite of an unstopped suit.

VUL. VS.
NOT VUL.

You

1♣ — 1♠ — Pass — 2♣
Pass — ?

♠ A Q 8 7 6
♡ Q 2
◇ A K 7 3
♣ J 7

Two diamonds. You have a fine hand and will make sure of reaching game eventually. Note that partner's cue bid is forcing to two spades, so you can begin by showing a distributional feature without fear of being dropped. You can catch up on your strength later.

NO ONE VUL.

You

1◇ — 1♡ — Pass — 2◇
Pass — ?

♠ A 7 6
♡ K Q J 9 5
◇ 4 2
♣ K 7 6

The one thing you must not do is rebid two hearts. Partner could pass. I would try two spades and hope that partner doesn't get carried away. If he raises hearts or introduces notrumps, I raise to game.

NO ONE VUL.

You

1♠ — 2♣ — Pass — 2♠
Pass — ?

♠ Q 10 7
♡ 4 2
◇ A J
♣ A Q 10 9 7 3

Two notrumps. You need have no qualms about your values and should show your stopper. Don't worry about the lack of a heart stopper. You can't have everything.

NO ONE VUL.

You

1♡ — 2♣ — Pass — 2♡
Pass — ?

♠ 4
♡ Q J 7 2
◇ 4 2
♣ A Q J 10 8 7

Three clubs. True, you have a heart stopper, but your hand is a bit weak for notrumps. Also, you are looking at two unstopped suits, not one.

VUL. VS.
NOT VUL.
                    You
                    1♣ — 1♠ — Pass — 2♣
                    Pass — ?

♠ Q J 10 8 7   Two spades in spite of the club stopper. You
♡ K 8 7   need something like the strength of an open-
◇ 4 2   ing bid for two notrumps. A balanced hand
♣ A 6 5   does not qualify per se. If over two spades,
                  partner cue bids again, or if he bids three
diamonds, you can bid three notrumps. He will assume a
weakish hand and should not get unduly excited.

VUL. VS.
NOT VUL.
                    You
                    1♣ — 1♠ — Pass — 2♣
                    Pass — ?

♠ A Q 10 8 6   You can't bid two spades, as this could be
♡ A 2   passed. You could bid two diamonds, intend-
◇ K 6 3   ing to catch up on values later, but you do
♣ J 8 7   have a balanced hand suited to notrumps.
                  The only drawback is no club stopper. For
partnerships wishing to devote a little discussion to system you
can try this convention. Cue bid three clubs. This, as a response
to a cue bid, means: I have values to bid at this level and I have
at least half a stop in the cue bid suit. It also tends to show a
balanced hand as you would show your distribution if you had a
second suit. With suitable values, you would cue bid on any of
these holdings:

                    Q x
                    J x x
                    K x x
                    A x x   etc.

When partner has a half stopper himself, he can bid notrumps if
he wishes. This means that you can bring to light stoppers like

                    Q x opposite J x x

and you can play in notrumps from the right side when you
have

A x x opposite Q x
or   K x x opposite Q x
or   K x x opposite J x x

Note that when you have a full stopper, you can bid notrumps yourself if partner can't. An extension of this convention can be used when RHO doubles partner's cue bid. When holding something in their suit, you can redouble. This is an excellent understanding to have as it presents you with a descriptive bid with no loss of bidding room. Do remember however, that you need a goodish hand for this action. A stopper or a half stopper does not of itself warrant a redouble.

VUL. VS.
NOT VUL.   *You*
                   1◇ − 1♠ − Pass − 2◇
                   Pass − ?

♠ A Q J 8 7 6   Three spades. This shows extra values, a good
♡ 3   six card suit, and is a game force. You could
◇ 8 7 5   have a much bigger hand for this bid. Oppo-
♣ A J 5   site a minimum cue bid, you want to be in
                    game. You are not jumping because you have
a six card suit. You are jumping because you have a six card suit
plus a good hand.

NO ONE VUL.   *You*
                   1♡ − 2◇ − Pass − 2♡
                   Dbl. − ?

♠ 8 7   Redouble. A good hand with an interest in
♡ A 6 2   hearing partner bid notrumps if possible.
◇ K Q J 10 8 3
♣ Q 10

NO ONE VUL.

You
1♣ — 1◊ — 1♠ — 2♣
Pass — ?

♠ 8 2
♡ A 6 5
◊ A K Q 10 8 5
♣ 4 2

While you consider two hearts, three diamonds is a more natural and descriptive bid. This jump is forcing to four of something, so it's possible to stop short of game. This is only the case when your suit is a minor.

NO ONE VUL.

You
1♠ — 2◊ — Pass — 2♠
Pass — ?

♠ 8 7 3
♡ A 2
◊ K Q J 10 8 7
♣ K 5

Some of the time, it is impractical to jump when partner cue bids because it will get you past three notrumps. If this is the case, you may wish to manufacture some other call. I would try three clubs here. If partner bids three diamonds, I'll try three hearts, looking for three notrumps.

NO ONE VUL.

You
1♠ — 2◊ — Pass — 3◊
Pass — ?

♠ Q 4
♡ A 2
◊ A Q J 10 8 3
♣ Q 7 5

When partner has raised, as in this auction, you can consider a cue bid is an effort to reach three notrumps. Short of space, you can't assign more than one possible meaning to the cue bid. I suggest this scale:

1. NT equals a full stopper.
2. A cue equals a half stopper.
3. Another suit equals no stopper.

With this hand, you could bid three spades as you search for three notrumps. If you had the heart queen instead of the spade queen, you could bid three hearts.

NO ONE VUL.   1♡ — 2◇ — Pass — 3◇
                     Pass — ?

♠ J 10   In keeping with our guidelines, your bid here
♡ 8 6   would be three spades. This isn't intended as a
◇ A Q 10 8 7   psyche. It's simply the only bid left to explore
♣ A K Q 9   the possibility of three notrumps. Cue bidding
                  three hearts would imply a half stopper.

I offer no guarantee. But you will find that some reasonably concise definitions will work far better in general than a go-as-you-please guessing game.

This next section is offered with an apology. I would like to present a number of hands on cue bids with complete auctions. This I can do. But for reasons of space, I cannot give each one the full treatment it deserves, and so discussion will be necessarily curtailed.

12

QUIZ ON RESPONDING
TO OVERCALLS

I suggest you "select" one hand or the other and bid it in line
with the auction. I.e., note opponents' and partner's bids,
decide on your own and then compare it with the actual call.
You can, if you wish, bid all the East hands first, then, later,
bid the West hands in similar fashion.

Sometimes, you will see a bid followed by another in paren-
theses. These are bids which could reasonably have been chosen
as alternatives. Do keep in mind however that partner is bidding
in the light of your first bid, unaware of any other.

NOT VUL. MATCHPOINTS.

West	East
♠ J 8 7	♠ A Q 10 9 5 2
♡ K Q 10 9 4	♡ J 3
◊ K 6 3	◊ A Q 7
♣ 4 2	♣ 10 5

South	West	North	East
1♣	1♡	2♣	3♠
Pass	Pass (4♠)		

NOT VUL. MATCHPOINTS.

West	East
♠ Q 2	♠ A J 10 8 7 3
♡ A Q 6 5 4	♡ 8
◊ K 10 3	◊ A Q J 4
♣ 5 4 2	♣ K 3

South	West	North	East
1♣	1♡	Pass	2♣
Pass	2♡	Pass	2♠
Pass	3♠	Pass	4♠

VUL. IMP'S.

West	East
♠ A Q 10 8	♠ K 7 6 5
♡ 3 2	♡ A 5
◇ A J 8 7	◇ 10 5
♣ K 5 4	♣ A 10 8 6 2

South	West	North	East
1◇	1♠	Pass	2◇
Pass	2NT	Pass	3♠ (4♠)
Pass	3NT	Pass	4♠

NOT VUL. MATCHPOINTS.

West	East
♠ K J 8 7 5	♠ Q 10 2
♡ 4 2	♡ A 8 6 5 3
◇ A J 3	◇ 10 5 2
♣ 10 6 5	♣ A J

South	West	North	East
1◇	1♠	Pass	2◇
Pass	2♠	Pass	Pass
Pass			

NOT VUL. MATCHPOINTS.

West	East
♠ K J 8 7 5	♠ A 9 2
♡ 4 2	♡ A 8 6 5 3
◇ A J 3	◇ 10 5 2
♣ 10 6 5	♣ A J

South	West	North	East
1◇	1♠	Pass	2◇
Pass	2♠	Pass	3♠
Pass	Pass	Pass	

NOT VUL.

West	East
♠ 8 7 2	♠ Q J 4
♡ A Q 10 9 8	♡ K 7 5 2
◇ A 6 5	◇ 8 3
♣ 4 2	♣ A K 8 5

South	West	North	East
1♣	1♡	Pass	2♣
Pass	2♡	Pass	3♡
Pass	4♡	Pass	Pass
Pass			

VUL.

West	East
♠ J 2	♠ Q 10 8 3
♡ K Q J 8 7 5	♡ A 6 4
◇ A Q 8	◇ 4 2
♣ 10 5	♣ A 9 8 7

South	West	North	East
1♣	1♡	Pass	2♣
Pass	3♡	Pass	4♡

NOT VUL.

West	East
♠ 7 2	♠ Q 8 5
♡ A Q 9 6 3	♡ K 2
◇ K J 4	◇ 8 7 5
♣ Q 9 7	♣ A K J 4 2

South	West	North	East
1◇	1♡	Pass	2◇
Pass	2NT	Pass	3NT

NOT VUL.

West
♠ K Q 10 7 6
♡ 4 3 2
◇ 8 6
♣ A 5 4

East
♠ 8
♡ 10 6 5
◇ A K Q J 9 5
◇ K J 3

South	West	North	East
1♡	1♠	Pass	2♡
Pass	2♠	Pass	3◇
Pass	(3♠,3♡)	Pass	4◇
Pass	Pass	Pass	

Unlucky, but more or less unavoidable.

VUL.

West
♠ K 4 2
♡ A 10 7
◇ K Q J 8 4
♣ Q 2

East
♠ Q 5
♡ K J 8 4
◇ A 10 9 3
♣ J 10 5

South	West	North	East
1♣	1◇	Pass	2♣
Dbl.	Rdbl.	Pass	2◇
Pass	3◇	Pass	3NT
Pass	Pass	Pass	

VUL.

West
♠ A Q 10 7
♡ A 6 5 4
◇ K J 2
♣ 8 7

East
♠ K 6 5
♡ Q 2
◇ A 9 8 7
♣ Q 9 4 2

South	West	North	East
1♡	1♠	Pass	2♡
Pass	3♡	Pass	3NT
Pass	Pass	Pass	

VUL.

	West			East
	♠ A K J 8			♠ 10 6 2
	♡ A 2			♡ K Q J 8
	◇ 10 8 7 6			◇ J 5 4
	♣ J 5 4			♣ A Q 3

South	West	North	East
1◇	1♠	Pass	2◇
Pass	3◇	Pass	3NT
Pass	Pass	Pass	

NOT VUL.

	West			East
	♠ Q 10 8 7 5			♠ J 9 6 2
	♡ A Q 5 4			♡ 3
	◇ 4			◇ K 10 9 5 3
	♣ K 8 7			♣ A 4 2

South	West	North	East
1♣	1♠	Pass	3♠
Pass	4♠	Pass	Pass
Pass			

VUL.

	West			East
	♠ A 9 7 6 5			♠ 4
	♡ A Q 2			♡ 10 8 5 4
	◇ K J 3			◇ A Q 10 6 4 2
	♣ 4 2			♣ K 5

South	West	North	East
1♣	1♠	2♣	2◇
Pass	3♣	Pass	3NT
Pass			

VUL.

	West			East
	♠ 8 2			♠ K 5 3
	♡ 8 2			♡ A Q 7 3
	◇ A Q J 10 8 7			◇ K 9 4 2
	♣ A J 4			♣ 8 3

South	West	North	East
1♠	2◇	Pass	2♠ (2NT)
Pass	3♣	Pass	3NT
Pass	Pass	Pass	

VUL.

	West			East
	♠ 4 2			♠ K 7
	♡ K 2			♡ J 9 5
	◇ A Q 8 7 6 5 2			◇ K 4 3
	♣ A 8			♣ Q 6 5 4 2

South	West	North	East
1♠	2◇	2♠	3◇
Pass	3♡	Pass	3NT
Pass	Pass	Pass	

NOT VUL.

	West			East
	♠ A Q 10 4 3			♠ J 2
	♡ J 5 4			♡ A Q 10 8
	◇ K 8			◇ 7 3 2
	♣ 5 4 2			♣ K Q J 9

South	West	North	East
1◇	1♠	2◇	Dbl.
Pass	2♡	Pass	3◇
Pass	3♡	Pass	Pass
Pass			

VUL.

West	East
♠ K 10 8 7 5	♠ Q 2
♡ K J 2	♡ A Q 8 7
◇ Q J 8	◇ 7 4 2
♣ A 7	♣ K Q J 9

South	West	North	East
1◇	1♠	2◇	Dbl.
Pass	2♡	Pass	3◇
Pass	3NT	Pass	Pass
Pass			

NOT VUL.

West	East
♠ A 8 7 5 2	♠ Q 2
♡ K J 3	♡ A Q 8 7
◇ 4 2	◇ 10 7 3
♣ A 6 2	♣ K Q J 9

South	West	North	East
1◇	1♠	2◇	Dbl.
Pass	2♡	Pass	3◇
Pass	4♡	Pass	Pass
Pass			

NOT VUL.

West	East
♠ 8 6 5	♠ K 7 4 2
♡ A Q 10 8 4	♡ J 9 7
◇ K 9 7	◇ A J 5
♣ Q 2	♣ K 5 4

South	West	North	East
1♣	1♡	Dbl. (Neg.)	2♣
Dbl.	Pass	Pass	2♡
Pass	Pass	Pass	

VUL.

West			East
♠ A Q 8 7 5			♠ K 6 4
♡ J 2			♡ K Q 5 4
◊ A K 9			◊ J 7
♣ 4 3 2			♣ Q J 8 5

South	West	North	East
1♣	1♠	Pass	2♣
Pass	2◊	Pass	2♠
Pass	3♣	Pass	3NT
Pass	Pass	Pass	

NOT VUL.

West			East
♠ Q J 10 7 5			♠ K 6 4
♡ K 2			♡ A 8 6 3
◊ A K 8 5			◊ J 6 4
♣ 4 2			♣ K 7 5

South	West	North	East
1♣	1♠	Pass	2♣
Pass	2◊	Pass	2♠
Pass	3♠ (4♠)	Pass	Pass
Pass			

NOT VUL.

West			East
♠ A Q 8 7 5			♠ K 6 4 2
♡ K 5 4			♡ A 7 2
◊ A Q 4 2			◊ K J 3
♣ 3			♣ 9 7 2

South	West	North	East
1♣	1♠	Pass	2♣
Pass	2◊	Pass	2♠
Pass	4♣!	Pass	4♡
Pass	4NT	Pass	5◊
Pass	6♠	Pass	Pass
Pass			

The splinter bid of four clubs, showing a singleton, is normally used by the opening bidder's side. On occasion, however, it can be used by the defending side as well.

NOT VUL.

West	East
♠ K 10 7 6	♠ 4 3
♡ 4 3	♡ K J 7
◇ A Q 10 8 6	◇ K 7 5 4
♣ A 3	♣ K J 8 2

South	West	North	East
1♠	2◇	Pass	2♠
Pass	2NT	Pass	3◇
Pass	Pass	Pass	

NOT VUL.

West	East
♠ A J 8 7 5	♠ Q 2
♡ K 5 4	♡ 9 3
◇ K Q 7	◇ A 10 8 5
♣ J 5	♣ K Q 4 3 2

South	West	North	East
2♡	2♠	Pass	3♡
Pass	3NT	Pass	Pass
Pass			

VUL.

West	East
♠ A 10 8 6 5	♠ 3
♡ A 7 6	♡ 4 2
◇ K 5 4	◇ A Q 9 7 6 3 2
♣ 10 7	♣ Q 5 4

South	West	North	East
1♡	1♠	Pass	2◇
Pass	3◇	Pass	3♡
Pass	3NT	Pass	Pass
Pass			

NOT VUL.

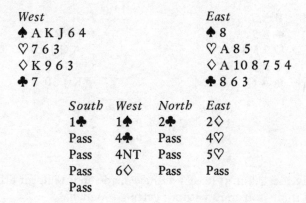

	West			East
	♠ A K J 6 4			♠ 8
	♡ 7 6 3			♡ A 8 5
	◇ K 9 6 3			◇ A 10 8 7 5 4
	♣ 7			♣ 8 6 3

South	West	North	East
1♣	1♠	2♣	2◇
Pass	4♣	Pass	4♡
Pass	4NT	Pass	5♡
Pass	6◇	Pass	Pass
Pass			

NOT VUL.

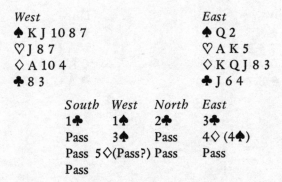

	West			East
	♠ K J 10 8 7			♠ Q 2
	♡ J 8 7			♡ A K 5
	◇ A 10 4			◇ K Q J 8 3
	♣ 8 3			♣ J 6 4

South	West	North	East
1♣	1♠	2♣	3♣
Pass	3♠	Pass	4◇ (4♠)
Pass	5◇(Pass?)	Pass	Pass
Pass			

Very tough. If West had a singleton club, a slam might be on, so East is quite right to force. On the actual layout, four spades is the only makeable game, and even that isn't cold.

VUL.

	West			East
	♠ 8 5			♠ J 4 2
	♡ 9 5 4			♡ A Q J 10
	◇ K Q J 9 7			◇ 8 2
	♣ A Q 5			♣ K J 10 7

South	West	North	East
1♠	2◇	Pass	2♠
Pass	3◇	Pass	Pass
Pass			

Hardly ideal, but at least you have made an intelligent effort to reach three notrumps without getting too high.

VUL.

	West			East
	♠ K 3			♠ 9 5
	♡ 4 2			♡ A J 3
	◇ A Q J 8 7 6			◇ K 10 3
	♣ 8 7			♣ A Q J 4 2

South	West	North	East
1♠	2◇	Pass	2♠
Pass	3◇	Pass	3♠*
Pass	3NT	Pass	Pass
Pass			

*Try again.

NOT VUL.

	West			East
	♠ K 2			♠ A 8 7
	♡ A 8 7			♡ 6 4
	◇ K J 10 7 6 5			◇ A 4 3 2
	♣ 4 2			♣ A K 6 5

South	West	North	East
1♠	2◇	Pass	2♠
Pass	3◇	Pass	3♠
Pass	3NT	Pass	4◇
Pass	4♡	Pass	6◇
Pass	Pass	Pass	

NOT VUL.

	West			East
	♠ 7 2			♠ A K J 8 4
	♡ Q J 8 7 6 4			♡ 10 5 3
	◇ 10 2			◇ K 7 6 5
	♣ A K 7			♣ 4

South	West	North	East
1♣	1♡	1♠	2♣
Pass	2♡	Pass	Pass
Pass			

East should not get excited.

NOT VUL.

	West			East
	♠ K Q 8 7 5 2			♠ J 9 6 3
	♡ 7 3			♡ A K 8 5
	◇ 3			◇ 10 9 4 2
	♣ A 10 8 6			♣ 7

South	West	North	East
1◇	1♠	2♣	2◇
Pass	3♠	Pass	4♠
Pass	Pass	Pass	

One of the exceptions where East can use a cue bid after opponents make a two over one response. Here, it can only mean a good fit for partner's overcall. Note that three spades by East, after two clubs, would be pre-emptive.

NOT VUL.

	West			East
	♠ 10 2			♠ 9 8 5 3
	♡ K Q 7			♡ A J 9 5
	◇ A J 10 9 7 5			◇ 4
	♣ J 10			♣ A Q 8 6

South	West	North	East
1♠	2◇	Pass	2NT
Pass	Pass (3◇)	Pass	Pass

East should not cue bid because he wouldn't know what to do if partner rebids three diamonds. Better to make a constructive, if unorthodox bid which keeps the auction simple.

NOT VUL.

West	East
♠ 10 2	♠ 9 8 5
♡ K Q 7	♡ A J 9 5
◇ A J 10 9 7 5	◇ 4
♣ J 10	♣ A Q 8 6 5

South	West	North	East
1♠	2◇	Pass	3♣
Pass	Pass	Pass	

9 8 5 of spades is not close enough to a spade guard to pretend otherwise and the cue bid may create problems in the next round. Besides, you really ought to have a lot more.

VUL.

West	East
♠ A 8 7	♠ J 3
♡ K 7	♡ 4 2
◇ Q 10 8 3	◇ A K 7 2
♣ K J 8 4	♣ A 10 5 3 2

South	West	North	East
1♡	Dbl.	2♡	Dbl.
Pass	3♣	Pass	3♡
Pass	3NT	Pass	Pass
Pass			

East couldn't cue bid initially because West would have interpreted it as showing interest in spades. It would then be impossible for East to locate a heart stopper.

Part III
Continuing the Auction

13
OVERCALLER'S REBIDS

So far we have studied two areas of bidding: the overcall and the response to the overcall. Subsequent developments are yet to be discussed.

Why has this preliminary phase of the auction called for so much space? Because it is so often critical. In deciding whether or not to overcall a player faces the dangers of the unknown for he has less to go on than at any other stage of the auction. He would like to await further information, but he may not receive the information he needs, and anyway, by the time he gets it, the bidding will be too high. A decision must be made on the spot.

To a lesser extent, responder is under a similar disadvantage. If he can raise partner's suit there's no problem for a fit has been found. But the decision to introduce a new suit, when so little information is available, requires careful consideration. Many factors must be taken into account. Hence the space devoted to the first round of defensive bidding.

Thereafter life will be easier. Defenders have exchanged information, each one having had the opportunity to show his values and his suits. Opponents, too, have spoken again, filling in the picture. So you have a good idea of what is happening around the table.

This doesn't mean that once you survive the first round of bidding the rest will be a cakewalk. Far from it. Once in a while, it is true, your overcall will be followed by an uncontested auction, but most of the time opponents will fight you tooth and nail. Having opened the bidding they will doubtless think that the hand belongs to them and they will not let you steal the contract tamely.

By the time opener has made his first rebid a distinct trend can usually be discerned. At times one side or the other has gained right of way and the rest of the auction is uneventful. At others, the two sides are evenly matched and neither will give way. It's a fight to the end.

On occasion the course of the bidding is eminently predictable and likewise the fate of the contract, which hinges on how well or badly his suits break for declarer. Looking at your own cards you can tell what's in store for him.

Following the auction you should observe closely the swiftly changing scene. It will greatly help your judgment in competitive situations.

Remember when the bidding went 1♣—Pass—2♣ and I told you to bid almost regardless of your hand?

Remember when the bidding went 1♠—Pass—2◇ and I told you to pass almost regardless of your hand?

These two auctions represented the extremes of safety and danger, other auctions falling somewhere in between. The key to every decision was the nature of the auction.

As the bidding proceeds and you gain additional information you may find these guidelines useful.

When the hand belongs to opponents it is generally wise to give up early. Only a good fit and unmistakeable playing tricks can justify contesting the auction further. High cards are not enough.

When the balance of power is uncertain you can be more aggressive, but only within narrow limits. You are still at a disadvantage for it is easier for them to double you than for you to double them. They start off with values implicit in a sound opening whereas yours are based on a less solid overcall. There is, moreover, an overriding consideration: if there's no game for opponents a score of minus 200, let alone minus 300, will bring the roundest of zeros. On part-score hands you can afford no luxuries.

When both sides have a fit, press on. And remember that if opponents have a fit, you should have one, too, so look for it and don't sell out too cheaply.

Most of your decisions will revolve around the wisdom of making an overcall or responding to partner's. So long as you are satisfied that you did the right thing on the first round you will be well placed in those that follow. There will still be decisions to take, but no longer will you be bidding in the dark.

CASE 1

YOU OVERCALL. PARTNER PASSES.

Your first thought should be that partner is either broke or that his values are such that he could not adequately express them. You can make an educated guess as to which it is from the nature of opponents' auction. Is it strong or is it weak? Or is that not clear? If it's weak, you can reasonably infer that partner has some values, and if that's all you need, you can compete further. If on the other hand, opponents' bidding is strong or unclear, you would do well to pass unless you have enough to bid again on your own.

Should you rebid your own suit? Perhaps, but there are distinct dangers.

1. If LHO bid 1NT over your overcall, there is a good chance he can double you if you continue.

NO ONE VUL.   *You*
      1♣ − 1♠ − 1NT − Pass
      Pass − ?

♠ K J 7 6 5 4 It looks easy to rebid 2♠, and many would.
♡ A Q 8   But with poor spade spots the knowledge that
♢ K J 4   LHO has a spade stop should deter you. Your
♣ 3   dummy rates to have 1¼ spades and 4½ points.
       This is the sort of hand of which −300's
and −500's are made. At matchpoints you could survive 2♠ against conservative opponents because they might not double when they should or because they might defend poorly or because someone might decide to raise clubs. At IMP's you should clearly pass. To bring this up to a 2♠ call would require the 10 and 9 of spades or the A J 10 of diamonds. Something worth another trick.

2. If LHO has made a two over one response, you have little reason to rebid your suit. Opponents will bid on anyway and

you will merely be offering them the option of doubling you. Only against people who make very light or even ridiculous two-over-one responses should you consider rebidding your suit.

NOT VUL.
VS. VUL.   *You*

            1♡ — 1♠ — 2♣ — Pass
            2♡ — ?

♠ Q 10 8 7 6 5   This is a fine one spade overcall. It is equally a
♡ A 4 2   fine pass over two hearts. The auction screams
◇ K Q   that partner is broke. If he is short in spades
♣ K 10   as well, you will go for a ride.

NOT VUL.
VS. VUL.   *You*

            1♡ — 1♠ — 2♣ — Pass
            2♡ — ?

♠ K Q J 9 7 6   Two spades would be okay here. You have a
♡ 3   good suit and distribution. If partner wants
◇ A 10 7 5   to save, that's fine. Perhaps he can raise to
♣ 4 2   three spades and you will save.

3. If LHO has made a one-over-one response, you can hope for something in partner's hand, but you should still lean in the direction of safety first.

4. Only when there has been a finite sequence where both opponents have shown limited values, should you be optimistic.

NO ONE VUL.   *You*

            1♡ — 1♠ — 2♡ — Pass
            Pass — ?

♠ Q J 9 7 6 5   Here, for a change, you can rely on partner
♡ 4 3   for a tidbit or two. I would expect him to
◇ A K 7   have something like six points and a couple
♣ A 10   of spades. Typical would be this hand:

                ♠ 8 3
                ♡ Q 9 5
                ◇ J 8 7 6 5
                ♣ K 9 4

With this, we can make one or two spades and expect more often than not to push opponents to three hearts. Note that I gave partner the heart queen which was wasted rather than the diamond queen. That card would give you a play for three spades.

Observe that all examples of rebidding your suit were at the two level. It's a rare hand that can overcall one of a suit and then find sufficient justification to bid at the three level opposite a passing partner. One reason for this is that there are not many "weak auctions" by opponents which would force you to the three level. Most of their limited sequences leave you room for a simple rebid. The times you find yourself contemplating a three level rebid are when opponents have good hands, and this should warn you.

NO ONE VUL.   *You*

1♣ − 1♡ − 1♠ − Pass
2♣ − ?

♠ J 7 2
♡ A K 10 8 7 5
♢ A Q 2
♣ 3

Three hearts with tempered enthusiasm. This is the "weak" auction where you might overcall at the one level and subsequently try again at the three level. Note that LHO is still unlimited, so yours is not an entirely safe move. If you were to remove one spade and add a club, then pass would be best. As the hand stands, the J 7 2 of spades suggests a fit.

There will be far more occasions for rebidding your suit at the three level after making a two level overcall. This is because there is a frequent "limited auction" which affords you that second chance.

VUL. VS. NOT.   *You*

1♠ − 2♡ − 2♠ − Pass
Pass − ?

♠ K 8 7
♡ A Q 10 9 8 6
♢ A Q 4
♣ 3

Here is the typical "limited auction" by opponents on which you can reasonably rebid your suit at the three level with a passing partner. On this hand you can even hope for a fit because of your three spades.

NO ONE VUL.   *You*
                1♡ — 2◇ — 2♡ — Pass
                Pass — ?

♠ A J 2
♡ 4 2
◇ K Q J 9 8 7
♣ A 8

Again, three diamonds. You have no reason to expect a fit, but partner can easily have a useful card or two. I would expect to make three diamonds as often as not. Note that after:

                You
                1♠ — 2◇ — 2♡ — Pass
                2♠ — ?

bidding three diamonds would be very unwise.

When partner passes, should you introduce a new suit?

You are in the same position as when you decide whether to rebid your first suit. You draw inferences from the auction and consider the values left to partner.

NO ONE VUL.   *You*
                1♣   — 1♠ — 1NT — Pass
                Pass — ?

♠ K J 8 7 5
♡ 3
◇ A Q 6 5
♣ K 4 2

Whereas the auction has strongly warned you off spades, there is far less objection to bidding a new suit. Two diamonds is fully justified.

NO ONE VUL.   *You*
                1♡ — 1♠ — 2♣ — Pass
                2♡ — ?

♠ K Q 8 7 5
♡ K 2
◇ A J 9 7 5
♣ 3

In practice, any time you wish to bid a new suit after LHO has made a two-over-one response, you will have to do so at the three level. It's rarely worth it. This hand certainly isn't. Your suits are somewhat moth-eaten and require good support. A sound diamond bid would look like one of these hands

♠ A J 9 8 7 6   ♠ K Q J 10 7
♡ 4   ♡ 4 2
◇ K Q J 10 7   ◇ A K J 10 3
♣ 3   ♣ 4

and I wouldn't feel any too optimistic about the second hand.

VUL. VS. NOT.   *You*
                     1♡ − 1♠ − 2♡ − Pass
                     Pass − ?

♠ K Q 8 7 5   Three diamonds. When opponents have a fit
♡ K 2   and limited values, you bid on any excuse.
◇ A J 9 7 5   Contrast this with the previous hand and the
♣ 3   one below.

VUL. VS. NOT.   *You*
                     1♣ − 1♡ − 1♠ − Pass
                     2♣ − ?

♠ K 2   Two diamonds. While certainly correct, this is
♡ K Q 8 7 5   slightly more dangerous than the three dia-
◇ A J 9 7 5   mond bid on the previous hand.
♣ 3   Why is two diamonds dangerous? Because
                   the auction is still "live". LHO has an un-
limited hand and RHO is undefined. All we know is that RHO
has less than seventeen points and a club suit. Compare this with
the

                     1♡ − 1♠ − 2♡ − Pass
                     Pass − ?

sequence on the previous hand. Very different situations. On
one hand opponents are limited with a fit. On the other they are
unlimited with no fit.

NO ONE VUL.   *You*
                     1◇ − 1♡ − 1♠ − Pass
                     2◇ − ?

♠ K 2   Getting a little sticky. It's a dangerous auction
♡ K Q 8 7 5   and we're getting high. Not vul. at match-
◇ 3   points you could bid three clubs, but then at
♣ A J 9 7 5   matchpoints anything goes.

NO ONE VUL.   *You*
                   1◇ — 1♡ — 1♠ — Pass
                   2♠ — ?

♠ K 2   Three clubs without a doubt. Opponents have
♡ K Q 8 7 5   a fit and one of them has a limited hand. It's
◇ 3   true that LHO can have extra values, but the
♣ A J 9 7 5   concept of bidding more when they have a fit
                   should prevail.

NO ONE VUL.   *You*
                   1♣ — 1♠ — 2♡ — Pass
                   3♡ — ?

♠ K Q J 8 7 6   Don't carry things too far. It's true that they
♡ 4 2   have a fit, but their announced values are too
◇ K 10 3   substantial for you to persist. LHO will bid
♣ A 2   four hearts most of the time and a three spade
                   call by you will merely give him the option of
                   doubling.

NO ONE VUL.   *You*
                   1♡ — 1♠ — 2◇ — Pass
                   3◇ — ?

♠ A Q 9 7 5   Again. They have a fit, but they also have
♡ 4   strength and are still unlimited. Four clubs
◇ K 3   would be foolhardy.
♣ A Q 7 6 5

NO ONE VUL.   *You*
                   1♡ — 1♠ — 2♡ — Pass
                   3♡ — ?

♠ A Q 9 7 5   If you feel that on the previous hand four
♡ 4   clubs was asking for trouble, while on this
◇ K 3   one, it's automatic, you are definitely on the
♣ A Q 7 6 5   right track. Here they have a fit and they are
                   both limited.

Some players, by the way, treat the three heart bid as pre-
emptive. They anticipate further action by you and are making
life more difficult. When this is so, your expectancy from

partner is even greater.

When RHO has rebid one notrump, you have to be slightly wary because LHO will be well placed to double you. That 1NT is very descriptive and LHO can judge the hand far better than if RHO had rebid his own suit.

NO ONE VUL.   *You*

               1♣ — 1♡ — 1♠ — Pass
               1NT — ?

♠ 6 2
♡ K Q 10 8 7
♢ A Q 6 5
♣ K 2

Two diamonds, but it's close. With a fifth diamond, you wouldn't need the club king as your playing strength would be much greater.

So far partner has invariably passed. While we wait for him to enter the auction let us look again at our guidelines for they will serve us as faithfully in the future as they have done in the past.

What is the state of the auction? Have opponents found a fit? Have they shown strength? Have both disclosed the limits of their holdings? Has either of them done so?

I am well aware that I am repeating myself and I do so deliberately for the importance of these factors, which determine the state of the auction, cannot be overemphasised. In competitive situations a player should constantly stretch his antennae, feeling how far he can go and when he should draw back.

Study the truism: competitive bidding is *competitive* bidding. It is not *constructive* bidding. The primary purpose is not to bid games or slams but to obstruct opponents by contesting the auction. If you find a fit you may, of course, explore the chances of game, but your main purpose is to push opponents a trick or two higher, a trick *too* high. It follows that some of your bids will not have the same encouraging implications as they would have, had you opened the bidding. Remember: the side which opens *expects* the hand to belong to them. The side which intervenes *hopes* that it belongs to them, accepts most of the time that it doesn't and bids accordingly.

CASE 2

YOU OVERCALL.
PARTNER BIDS A NEW SUIT.

When you overcall, you naturally hope to initiate a constructive dialogue with partner. Very seldom can you compete effectively opposite a passing partner. To this end, there are three contributions he can make: raise your overcall; bid notrumps; bid a new suit.

When partner bids a new suit, you should view it with mixed feelings. On the plus side, you should be happy that partner has some values and if you fit his suit, your side will be well placed for further action. On the minus side, partner's bid shows limited values, or he would make a stronger bid, and he doesn't care for your suit. Further action by you should allow for a misfit, even though partner is not broke.

Should you introduce the fourth suit? Usually this is not a bad idea, because most situations in which you might do this follow weak or limited auctions by opponents.

NO ONE VUL.   *You*
                1♣ — 1♠ — 2♣ — 2♡
                3♣ — ?

♠ A 10 8 7 5   Bid. They have a fit, so you should have a fit,
♡ J 2   and you have an easy method of finding it.
◇ K Q 9 6 3   Three diamonds. Note that you are not
♣ 4   promising a big hand. Contrary to the principles in opening, you can raise the level on
rather weak hands when it is "safe" to do so. If you had opened the bidding with a spade, a three club or three diamond rebid by you over two hearts would show a very good hand. Here in a competitive framework a similar sequence shows a hand that's not even worth an opening bid.

There is another important point to be made here. I've said that the "state" of the auction is all important and your bids must always be made with the safety factor in mind. This leads to another interesting conclusion which can be treated as one of the basic axioms of competitive bidding.

1. When opponents have good hands, your partner will always be minimum for whatever action he takes.

2. When opponents have minimum and limited hands, partner may well have a maximum for his actions.

You

1♣ — 1♠ — 2♣ — 2♡

Partner can have a fair hand just short of a strong response.

You

1♣ — 1♠ — 2♢ — 2♡

Partner will always have a good suit with very few high cards. He cannot have a good hand.

NO ONE VUL.   *You*

1♣ — 1♠ — Pass — 2♡

3♣ — ?

♠ A 10 8 7 5
♡ J 2
♢ K Q 9 6 3
♣ 4

Three diamonds again. East has shown a good hand but LHO is presumed to be weak. Note that LHO may have a good hand with spades, hoping to be able to double, but that fear should only dissuade you from rebidding spades. Other things being equal, you should feel quite comfortable bidding diamonds. This assumes that opponents are using the negative double. If they are not, LHO cannot have a spade stack with a good hand besides or he would have made a penalty double. Regardless of whether they are or are not using negative doubles, this is a three diamond bid.

NO ONE VUL.   *You*

1♣ — 1♠ — 1NT — 2♡

3♣ — ?

♠ A 10 8 7 5
♡ J 2
♢ K Q 9 6 3
♣ 4

Three diamonds still, but unenthusiastically. LHO's 1NT is not weak. It shows definite high card strength. RHO is showing signs of something extra too, although it may be in the form of distribution. In favour of bidding three diamonds is the fact that you have two hearts, partner's suit, and one club, and not one heart and two clubs. Your spade holding will play well in diamonds or for that matter, in hearts. You have the ace, not the king or queen-jack or king-jack. Partner, with no apparent interest in spades, may well have a singleton, and if so, he will be pleased to find you with the ace.

NO ONE VUL.   *You*
                    1♣ — 1♠ — 1NT — 2♡
                    3♣ — ?

♠ K Q J 7 5   This hand is the complete antithesis of the
♡ 3   previous hand. While you might still consider
◇ K J 8 6 5   a matchpoint three diamond call, you should
♣ Q 10   pass any other time. Look at the minuses:

      1. Partner doesn't care for spades, so your strength is largely wasted.

      2. Your singleton heart will not be an asset.

      3. Your clubs are worth nothing.

Here is a possible hand for partner. Note how it plays opposite either of the two previous hands.

♠ 3	♠ A 10 8 7 5	
♡ K Q 10 9 6 5	♡ J 2	
◇ 10 7 4	◇ K Q 9 6 3	
♣ 9 6 3	♣ 4	

                        ♠ K Q J 7 5
                        ♡ 3
                        ◇ K J 8 6 5
                        ♣ Q 10

Opposite the first hand, you expect to go one down, but might well pull it off against soft defence. But the second hand is a disaster. True, you found a poor dummy, but the way the hand would play for you was predictable. A useful point emerges. When partner does not care for your first suit, you should seriously devaluate holdings not headed by the ace. Other combinations are worth much less when not facing a fit.

      Should you bid notrumps?

      Some of the time, partner will bid a suit after your overcall, and your options will include some number of notrumps. At the one level, the bid is reasonably commonplace and needs only to be defined. I would expect it to show from eleven to fifteen points and no liking for partner's suit. It is not a sign-off in that you can't stand what partner has bid. It does require certain values.

NO ONE VUL.

You

1♣ — 1♡ — Pass — 1♠
Pass — ?

♠ 8 2
♡ A Q 10 7 6
◇ Q 8 2
♣ K J 4

One notrump. Sound, but a minimum for the call.

NO ONE VUL.

You

1♣ — 1◇ — Pass — 1♡
1♠ — ?

♠ Q 10 7
♡ 9 7
◇ K Q J 8 7
♣ A J 7

One notrump. When RHO rebids, you need more than a minimum.

NO ONE VUL.

You

1♣ — 1♡ — Pass — 1♠
Pass — ?

♠ 3
♡ K Q 10 8 7
◇ 8 6 3
♣ A 6 4 2

Pass. No need to continue. Rebidding two hearts would show a better suit, and one no-trump a better hand. When you overcall, you always hope for something good to happen, but when it doesn't you should be prepared to give up.

BOTH VUL.

You

1♣ — 1♡ — Pass — 1♠
Pass — ?

♠ 8
♡ K Q J 7
◇ K 6 5
♣ A 10 8 7 5

One notrump. Clearcut. Your bid does not promise any kind of spade support and partner should hesitate to rebid a questionable suit.

Notrump calls at the two level are somewhat rarer. You're a trick higher and that requires extra values. There are two auctions when you should forget about it immediately. When LHO bids 1NT after your overcall, or when LHO bids a new suit at the two level, desist.

NO ONE VUL.   *You*
                     1♣ — 1♠ — 1NT — 2♡
                     Pass — ?

♠ A Q 10 8 7   Pass. Partner has a good heart suit and nothing
♡ Q 2   else.
◇ K 6 5
♣ K Q 5

NO ONE VUL.   *You*
                     1♣ — 1♠ — 2◇ — 2♡
                     Pass — ?

It doesn't matter what you have. Two notrumps is wrong 99% of the time — at least.

NO ONE VUL.   *You*
                     1♣ — 1♠ — Pass — 2◇
                     Pass — ?

♠ Q 10 8 7 6   Two notrumps. You bid two notrumps when
♡ K 3   opponents show weak hands. LHO will have
◇ K 9   passed usually, so you can hope to find partner
♣ A Q 8 7   with a maximum for his bid. To have any idea
                 where the tricks are coming from, you will
need a semi fit or better for partner's suit. If you don't like his suit, and he doesn't like yours, it's going to be tough going. Therefore, if you don't like his suit, you need a much better hand to bid two notrumps. Note that two notrumps is encouraging. There is no such thing as running from partner's suit to notrumps just because you don't like it.

NO ONE VUL.   *You*
                    1♣ — 1♡ — 2♣ — 2◇
                    Pass — ?

♠ Q J 8   This is a very good hand in high card points.
♡ K Q J 8 7   But from a trick taking point of view, it's a
◇ K Q 10   trap. You could bid two or three notrumps,
♣ A 2   but where would the tricks come from? They
                     will lead a club, knocking out your stopper,
and as soon as they get in, they will run enough tricks to set
you. To succeed, you will need nine fast ones. Now if partner
has two red aces, fine. But if he has any of the following hands,
notrumps will fail.

                    ♠ A x x
                    ♡ x x
                    ◇ A 10 x x x x
                    ♣ x x

Note that partner even has a sixth diamond. And yet game
requires a spade finesse into the opening bidder.

                    ♠ K x
                    ♡ x x
                    ◇ A x x x x x x
                    ♣ x x

Three notrumps will down, even though partner has seven diamonds.
    I don't claim to have the answer to this hand. The reason for
presenting it is to show some of the objections to bidding notrumps in similar situations.

NO ONE VUL.   *You*
                    1♣ — 1♠ — 2♣ — 2◇
                    Pass — ?

♠ 8 7 6 5 4 2   This hand, with far fewer high card points is
♡ A Q   closer to producing three notrumps because
◇ K 10 3   the tricks are ready-made. With luck, you can
♣ K 8   grab your nine tricks without letting op-
                    ponents in.
    This hand and the one before show clearly the problems

you face when considering notrumps in an auction where opener's suit has been raised. You can anticipate the lead and so judge what tricks you have and whether you will be able to get at them in time.

When partner bids a new suit, should you rebid yours?

There are certainly times where you want to rebid your suit, but the considerations are somewhat different from other rebids.

Firstly, you expect partner not to like your suit, so there is no future in rebidding anything less than a fair six card suit. When you rebid your suit, you do so because you have something positive to say, not because you don't care for partner's.

Secondly, bear in mind that LHO may be waiting to double you. This happens frequently against opponents playing the negative double and should discourage you from rebidding five card suits.

When should you rebid your suit and what does it mean?

1. RHO passes.
2. RHO bids.

Let's examine each case in turn.

NO ONE VUL.   *You*
                       1♣ — 1♠ — Pass — 2◊
                       Pass — ?

♠ K Q 10 8 7 6   Two spades. It's important to note that your
♡ K 4 2   bid shows a good suit. It's not made because
◊ 7   you don't like diamonds.
♣ A 6 3

NO ONE VUL.   *You*
                       1♣ — 1♡ — 1♠ — 2◊
                       Pass — ?

♠ J 8   Two hearts. Two diamonds would obviously
♡ K Q J 10 7 6   be a fine contract, so you need a very good
◊ K 4 2   suit of your own to rebid it. You do not
♣ Q 2   intend two hearts as an escape. You are show-
                  ing a good suit. As your support for partner
gets better, the quality of the suit you rebid must also get better.

NO ONE VUL.   *You*
1♣ — 1♡ — Pass — 2◇
Pass — ?

♠ A 7 6
♡ Q 10 8 6 5
◇ 2
♣ K 7 5 4

Pass. Your suit is poor and your hand is a minimum. Add a sixth heart and you should still pass.

BOTH VUL.   *You*
1♣ — 1♠ — 2♣ — 2♡
Pass — ?

♠ K Q J 10 7 6
♡ Q 5
◇ A 10 8 6
♣ 3

This suit is clearly worth rebidding and the only question is how high. I'd try four spades but would hardly quarrel with three. What has happened that makes this hand worth a jump when it was worth only an overcall in the first place is:

1. Your heart queen has become a significant value.

2. Partner has some strength.

3. Partner probably has little in clubs, so whatever he has will be working for you.

NO ONE VUL.   *You*
1♣ — 1♠ — 2♣ — 2♡
Pass — ?

♠ K Q J 10 8 7
♡ 3
◇ A 10 5 4
♣ Q 2

Only two spades. The difference between the doubleton club queen here and the doubleton heart queen on the previous hand is enormous. It could easily come to three or four tricks.

NO ONE VUL.   *You*
1◇ — 1♠ — 2◇ — 3♣
Pass — ?

♠ Q J 10 8 4 2
♡ A K 2
◇ 7 2
♣ 9 2

You should be less inclined to remove partner's suit when he bids it at the three level than at the level of two.

BOTH VUL.   *You*
                        1♡ – 1♠ – 2♡ – 3♣
                        Pass – ?

♠ K Q J 7 6 2   Still best to pass. With the auction at the three
♡ Q 2   level, it is dangerous to continue. There is less
◊ A 4 2   space to look for your best fit. Add the spade
♣ 3 2   ten, and you could rebid them. Without it,
                     caution is best.

When opener rebids, you are not compelled to persist, so
further action by you requires a little extra. Rebidding your suit
is a bit dangerous, remember, because LHO may be lying in wait
(negative double) while partner doesn't like your suit. So you
do require a good six card suit as a minimum. Strangely, you do
not need much extra in the way of high cards so long as the
suit quality is adequate. This advice, by the way, is for rebids at
the two level only. Three level auctions require more.

NO ONE VUL.   *You*
                        1♣ – 1♡ – Pass – 1♠
                        2♣ – ?

♠ 8 7   Pass. The suit is good enough but the hand is a
♡ K Q J 7 6 5   bare minimum.
◊ Q 5 4
♣ J 3

NO ONE VUL.   *You*
                        1♣ – 1♡ – Pass – 1♠
                        2♣ – ?

♠ Q 3   Two hearts. The spade queen is now quite
♡ A Q J 10 8 6   valuable and there is nothing wasted.
◊ Q 10 2
♣ 9 6

BOTH VUL.   *You*

1♣ − 1◇ − 1♡ − 1♠

2♣ − ?

♠ 9 6 2

♡ A 2

◇ K Q J 10 8 3

♣ 4 2

I would bid two diamonds, intending if they bid two hearts, to continue to two spades. When your maximum is a part-score, you may as well stick to the best suit. If RHO had rebid two hearts, you could have chosen two spades.

VUL. VS. NOT.   *You*

1♣ − 1♠ − 2♣ − 2◇

3♣ − ?

♠ K Q J 10 8 2

♡ K 3

◇ A 10 4

♣ J 2

You can bid three diamonds, raising partner, or you can rebid three spades. Or you can pass I suppose, but that would be unreasonable. I would choose three spades showing both a good suit and extra values. A three diamond raise would be only competitive showing a fit and no more. Clearly an underbid. If RHO had not bid three clubs, it would have been a three spade bid also. But being a jump, it would have been a better description of the hand.

Partner bids a new suit after your overcall. Should you raise?
Whenever as a defender you bid a new suit, the best thing that can happen is to hear partner raise it. That, above all, can pave the way to a successful defence. When your hands fit, you can exert heavy pressure. When they fit really well, you can throw opponents off balance, take their contracts from them by barefaced robbery, or else, outgun them by making more tricks than they can, despite their preponderance of high cards.

    Should you raise partner? Yes. Yes. Yes. For two hundred pages now, we've been looking at ways to get into the auction. Some were dangerous but we ran risks, in the hope of finding a fit. Now that the fit has been found, the dangers are past and it is safe to bid. Seize the chance.

NO ONE VUL.   *You*
                        1♣ − 1◇ − Pass − 1♠
                        Pass − ?

♠ Q 8 7   A sound minimum raise to two spades.
♡ 10 2   Partner has five or more spades with enough
◇ A K 10 7 5   points to make game possible. Passing would
♣ K J 4   be a serious error.

NO ONE VUL.   *You*
                        1♣ − 1◇ − Pass − 1♡
                        Pass − ?

♠ 8 7 2   Marginal whether you raise or pass. Opponents'
♡ A 9 6   silence suggests partner will probably bid
◇ K Q 8 7 4   again. Best to pass. Note that partner can't
♣ J 2   really have enough for game or he would have
                     made a stronger bid.

NO ONE VUL.   *You*
                        1♣ − 1◇ − Pass − 1♠
                        2♣ − ?

♠ K 8 7   Two spades. In competitive auctions, you
♡ 10 6 4   must raise partner when you have a fit. Had
◇ A Q 10 8 3   opener passed you would also have passed.
♣ 4 2   But he didn't. When you raise partner, the
                     concept of free bids has little meaning. You
raise to show a fit, not to show a good hand. Points don't count
for nearly as much as your liking or otherwise for partner's suit.
He would far, far rather know that you fit his suit than that
your overcall was minimum or maximum.

NO ONE VUL.   *You*
                        1♣ − 1♡ − Pass − 1♠
                        2♣ − ?

♠ K 8 7   Three spades. A straightforward game try. If
♡ A Q 6 5 4   anything, this is an underbid.
◇ A 6 4 2
♣ 3

NO ONE VUL.   *You*
　　　　　　　　　　1♣ — 1◇ — 1♡ — 1♠
　　　　　　　　　　1NT — ?

♠ Q 8 7　　　　　　Two spades. While it's possible that you could
♡ A 4 2　　　　　　beat one notrump, you should have little
◇ A J 8 7 2　　　　trouble making two spades. What's more, you
♣ 4 2　　　　　　　keep LHO from bidding two clubs.
　　　　　　　　　　　　　　Note that when RHO rebids 1NT, he shows
a stopper in your trump suit. This isn't serious, but it means
that games which require a successful trump finesse will fail.

NO ONE VUL.   *You*
　　　　　　　　　　1♣ — 1◇ — 1♡ — 1♠
　　　　　　　　　　1NT — ?

♠ A 10 2　　　　　　Two spades again. When you have a fit, you
♡ 4 2　　　　　　　should nearly always raise unless there is clear
◇ A J 9 6 5　　　　reason not to. Had RHO passed instead of
♣ 9 6 2　　　　　　rebidding 1NT, you might have considered
　　　　　　　　　　passing for fear that partner might expect
more. But after opener's 1NT rebid, the raise to two spades is
clearcut. Note that partner will be able to play the trump suit to
advantage. Whatever honours are missing will be in the opener's
hand. If RHO has the K x x of spades, he will be disappointed
to find the ace over him.

BOTH VUL.   *You*
　　　　　　　　　　1♣ — 1♠ — 2♣ — 2◇
　　　　　　　　　　3♣ — ?

♠ A Q 10 8 6　　　　Three diamonds. This is a minimum and
♡ 4 2　　　　　　　many players wouldn't overcall in the first
◇ K J 3　　　　　　place. Yet when partner volunteers two
♣ 7 6 3　　　　　　diamonds, it becomes so good that even game
　　　　　　　　　　is not out of the question. Passing three
clubs is ultra-conservative. True, you have a minimum, but
everything is working overtime.

BOTH VUL.   *You*
                      1♣ — 1♠ — 2♣ — 2◊
                      3♣ — ?

♠ K Q 8 6 2   Three diamonds, but with none of the enthus-
♡ Q J 3   iasm of the previous example. This hand,
◊ K Q 4   with no aces, the wasted club queen, exactly
♣ Q 8   two clubs, soft hearts, etc. won't yield many
                      tricks in play.

NO ONE VUL.   *You*
                      1♣ — 1♠ — 2♣ — 2♡
                      3♣ — ?

♠ K 10 8 7 6   Bid four hearts. The only reason this hand is
♡ K 4 2   included is that I've seen people actually pass!
◊ A Q 10 7
♣ 3

So far, the auctions have been safe in that opponents have
limited their hands. When this is so, you feel that your side may
have a game and you bid with this in mind. On other sequences,
your side will have no game, short of miracle fits, and then
your bidding will be purely competitive with no thought of
game.

NO ONE VUL.   *You*
                      1♣ — 1♠ — 2◊ — 2♡
                      3◊ — ?

♠ A Q 10 7 2   Three hearts. Not because you expect to make
♡ J 10 5   it, still less because you hope to get to game.
♡ 4   On this auction, partner won't have many
♣ 8 6 5 2   high cards. If he bids four hearts, he will do it
                      as a sacrifice.

NO ONE VUL.   *You*
                      1♣ — 1♠ — 2◊ — 2♡
                      3◊ — ?

♠ K Q 8 7 6   Pass. You have only defensive values and
♡ Q 4 2   shouldn't invite partner to save.
◊ Q 3
♣ K 7 4

NOT VUL.
VS. VUL.

	You
	1♣ − 1♠ − 2◇ − 2♡
	3♣ − ?

♠ A Q 10 8
♡ K 6 5
◇ 4 3 2
♣ 4 3 2

Three hearts. Partner has a good suit and you have no wasted values. If you would not have overcalled in the first place, that's fine. But, if you did make a matchpoint decision to overcall, you should not back out now.

VUL. VS. NOT.

	You
	1◇ − 1♠ − 2♣ − 2♡
	3◇ − ?

♠ A Q 8 6 5 4
♡ 10 7 5 4
◇ K 4
♣ 2

Four hearts. Remember that this is a very dangerous moment for partner to introduce a new suit. It must be a good one. This is the sort of hand you need to bid game when opponents have shown most of the high cards. You have shape. You have good trump support. And you have no wasted high cards. Every one of them is working. This is because your side will seldom have more than 15 points when an opponent makes a two-over-one response.

VUL. VS. NOT.

	You
	1◇ − 1♠ − 2♣ − 2♡
	3◇ − ?

♠ K J 8 7 2
♡ Q J 4
◇ Q 3
♣ K 10 5

Once again. Pass. Your spades are suspect, your clubs and diamonds are worthless, and your distribution is vile. When the state of the auction spells danger, do not make questionable bids. On this vulnerability it would be suicidal.

NO ONE VUL.   *You*

    1◇ — 1♠ — 2◇ — 2♡
    3◇ — ?

♠ K J 8 7 2   Here is the same hand again but with a differ-
♡ Q J 4   ent auction and with different vulnerability.
◇ Q 3   On this sequence, three hearts would be
♣ K 10 5   acceptable. Note the difference. On the
                   second auction opponents are limited. On the
first auction they were not.

On the second auction, partner may have a few extra values.
On the first this was unlikely. On the second auction your club
king is worth full value. On the first it was of no value.

On the second auction, your worst result is down one
doubled. On the first it was down four doubled. On the second
auction, you aren't vul., on the first auction, you were.

On the second auction, no one will be inclined to double
you. On the first, both opponents would have been delighted.

I could go on.

Once again, the state of the auction is the deciding factor.
On the last two examples you would have known each time why
it was right or wrong to bid again.

NO ONE VUL.   *You*

    1♡ — 1♠ — 2♣ — 2◇
    2♡ — ?

♠ Q J 6 5 4   You could bid three diamonds, but nothing
♡ Q 2   much will come of it. Opponents will con-
◇ K Q 6 4   tinue, probably to four hearts, and you don't
♣ K 2   really want partner to save in five diamonds.

As usual, when opponents produce a strong
sequence, you should be influenced by the number of questionable cards you hold. Here your only certain values are the
king and queen of diamonds. And even the queen may be over-
valued.

VUL. VS. NOT.   *You*
                       1♡ — 1♠ — 2♣ — 2◇
                       2♡ — ?

♠ A Q 6 5 4   To start with, this hand is not worth a vulner-
♡ 3   able overcall. But if you somehow miscounted
◇ J 10 6   it and heard the given auction, you would not
♣ 8 6 5 4   be far wrong to bid three diamonds. You have
                 an attacking hand with no wasted cards.
The enormous increase in value due to a discovered fit justifies
a second bid on a hand barely worth the first one.

Partner bids a new suit after your overcall. Should you pass?
The only important point here is that you can indeed pass if
you think it best. A bid by you is encouraging in that you are
looking for something. You should not run from partner's suit
just because you don't like it.

NO ONE VUL.   *You*
                      1♠ — 2♣ — Pass — 2♡
                      Pass — ?

♠ A 6 2   Pass. You want better clubs to rebid them
♡ 3   and a better hand to try notrumps. Your
◇ Q 5 4   singleton heart will be a bigger liability in
♣ A Q 10 6 5 4   notrumps than in hearts.

BOTH VUL.   *You*
                      1♡ — 1♠ — Pass — 2◇
                      Pass — ?

♠ K Q 8 7 6   Pass again. Some of the time you must be
♡ K 2   content to show part of your hand. Two
◇ 7   diamonds is not forcing.
♣ K 9 6 5 4

NO ONE VUL.   *You*
                1♡ — 1♠ — 2♡ — 3♣
                Pass — ?

♠ Q 10 8 7 6 5   Pass. This should be a fine spot if you are
♡ A J 2   allowed to stay there. Rebidding spades or
◇ 4 2   notrumps would be poor.
♣ K 3

NO ONE VUL.   *You*
                1♡ — 2◇ — 2♡ — 3♣
                Pass — ?

♠ A 8 7   Pass. No reason to expect diamonds to be
♡ K 5 4   better than clubs. You have a decent overcall
◇ K Q 10 8 7 6   which didn't improve when partner bid
♣ 3   clubs. You can pass. Do so.

CASE 3

YOU OVERCALL.
PARTNER MAKES A JUMP SHIFT.

This one is pretty easy. Partner's jump is either strong and
invitational or it is weak and pre-emptive. The important point
is to know which it is.

Type one. Partner's bid is strong. When you overcall, and
LHO passes, raises, or bids a new suit at the one level, partner's
jump will show a good hand. You are allowed to pass this, but
only on a minimum *and* a misfit.

NO ONE VUL.   *You*
                1♣ — 1♡ — Pass — 2♠
                Pass — ?

♠ 9 2   Two notrumps. Slightly better than a mini-
♡ A Q 10 7 6   mum, no apparent misfit, and a club stopper.
◇ Q J 7
♣ K 10 5

BOTH VUL.

You

1♣ — 1♠ — 2♣ — 3♡

Pass — ?

♠ Q J 9 7 6 5
♡ 4
◇ Q 2
♣ A 6 5 4

Pass. Even though you have a club stopper, you have a minimum. As long as it is understood that you can pass, those hands where it is correct to do so are fairly clearcut.

NO ONE VUL.

You

1♣ — 1◇ — 2♣ — 3♠

Pass — ?

♠ Q 2
♡ 8 6 5
◇ A K Q 8 3
♣ 9 6 4

Bid four spades. You have a fine hand with a fit and ready made tricks.

NO ONE VUL.

You

1♡ — 2♣ — 2♡ — 3♠

Pass — ?

♠ 10 2
♡ 3
◇ A 8 6 5
♣ A Q 10 8 6 5

Bid four spades. Partner has shown six or five very good spades so 10 2 is adequate support. Your hand is a minimum, but it will be useful nonetheless. Compare it with the next example.

NO ONE VUL.

You

1♡ — 2♣ — 2♡ — 3♠

Pass — ?

♠ 10 7
♡ Q 3
◇ K J 7
♣ K Q J 10 8 7

Pass. This time you have many more losers than before. The heart holding is the worst possible and you have no aces. Best to go quietly. But, note that you are not passing because you have only two spades, but because you have a poor holding which grew poorer still when hearts were raised.

BOTH VUL.

You
1♡ − 2♣ − Pass − 3♠
Pass − ?

♠ 10 6 2
♡ 3
◇ 4 3 2
♣ A Q J 8 7 2

You wouldn't make a vulnerable two club bid on this hand, but if somehow the auction had gone as indicated, you would raise to four spades with the utmost confidence.

BOTH VUL.

You
1♣ − 1♡ − Pass − 2♠
Pass − ?

♠ 3 2
♡ A K Q 8 7
◇ A 5 4
♣ J 4 2

Three clubs. Game is almost sure, but what in isn't clear. You hope that partner can bid three notrumps. But failing that, four hearts or four spades could be the right spot.

NO ONE VUL.

You
1♣ − 1♠ − 2♣ − 3♡
Pass − ?

♠ A Q 10 8 7 6
♡ 3
◇ A J 7 6
♣ Q 2

Three spades. The question is whether or not a rebid of your suit is forcing when partner makes a jump shift. There are probably good reasons for playing it as non-forcing, but my own feeling is that it should be forcing. This hand is shown only to let you ponder over the question.

NO ONE VUL.

You
1♣ − 1♠ − 2♣ − 3♡
Pass − ?

♠ Q J 8 7 6 4 2
♡ −
◇ K 8 7 5
♣ Q 8

Probably pass is best. If you play three spades as non-forcing, you could bid that, but that is not the recommended treatment.

NO ONE VUL.   *You*
                    1♣ — 1♠ — Pass — 3♡
                    Pass — ?

♠ K J 8 7 2   Pass. Is a new suit after partner's jump shift
♡ 3   forcing? Without getting into an involved
◇ A 10 9 7 4   discussion, I suggest that it should be forcing.
♣ Q 3   Here you have a minimum hand. Three hearts
                 is likely to be a good enough contract. Leave
it alone.

   Type two. Partner's jump is pre-emptive. When you overcall,
and LHO bids notrumps or a new suit at the two level or higher,
a jump shift by partner is weak. Most of the time, your side will
be poorly placed to find a makeable contract because opponents
have most of the high cards. Usually your best strategy will be
to pass and hope that partner's pre-empt has upset opponents'
exchange of information. On occasion, though, you may be
able to continue the auction, but only when you have a fit.

NO ONE VUL.   *You*
                    1♣ — 1♠ — 1NT — 3◇
                    Pass — ?

♠ K 10 8 7 6   Pass. No other choice. Once you realise what
♡ A Q 3   opponents have shown it is clear that partner
◇ 8   is weak. There is no future for this hand other
♣ A J 5 4   than in three diamonds. What does partner
                 have? Perhaps:

                      ♠ 3
                      ♡ J 10 4 2
                      ◇ Q J 10 8 7 6 5
                      ♣ 7

or some similar concoction.

NO ONE VUL.   *You*
                     1♣ — 1♠ — 2◇ — 3♡
                     4♣ — ?

♠ A Q 8 7 6 5   Pass again. This is easy once you accept that
♡ 3   partner is weak. His three heart bid may have
◇ K 7 5   kept them out of a cold three notrumps.
♣ A 4 2   Why bid and ruin partner's good work?

VUL. VS. NOT.   *You*
                     1♣ — 1♠ — 2◇ — 3♡
                     Pass — ?

♠ K Q 10 8 7   Still pass. In no circumstances should you try
♡ 2   three notrumps. There's a good chance that
◇ K 9 7   LHO is about to bid three notrumps, and with
♣ K Q 7 3   a better chance of making it than you have.

NO ONE VUL.   *You*
                     1♣ — 1♠ — 2◇ — 3♡
                     Pass — ?

♠ Q J 10 8 7 6 5   Even with this hand, a pass might be best. If
♡ —   you do decide to bid three spades, however,
◇ K 8 7   it should be treated as non-forcing.
♣ A 5 4   As for bidding another suit, you probably
                     shouldn't. Much of the time there won't be a
fourth suit to bid. But if it should ever happen, it should be
non-forcing.

So far all the hands in this section have been misfits and the
proper action after partner's jump shift was a pass.

On some hands however, you will have a fit and it will be
correct to bid. Your purpose, however, will be to pave the way
to a worthwhile sacrifice, rather than to makeable contract.

NO ONE VUL.   *You*
                     1♣ — 1♠ — 2◇ — 3♡
                     Pass — ?

♠ A Q 8 7 6   Bid four hearts. A case could be made for
♡ K 6 4   five hearts. You have a fit, an attacking hand,
◇ 7 6 5 4   and no reason to think that you can defeat
♣ 9   any game contract, or, for that matter, a

slam, but you can make a useful bid which takes up bidding space. Make no mistake, this hand belongs to opponents.

NO ONE VUL.   *You*

1♡ – 1♠ – 2♣ – 3◇

3♡ – ?

♠ A Q 6 5 4   Bid five diamonds. Opponents surely have a
♡ 9   game and maybe a slam. As with most pre-
◇ Q 10 8   emptive actions, by bidding the maximum
♣ 10 8 7 5   immediately, you force them to guess. If you
                pass or bid four diamonds now and later
bid five diamonds, opponents will have exchanged more information and can better judge the situation. Bidding five diamonds directly creates problems and shuts out cue bids and Blackwood.

As long as your understandings are clear as to which jumps are weak and which are strong, there shouldn't be any problems.

CASE 4

YOU OVERCALL, PARTNER RAISES.

Of all the things that can happen when you overcall, this is about the best. When you make any defensive bid at all, you always hope for a fit, and when partner raises you will have found one. Now it remains to exploit this to its fullest.

When you have a fit, you still have problems, mostly pleasant ones.

After a simple raise by partner, you have to decide:
1. Do you have a sure game?
2. Do you have a potential game?
3. Should you compete?
4. Should you double?
5. Should you quit?
6. Should you save?

By now, you know that the answers to these questions will depend largely on the state of the auction. On some sequences, game will be unlikely or impossible and your action will be competitive or save orientated. Other sequences will leave open the possibility of game and you will have genuine cause for optimism.

When can you be optimistic?

On sequences where LHO has passed, raised opener, or introduced a new suit at the one level, you can feel that your side has a distinct interest in the hand. This doesn't mean that the hand belongs to you, but that the possibility exists. Since LHO's bid does not show many points, more are left for your side.

   1. Do you have a sure game?

NO ONE VUL.   *You*
                    1♣ — 1♠ — 2♣ — 2♠
                    Pass — ?

♠ A Q 8 7 6   Bid four spades. Quite routine. This hand
♡ A Q 5   will make game easily. If opponents save, you
◇ K J 7 2   have to decide what to do, but that will come
♣ 3   later. In the play, you will benefit from the
                 descriptive bids of both opponents, which
                 should help you to place the cards.

VUL. VS. NOT.   *You*
                    1♣ — 1♠ — Pass — 2♠
                    3♣ — ?

♠ A J 8 7 6 5 In this sequence game is possible and I would
♡ K 8   bid four spades at once. Oddly enough, had I
◇ K 10 8 7   opened one spade I would have probably
♣ 7   passed a simple raise to two spades. Here,
                 however, I know that the cards will be well
placed for me. It's almost as if I had another ace. I also know that partner is unlikely to have wasted strength in clubs.

NO ONE VUL.   *You*
                   1♣ − 1◊ − 1♡ − 2◊
                   Pass − ?

♠ 4 2   Three notrumps. When your major suit over-
♡ A K 3   call is raised, you usually avoid notrumps.
◊ A Q 6 5 4 2   But when your overcall is in a minor, you
♣ K 3   may well make the switch. This hand looks
                   like yielding at least nine notrump tricks
while offering no such assurance about five diamonds. Note that
the spade suit is not a threat. Neither opponent has five. Partner
therefore has three and probably more.

If LHO had not bid 1♡, but had passed instead, he might
indeed have five spades without the values to bid them. It is
actually more dangerous to bid three notrumps when LHO
passes throughout than when he bids 1♡.

2. Should you make a game try?

When the auction is safe there is a real chance that your
side has a game. If you think so, make a game try.

NO ONE VUL.   *You*
                   1♣ − 1♠ − 2♣ − 2♠
                   Pass − ?

♠ Q 10 8 7 2   With the opening bid on your right, it looks
♡ K 2   as if your finesses will work. Try three
◊ A Q 8 3   diamonds.
♣ K 2

VUL. VS. VUL.   *You*
                   1♣ − 1◊ − 1♡ − 2◊
                   Pass − ?

♠ 8 2   Two notrumps. Partner can have more than
♡ K 9   if he had raised an opening bid. Two notrumps
◊ A Q 10 8 7   allows him to pass, raise, or return to three
♣ A Q 10 5   diamonds. Don't worry about the two small
                   spades. In competitive sequences science
                   comes second to pragmatism.

NO ONE VUL.   *You*
                     1♡ − 2◊ − Pass − 3◊
                     Pass − ?

♠ A 8 7   I would try three spades. Three notrumps or
♡ 4 2   five diamonds are possible and three spades
◊ A Q 8 7 6 5   caters for both. If partner raises spades, you
♣ A 4   retreat to five diamonds.

BOTH VUL.   *You*
                     1♣ − 1♠ − 2♣ − 2♠
                     Pass − ?

♠ Q 9 7 6 5   Three spades. It's useful to play so that when
♡ 3   RHO passes, the three spade bid asks for good
◊ A Q 10 9   trumps. Had RHO bid three clubs, the three
♣ A Q 2   spade bid would have been competitive.

NO ONE VUL.   *You*
                     1◊ − 1♠ − 2◊ − 2♠
                     3◊ − ?

♠ A Q 9 7 6   You would like to make a game try, but there
♡ Q 3   is no clearcut game try available. You would
◊ 4 2   like three spades to show a promising hand,
♣ A K 10 5   but as you will see in the next section, that
                     bid is best treated as a competitive effort.
This leaves three hearts as the only legal bid left which can be
construed as a game try. Scientific? Yes. But not unreasonable.

BOTH VUL.   *You*
                     1♡ − 1♠ − 2♡ − 2♠
                     3♡ − ?

♠ K 10 7 6 5   More problems. Again, you would like to
♡ 4 2   make a game try, but the only bid available
◊ A Q   is three spades. And that is competitive. Or
♣ A Q 8 7   is it?
                     Here are some possible solutions:
     1. Play so that when there is no game try available, three
spades would be invitational and not competitive.
     2. Play so that a double is an artificial game try and three

spades remains competitive. This loses the penalty double and runs the risk that someone will forget the convention.

3. Perhaps you should play a double as a game try only when they have established a fit.

Anything will work as long as you keep track of what's happening.

3. Should you compete?

On auctions where it is "safe" to continue, you should feel free to do so. Only when it is clearly wrong to continue should you give up.

NO ONE VUL.   *You*
                   1♣ — 1♡ — 1♠ — 2♡
                   2♠ — ?

♠ 8 2   Three hearts. This is a typical competitive
♡ A Q 10 6 5   action. RHO has rebid, so your three heart
◊ K Q 9 3   bid is defined as competitive. You have only a
♣ 4 2   normal overcall, but it is of an attacking
                nature with few defensive values. Opponents
have found what rates to be a good two level contract, so it behooves you to get them out of it.

NO ONE VUL.   *You*
                   1♣ — 1♠ — Pass — 2♠
                   3♣ — ?

♠ Q 10 9 7 3   You can bid three spades, but you should
♡ A 10 2   bear in mind that:
◊ K J 5 4   1. Your trump suit is poor.
♣ 3   2. There is no reason to think they have a
                fit.

3. They are at the three level. You have more chance of defeating a three level contract than a two level contract. At IMP's, this would be a pass.

NO ONE VUL.   *You*
1♣ — 1♠ — 2♣ — 2♠
3♣ — ?

♠ Q 10 9 7 3   Three spades here is far safer than on the pre-
♡ A 10 2   vious auction. There is a better chance that
◇ K J 5 4   partner's values won't be wasted in clubs and
♣ 3   opponents have a known fit.

VUL. VS. NOT.   *You*
1◇ — 1♡ — 1♠ — 2♡
3♣ — ?

♠ 5 3   Three hearts. A competitive bid only and
♡ A J 8 7 5 3   partner is not expected to do any further
◇ K 10 8 5   bidding. This hand offers many points of
♣ 3   interest.
           1. You are vulnerable, so you need addi-
tional safety to continue.
   2. A good six card suit which has been raised is a good basis
for competing.
   3. Opponents are at the three level so the need to compete
is less urgent.
   4. Opponents have no fit yet, which suggests caution.
   5. Your shape is attractive.

VUL. VS. NOT.   *You*
1◇ — 1♡ — 1♠ — 2♡
3♣ — ?

♠ Q 3   Good time to pass. You have a defensive
♡ K 10 9 5 4   hand. Your shape is undistinguished. Op-
◇ K J 3   ponents have no known fit. Your suit is poor.
♣ K 4 2   Your spade queen is of marginal value. You
           are vulnerable. This sequence and vulnera-
bility are the same as on the preceding hand, but that's as far as
it goes. I would rather bid four hearts on the previous hand
than three hearts on this one.

NO ONE VUL.   *You*
                     1♡ – 1♠ – 2♡ – 2♠
                     3♡ – ?

♠ J 10 8 7 6 5   The answer depends on your agreed treat-
♡ 3   ment. If you play three spades as encouraging,
◇ A 8 6   you have to pass. If you play it as competi-
♣ A 4 2   tive, you can bid. Part-scores have far more
                  importance than appears at first sight. At
matchpoints, +100 instead of +110 or +140 can be a zero.
And at IMP's, if you allow opponents to steal a part-score, you
lose from five to seven IMP's. Two such losses come to more
than a game swing of eleven IMP's.

Bidding methods should be attuned to the never-ending
battle for part-scores.

NO ONE VUL.   *You*
                     1♠ – 2♣ – 2♠ – 3♣
                     3♠ – ?

♠ 3   It looks reasonable to bid four clubs, but it is
♡ K J 2   not as simple as that. Opponents have been
◇ K 8 7   pushed to the three level which is one of the
♣ A Q 8 7 6 5   goals of competitive auctions. Having achieved
                  that, any further action must be fairly sound.
You should not be nearly as eager to get them to the four level
as to the three level.

   4. Should you double?

When you have established a fit, you should not rush to
double opponents. If LHO has introduced a new suit you can
be moderately aggressive with your doubles, but if they have a
fit, you should be very cautious.

NO ONE VUL.   *You*
                     1♡ – 1♠ – 2♡ – 2♠
                     3♡ – ?

♠ Q 10 8 7 6   Double here can work out, but three spades
♡ A Q 5 2   should be cold. Your decision will depend
◇ A 8 7   on your understanding of the double. If it is a
♣ 3   try, you couldn't use it anyway.

NO ONE VUL.   *You*
                1♡ — 1♠ — 2♡ — 2♠
                3♡ — ?

♠ A Q 8 7 6 5   Bid four spades. To double would be a serious
♡ K 6 5 4 2   error. In spite of your heart length, you have
♢ A   no spots. With such excellent game-going
♣ 3   potential, go for it.

                  You may have a hand close to a penalty
double. One of the deciding factors then might be whether
RHO's last bid was invitational or competitive. You might
decide to double a competitive bid but not an invitational one.

VUL. VS. NOT.   *You*
                1♢ — 1♠ — 2♢ — 2♠
                3♢ — ?

♠ K J 4 3 2   You have a good enough hand to compete
♡ K Q 3   to three spades, but it's nothing special.
♢ Q 2   Whatever you do, don't make a penalty
♣ A J 3   double. If this bid wouldn't occur to you,
                 go on to the next hand. But if it crossed your
mind, forget it. Any time you have a reasonable chance to make
something or to defeat something, play the hand.

NO ONE VUL.   *You*
                1♠ — 2♣ — Pass — 3♣
                3♠ — ?

♠ Q 10 8 3   This one you can take to the bank. When one
♡ A 2   hand is doing all the bidding for the other
♢ 3   side, or when they haven't found a fit, you
♣ A Q 8 7 6 5   can be very aggressive with your penalty
                 doubles. Had LHO raised to two spades
instead of passing, it would not be nearly so tempting to double.
On the given auction, your partner could have anything from
one to three spades. But if LHO has raised spades, your partner
will have one or none. This highlights the defensive and attacking potential of this hand according to the sequence.

After a Jump Raise:
When partner makes a jump raise, you have to decide whether to

pass or to continue to game, and your understanding of partner's
bid will help you decide.

NO ONE VUL.   *You*
                     1♣ — 1♠ — Pass — 3♠
                     Pass — ?

♠ K 10 7 6 5   Go on to four spades. You have shape and
♡ 3   useful high cards. Partner's bid shows four
◇ A 10 4 2   trumps plus some distribution. Note that
♣ K 10 3   when partner could have cue bid, but jumps
                     instead, he guarantees four trumps. This is
even more important on hands where you have overcalled on a
four card suit.

BOTH VUL.   *You*
                     1♡ — 1♠ — Pass — 3♠
                     Pass — ?

♠ A Q 10 3   An automatic four spade bid. The only
♡ A J 6 2   drawback is lack of a fifth trump. But as long
◇ K 6 5 2   as partner has four or more, you shouldn't
♣ 5   worry.

NO ONE VUL.   *You*
                     1♣ — 1♠ — Pass — 3♠
                     Pass — ?

♠ K Q 7 6 5   Opposite an invitational raise, you should
♡ Q 2   pass. Your hand is too porous.
◇ K J 5
♣ Q 8 7

BOTH VUL.   *You*
                     1♡ — 1♠ — 2♡ — 3♠
                     Pass — ?

♠ K 8 7 6 5   You have enough here to go on to four
♡ 4 2   spades, in spite of a weakish suit and drab
◇ A Q 8   distribution.
♣ A J 5   Note that a cue bid by partner would
                     be ambiguous here. It could be either a raise

of spades or a game force in some other suit. Because LHO's raise to two hearts has taken up a lot of room you should treat partner's cue bid as being a spade raise with a balanced hand.

14

WHEN GAME IS NOT POSSIBLE

After a Raise:
When you overcall and LHO bids notrumps or a new suit at the two level or higher, and your partner raises, you should assume that your side has no game. Either your trump suit will break badly, or you will be seriously outgunned pointwise. In either case, a game contract by you would be exceptional. When you can't expect game, it is reasonable to give up all invitational sequences and make all your bids competitive. It's easy to recognise when this applies, but essential to define your methods.

BOTH VUL.

You
1♣ — 1♠ — 1NT — 2♠
3♣ — ?

♠ A J 8 7 6 5
♡ K 10 5 4
◇ 3
♣ K 2

Three spades. When LHO is known to have a spade trick plus some additional high cards, you have to be cautious. Had LHO raised to two clubs instead of bidding 1NT, you would have bid four spades. But in the circumstances, a non-invitational three spades is best. Alternatively, you could try three hearts as a game try.

NO ONE VUL.

You
1♡ — 1♠ — 1NT — 2♠
3♣ — ?

♠ K J 7 6 5
♡ 7 6 5
◇ A Q 7
♣ K 2

This hand, good as it is, has drawbacks. Your suit is full of holes and your heart holding is depressing. I would rate three spades as barely acceptable at matchpoints, but on the understanding that you expect to go down. At IMP's this would be too dangerous. One thing you have going for you, if you do decide to bid, is that partner needs a good hand to raise after the one notrump. From his point of view, you might have overcalled on a four card suit, so he won't be bidding on three small with questionable values outside.

NO ONE VUL.   *You*
                   1♡ – 1♠ – 1NT – 2♠
                   3♣ – ?

♠ K Q 9 7   Double. This is the sort of good result which
♡ A 10 6 5   can occur when you make a well-judged
◇ 3   overcall on a four card suit.
♣ Q 10 9 7

NO ONE VUL.   *You*
                   1♠ – 2♡ – 2NT – 3♡
                   Pass – ?

♠ 4 2   Pass. Looks as if game were possible, but you
♡ A Q 10 6 5 4   should be warned by that two notrump bid.
◇ –   You expect to have two spade losers, and a
♣ A 8 6 5 3   heart loser, so you have to lose no clubs.
                   With a spade lead and trump return, three
hearts will be the probable limit. Who knows, you might yet
be doubled in three hearts.

NO ONE VUL.   *You*
                   1♡ – 1♠ – 2♣ – 2♠
                   Pass – ?

♠ A 10 7 6 5   Given the two club bid, the game should be
♡ K Q 7   out of the question. You might be willing to
◇ A 10 5 4   go as high as three spades, but no higher.
♣ 3   You can either pass or bid three spades at this
                   juncture. If you pass, LHO will surely do
something. Probably two notrumps or three clubs. Against
three clubs, you might compete with three spades, but against
anything else, you should pass. Once in a while, two spades will
be passed out, but that would be rare. All things considered, I
would pass now and probably later as well.

NO ONE VUL.   *You*

1♡ — 1♠ — 2♣ — 2♠

Pass — ?

♠ Q J 8 7 6 5

♡ A 6 4 2

♢ 4 2

♣ 7

This is a good example of a competitive three spade bid. If you can bid three spades with the assurance that partner will pass, you can make it difficult for LHO to continue. If they were vul., you could even bid four spades. Remember, partner should not raise on this sequence unless he has either good trumps or shape. A random seven or eight count with bad trumps is not worth a raise.

NO ONE VUL.   *You*

1♣ — 1♠ — 2♡ — 2♠

3♡ — ?

♠ A K 8 7 2

♡ K J 3

♢ Q 5 4

♣ Q 2

Clearly, pass. You have a defensive hand unsuited for competing. Partner's values are likely to include a singleton heart and that isn't much use to you.

BOTH VUL.   *You*

1♢ — 1♠ — 2♡ — 2♠

3♡ — ?

♠ A J 8 7 6 5

♡ 5 4 3 2

♢ K 3

♣ 2

Four spades. This could easily be a hand with game for both sides. Even if you don't make, it will be a good save more often than not. Note that your hand has improved immensely, whereas the one before remained unchanged or even lessened in value.

NOT VUL.

VS. VUL.   *You*

1♣ — 1♠ — 2♡ — 2♠

3♣ — ?

♠ A J 8 7 2

♡ 4 2

♢ K Q 7 6 5

♣ 2

With a good attacking hand, a save might be in order. But opponents have yet to find a fit and even with game values, they may have trouble making a game. Rather than bidding four spades, you can try three diamonds to give partner a chance to save or not, as he sees fit.

After a Jump Raise:

NO ONE VUL.

You
1♣ − 1♠ − 2♡ − 3♠
Pass − ?

♠ K Q 8 7 5
♡ K Q 4
♢ K J 7
♣ 4 2

Pass. How do you interpret partner's three spade bid? If you have decided to play it as pre-emptive, after a two-over-one by LHO, then your decision to pass is clearcut. If you play three spades as strong or invitational, then you should go on to game. In this sequence, you will rarely have a hand worth a strong raise, so using it as a weak obstructive bid makes a lot of sense. It only remains to remember what the bid means.

BOTH VUL.

You
1♣ − 1♡ − 2♢ − 3♡
Pass − ?

♠ K 10 7 6
♡ K 9 8 4 3 2
♢ 3
♣ K 2

This is the sort of hand where you should continue after a weak jump raise by partner. Very seldom will you do so as a result of high cards. Nearly always it will be on distribution with every high card working overtime.

SUMMARY

I make no claim to have covered the whole area of overcalls. High level decisions, slam methods, saves, have been barely touched upon. And the problem of what to do with really big hands, when RHO opens, has been ignored. These topics will have to wait for another book. What I have done has been to dwell on the early decisions both by the overcaller and his partner. A foundation has been created which will help make later decisions easier. Bids have been defined and common situations identified and I have put forward some suggestions, which will, I hope, prove useful.

Hands in the section which follows bring out the main points made in these pages. For considerations of space, detailed comment will not be possible, so most of the comment will be on subjects which have not come up before.

Part IV
Test What You Have Learned

QUIZ

The best way to tackle these quizzes is to take a card and cover up the last column showing the bids recommended for South, your hand. Follow the auction round by round and each time, as the scene changes, choose your bid.

Occasionally the recommended bid will be followed by another, or two others, in brackets

e.g.

                South
                4♠ (Double = 60) (Pass = 50)

This would show that 4♠ was the best bid with double worth sixty per cent and a pass fifty per cent. Perfection in bridge is unattainable and I do not expect my ideas to be accepted universally. Someone may give my second choice pride of place. Someone else may prefer a bid which I hadn't even considered. By and large, however, no one will reject my selections out of hand. My style is my own and may not suit everyone, but it has worked well for me, and if it suits you, it will work well for you, too.

A final word of advice: watch your values change with every bid round the table as the dangerous auctions and those that are safe are brought sharply into relief.

OVERCALLER (South)

NOT VS. NOT	West	North	East	South
♠ 8 7 6 4 2	–	–	1♣	1♠
♡ A 10 7	1NT	2♡	Pass	3♡ (4♡ = 80)
◇ 3	Pass	Pass	Pass	
♣ A Q 9 3				

NOT VS. VUL.	West	North	East	South
♠ K 8 6 5 3	—	—	1♣	1♠
♡ 3 2	2◇	2♠	3♣	Pass
◇ K J 3	3◇	Pass	Pass	Pass
♣ A 5 4				

When opponents pursue a strong auction, you need good suits and shape to continue.

VUL. VS. NOT	West	North	East	South
♠ Q 10 8 6 5 4	—	—	1♡	1♠
♡ A 9 3	2♡	2♠	Pass	Pass
◇ 4	3♡	Pass	Pass	3♠
♣ K 10 6	Pass	Pass	Pass	

NOT VS. NOT	West	North	East	South
♠ A 10 8 6 5	—	—	1♡	1♠
♡ 3	2♡	Dbl.*	Pass	4♣
◇ K 4	Pass	Pass	Pass	
♣ K 10 7 6 3				

*Responsive

NOT VS. NOT	West	North	East	South
♠ A Q 8 6 4 3	—	—	1♣	1♠
♡ J 8 4 2	2♣	Dbl.*	Pass	2♡
◇ Q 3	Pass	Pass	3♣	3♡
♣ 7	Pass	Pass	Pass	

*Responsive

VUL. VS. NOT	West	North	East	South
♠ K 7 5 4 3 2	—	—	1◇	1♠
♡ A 9 6	2◇	Dbl.*	Pass	2♡
◇ K 5 3	3♣	Pass	3◇	Pass
♣ 7	Pass	Pass		

*Responsive

NOT VS. VUL.	West	North	East	South
♠ K Q J 10 6 3	–	–	1♣	1♠
♡ 9 5 4	2♣	Dbl.*	Pass	2♠
◊ K 2	Pass	Pass	3♣	Pass
♣ 7 3	Pass	Pass		

*Responsive

VUL. VS. VUL.	West	North	East	South
♠ A K 8 7 5	–	–	1♣	1♠
♡ Q 5 4	2♣	Dbl.*	Pass	2♡
◊ K 2	Pass	3♡	Pass	4♡
♣ 8 5 3	Pass	Pass	Pass	

*Responsive

You haven't promised more than three hearts and you have a good overcall.

NOT VS. VUL.	West	North	East	South
♠ A Q J 10 8 7	–	–	1♣	1♠
♡ Q 2	2♣	Dbl.*	Pass	2♠
◊ K 7 3	Pass	Pass	3♣	3◊
♣ 9 5	Pass	Pass	Pass	

*Responsive

NOT VS. NOT	West	North	East	South
♠ K 10 7 6 4 3	–	–	1♣	1♠
♡ K 3	1NT	Pass	Pass	Pass
◊ A Q 2				
♣ Q 5				

VUL. VS. NOT	West	North	East	South
♠ J 10 8 7 6 4	–	–	1◊	1♠
♡ A K	2◊	Pass	Pass	2♠
◊ A 2	Pass	Pass	3◊	Pass
♣ K 4 3	Pass	3♠	Pass	Pass
	Pass			

Partner should have a few points and a couple of spades as well.

VUL. VS. VUL.	West	North	East	South
♠ A Q 6 4 2	—	—	1♡	1♠
♡ 4	2♣	Pass	2♡	Pass (3◇ = 30)
◇ K J 6 5 3	3♣	Pass	Pass	Pass (3◇ = 40)
♣ A 3				

NOT. VS. NOT	West	North	East	South
♠ Q J 8 6 2	—	—	1♡	1♠
♡ 8 7	Pass	2♡	Pass	2♠
◇ A Q 5	Pass	3♠	Pass	4♠
♣ K 9 5	Pass	Pass	Pass	

You have a maximum for a signoff in two spades and partner is stil interested.

VUL. VS. VUL.	West	North	East	South
♠ A Q 2	—	—	1♣	1♡
♡ A K 8 6 5	Pass	2♣	Pass	2♠
◇ 4 2	Pass	3◇	Pass	3♡
♣ 8 5 3	Pass	4♡	Pass	Pass
	Pass			

NOT VS. VUL.	West	North	East	South
♠ Q 2	—	—	1♣	1◇
♡ A 4 2	Pass	2♣	Dbl.	Rdbl.*
◇ K Q 8 7 5	Pass	2◇**	Pass	3♣***
♣ A 8 4	Pass	3◇	Pass	3NT
	Pass	Pass	Pass	

*Good hand with at least ½ a club stopper.
**Minimum hand for the cue bid. Diamond support.
***Insisting on game and trying to get partner to declare notrumps if he has anything in clubs.

NOT VS. NOT	West	North	East	South
♠ Q 8	—	—	1♣	1♡
♡ A K J 6 4	Pass	2♣	Pass	2♡
◇ J 10 3	Pass	2♠	Pass	3♠
♣ 8 7 3	Pass	4♠	Pass	Pass
	Pass			

NOT VS. NOT	West	North	East	South
♠ 4 2	—	—	1◇	1♡
♡ A Q 10 8 4	Pass	2◇	Pass	2♡
◇ J 8 7	Pass	3♣	Pass	3◇*
♣ K 10 5	Pass	3NT	Pass	Pass
	Pass			

*After partner's strong auction, you can try three notrumps.

NOT VS. VUL.	West	North	East	South
♠ Q 10 9 8 6 4	—	—	1♡	1♠
♡ 3	2♣	2◇	2♡	5◇ (4◇ = 80)
◇ A Q 8 2	Pass	Pass	Dbl.	Pass (3◇ = −10)
♣ 8 5	Pass	Pass		

They have a game. Make it hard for them to judge the auction.

VUL. VS. VUL.	West	North	East	South
♠ A J 8	—	—	1♣	1◇
♡ 4	1♡	1♠	2♡	3♠ (2♠ = 50)
◇ A 10 9 7 3	Pass	4♠	Pass	Pass
♣ K 9 7 5	Pass			

NOT. VS. NOT	West	North	East	South
♠ K 10 8 6 5 4	—	—	1♡	1♠
♡ Q 3	2◇	Pass	2♡	Pass
◇ K 9 5	3♡	Pass	Pass	Pass
♣ A Q				

Don't rebid on marginal hands when opponents show strength.

NOT VS. NOT	West	North	East	South
♠ K Q 10 8 4	—	Pass	1♡	1♠
♡ 3	2♡	3◇	3♡	4◇
◇ A Q 4 2	4♡	Pass	Pass	Pass
♣ J 8 5				

Opponents are limited. No reason to save.

VUL. VS. NOT	West	North	East	South
♠ A J 9 8 7	–	–	–	Pass
♡ 4	Pass	Pass	1♡	1♠
◇ 8 3	2♡	3♡	4♡	4♠
♣ A 10 9 7 5	Pass	Pass	Pass	

Don't worry that partner is a passed hand. He invites you. Having passed originally, you couldn't have more.

NOT. VS. NOT	West	North	East	South
♠ K Q 7 5 3	–	Pass	1♡	1♠
♡ A J 4	2♡	Dbl.*	Pass	3♣
◇ 7 4	3♡	Pass	Pass	Pass
♣ J 7 3				

*Responsive

Don't consider doubling. Be happy that the responsive double has helped you to push them to the three level.

NOT VS. NOT	West	North	East	South
♠ Q 10 8 5 3	–	Pass	1♡	1♠
♡ 3	2♡	Dbl.*	Pass	3♣
◇ Q 10 4	3♡	Pass	Pass	4♣
♣ A Q 9 5	Pass	Pass	Pass	

*Responsive

You have strength in clubs and diamonds. Your hands fit well. Don't be afraid that you may push them to game. They were content to stop in three hearts. Trust them.

NOT VS. NOT	West	North	East	South
♠ A K 8 7 4	–	–	1♡	1♠
♡ 8 5	Pass	3◇	Pass	3♡
◇ K J	Pass	4◇	Pass	Pass
♣ 10 7 5 2	Pass			

You tried. No luck. Give it up.

NOT VS. NOT	West	North	East	South
♠ A Q 6 5	—	—	1♣	1♠
♡ 3	Pass	2♣	Pass	2◇
◇ 10 7 5 3	Pass	2♠	Pass	3♣ (Pass = 80)
♣ A J 9 5	Pass	3♠	Pass	Pass
	Pass			

NOT VS. NOT	West	North	East	South
♠ A 10 7 5 2	—	—	1♡	1♠
♡ J 3	1NT	Pass	2♣	2◇
◇ K Q 8 6 4	3♣	3◇	4♣	Pass
♣ 8	Pass	Dbl.	Pass	Pass
	Pass			

NOT VS. VUL.	West	North	East	South
♠ A J 5 3 2	—	—	1♣	1♠
♡ A J 5	Pass	2♣	Pass	3♣
◇ 5 3	Pass	3◇	Pass	3NT
♣ K 9 7	Pass	Pass	Pass	

NOT VS. VUL.	West	North	East	South
♠ K Q 8	—	—	1♣	1♡
♡ J 10 8 7 6	Pass	2◇	Pass	Pass
◇ 4	Pass			
♣ A Q 6 2				

NOT VS. NOT	West	North	East	South
♠ J 8 7	—	—	1♣	1◇
♡ 8 3	1♡	1♠	2♣	2♠
◇ A K 10 8 4	Pass	3♠	Pass	4♠
♣ A 10 3	Pass	Pass	Pass	

NOT VS. VUL.	West	North	East	South
♠ A Q 8 7	—	—	1♡	1♠
♡ K 10 9 6 3	Pass	2◇	Pass	2NT
◇ J 3	Pass	3◇	Pass	Pass
♣ A 4	Pass			

VUL. VS. VUL.	West	North	East	South
♠ A J 10 8 4	—	—	1♣	1♠
♡ A Q 2	Pass	1NT	Pass	3NT
◇ K J 4	Pass	Pass	Pass	
♣ J 5				

NOT VS. VUL.	West	North	East	South
♠ K Q J 5	1♣	Pass	1♡	1♠
♡ A J 8 7 4	2♣	2♠	3♣	Pass (3♠ = 60)
◇ 3	Pass	3♠	Pass	Pass
♣ 10 6 3	Pass			

VUL. VS. NOT	West	North	East	South
♠ A K J 9 7	—	—	1♣	1♠
♡ K Q 4	1NT	Pass	Pass	Pass (2♠ = 10)
◇ Q 4				
♣ Q 10 7				

NOT VS. NOT	West	North	East	South
♠ A 8 7	—	Pass	1♡	2♣
♡ Q 6 4	2♡	2♠	Pass	Pass
◇ 8 3	Pass			
♣ A K 10 7 4				

Partner couldn't open, so pass and hope to buy it.

VUL. VS. VUL.	West	North	East	South
♠ K J 8 4	—	Pass	1♡	2♣
♡ 4 3	2♡	Pass	Pass	2♠
◇ 3	Pass	3♣	Pass	Pass
♣ A Q J 8 6 3	Pass			

NOT VS. NOT	West	North	East	South
♠ Q J 10 8 3	—	—	1♡	2♣
♡ 4	2◇	Pass	2♡	2♠
◇ 3	3♡	3♠	4♡	4♠
♣ K Q J 8 7 5	5♡	Pass	Pass	Pass (5♠ = 60)

NOT VS. NOT	West	North	East	South
♠ K 10 7 5 3	1♣	Pass	1♡	Pass
♡ Q 4 2	2♣	Pass	Pass	Pass
◇ 8 5				
♣ K J 3				

Not imperative to bid when RHO has responded and so many of your cards could be valuable in defence.

NOT VS. VUL.	West	North	East	South
♠ 8 2	—	—	1♠	2♡
♡ A Q 10 8 3	2♠	Pass	Pass	3◇
◇ K Q J 8	Pass	4◇	Pass	Pass
♣ 4 3	Pass			

When opponents have a fit and are both limited, it is safe to compete.

VUL. VS. VUL.	West	North	East	South
♠ 4	—	Pass	1♠	2♣
♡ K J 8 5	2♠	Dbl.*	3◇	4♡
◇ 8 5	4♠	Pass	Pass	5♡ (Pass = 80)
♣ A Q J 9 7 6	Pass	Pass	Pass	

*Responsive

VUL. VS. VUL.	West	North	East	South
♠ 4	—	Pass	1◇	2♣
♡ A J 8 5	2◇	2♠	Pass	3♣
◇ 9 4	Pass	Pass	Pass	
♣ K Q J 8 5 3				

There is no sensible way of introducing the heart suit into the bidding. Anyway, if partner had hearts, he might have made a responsive double.

NOT VS. VUL.	West	North	East	South
♠ K 3	—	—	1♠	2♣
♡ 8 6	Pass	2♠	Pass	3♣
◇ 9 7 5	Pass	3♡	Pass	3NT
♣ A Q J 10 8 5	Pass	Pass	Pass	

NOT VS. VUL.	West	North	East	South
♠ 8	—	—	1♠	2♣
♡ 8 5 3	2♡	3◇	3♡	5◇
◇ Q J 8	Dbl.	Pass	Pass	Pass
♣ A K 10 9 6 3				

NOT VS. VUL.	West	North	East	South
♠ 8	—	—	1♠	2♣
♡ 8 5 3	2♠	3◇	3♠	4◇
◇ Q J 8	4♠	Pass	Pass	Pass
♣ A K 10 9 6 3				

NOT VS. VUL.	West	North	East	South
♠ 8 3	—	—	1♠	2♡
♡ Q J 10 8 5 3	2♠	3♣	Dbl.	Pass
◇ A Q 7 5	Pass	Pass		
♣ J				

NOT VS. NOT	West	North	East	South
♠ 3	—	—	1♠	2♡
♡ A Q J 8 6	2♠	Pass	Pass	Dbl.
◇ A Q 4	Pass	3◇	3♠	Pass
♣ J 10 8 4	Pass	4♣	Pass	Pass
	Pass			

NOT VS. NOT	West	North	East	South
♠ Q 7 4	—	—	1♡	2♣
♡ 8 4	2♡	2♠	3♡	3♠
◇ K 4	Pass	Pass	Pass	
♣ A Q 10 9 7 2				

NOT VS. VUL.	West	North	East	South
♠ 8 4 3	—	—	1♠	2♡
♡ A K Q 8 5	2♣	Dbl.*	3♠	4♣
◇ 10	Pass	Pass	Pass	
♣ K 10 7 3				

*Responsive

NOT VS. VUL.	West	North	East	South
♠ 8 5 3	—	—	1♠	2◇
♡ K Q	2♡	Pass	2♠	Pass
◇ K Q 9 8 6 4	2NT	Pass	Pass	Pass
♣ A J				

NOT VS. VUL.	West	North	East	South
♠ 10 5 4	—	—	1♠	2♣
♡ 3	2♡	3♣	3♡	5♣
◇ K 10 6	5♡	Pass	Pass	Pass
♣ A Q 10 8 6 3				

Don't first pass, then decide to save. Do it now.

NOT VS. NOT	West	North	East	South
♠ 8	—	—	1♡	2♣
♡ 7 4	2♠	4♣*	4NT	6♣
◇ K 10 8 5	Pass	Pass	Dbl.	Pass
♣ A Q 9 7 5 3	Pass	Pass		

*Pre-emptive

VUL. VS. VUL.	West	North	East	South
♠ Q 4	—	—	1♠	2♣
♡ A 7 4	Pass	2♠	Dbl.	Rdbl.*
◇ 8 5	Pass	2NT	Pass	3♣
♣ K Q J 10 7 3	Pass	Pass	Pass	

*Something in spades

NOT VS. VUL.	West	North	East	South
♠ K 8 7	—	—	1◇	2♣
♡ J 2	2◇	Dbl.*	Pass	2♠
◇ 8 5	Pass	Pass	3◇	Pass
♣ A Q 9 8 7 5	Pass	3♠	Pass	Pass
	Pass			

*Responsive

VUL. VS. VUL.	West	North	East	South
♠ K Q 7	—	—	1♡	2♣
♡ 9 7	2♡	Dbl.*	3♡	3♠
◇ 7 2	Pass	Pass	Pass	
♣ A Q J 8 6 4				

*Responsive

NOT VS. NOT	West	North	East	South
♠ A K J 8	—	—	1◇	1♠
♡ 7 5	2◇	Pass	Pass	Pass
◇ 10 4				
♣ K 6 5 3 2				

While one spade is probably your most effective bid, it means that you can't show the club suit.

VUL. VS. VUL.	West	North	East	South
♠ K 10 8 5 3	1♣	Pass	2♣	2♠
♡ K 2	3♣	3♠	Pass	Pass
◇ A J 4	Pass			
♣ 10 6 5				

VUL. VS. VUL.	West	North	East	South
♠ A 3	1♡	Pass	2♡	3♣
♡ 8 5 3	Pass	Pass	3♡	Pass
◇ 8 4	Pass	Pass		
♣ A Q J 9 7 4				

NOT VS. VUL.	West	North	East	South
♠ K Q 8 6 5	1◇	Pass	2♣	Pass
♡ A Q 7	2◇	Pass	2NT	Pass
◇ K J 2	3NT	Pass	Pass	Pass
♣ 10 5				

NOT VS. NOT	West	North	East	South
♠ K 3	1♠	Pass	2♡	Pass
♡ 8 3	3♡	Pass	4♡	Pass
◇ A K 4	Pass	Pass		
♣ K J 9 7 5 3				

NOT VS. VUL.	West	North	East	South
♠ 8 5 3	1♠	Pass	2♣	2♡
♡ A Q J 10 8 6	2♠	3♡	3♠	4♡
◇ 7 5 2	4♠	Pass	Pass	5♡
♣ 9	Dbl.	Pass	Pass	Pass

Partner should not raise you on flimsy values. At IMP's, you might decide not to save.

NOT VS. VUL.	West	North	East	South
♠ 8 5	1♠	Pass	2◇	3♡ (4♡ = 80)
♡ Q J 10 9 7 5 3	3♠	4♡	4♠	Pass
◇ K 3	Pass	Pass		
♣ 6 4				

NOT VS. NOT	West	North	East	South
♠ K Q J 8 7 5 4	1♣	Pass	2♣	3♠
♡ A J 4	Pass	4♠	Pass	Pass
◇ Q 2	Pass			
♣ 7				

Jumps in this situation should show good hands.

NOT VS. NOT	West	North	East	South
♠ K Q 10 7 5	—	—	1♣	1♠
♡ K 5 4	2♣	Dbl.*	Pass	2♡
◇ Q 2	3♣	3◇	Pass	Pass
♣ J 7 5	Pass			

*Responsive

Partner has four hearts and probably six or seven diamonds.

VUL. VS. VUL.	West	North	East	South
♠ A J 10 8	1◇	Pass	1♡	Dbl.
♡ J 4 2	2◇	2♠	3◇	Pass
◇ 3	Pass	3♠	Pass	Pass
♣ A Q 8 5 4	Pass			

NOT VS. NOT	West	North	East	South
♠ 8 6 3	1♣	Pass	1♠	Pass
♡ K J 9 7 5	2♣	Pass	Pass	Pass
◇ A 3				
♣ K 5 4				

NOT VS. NOT	West	North	East	South
♠ K 10 8 6 4	1♡	Pass	1♠	2◇
♡ 3	2♡	Dbl.	Pass	Pass
◇ A Q 10 9 6	Pass			
♣ J 3				

NOT VS. VUL.	West	North	East	South
♠ Q 5	1♡	Pass	1♠	Pass
♡ K J 7	2♡	Pass	Pass	Pass
◇ K J 9 8 7				
♣ A 4 2				

VUL. VS' VUL.	West	North	East	South
♠ 8 6 5 4 2	1♣	Pass	1♡	1♠
♡ A Q 10 8	Pass	2♠	Pass	3♠
◇ A Q	Pass	4♠	Pass	Pass
♣ A 4	Pass			

NOT VS. NOT	West	North	East	South
♠ A 5 3	1◇	Pass	1NT	2♡
♡ Q J 10 8 7	3♣	3♡	Pass	Pass
◇ A 6 4	Pass			
♣ 5 4				

NOT VS. VUL.	West	North	East	South
♠ K 3	1♡	Pass	1NT	Pass
♡ Q 7 5	Pass	Pass		
◇ K Q 9 6 4				
♣ K 10 7				

VUL. VS. NOT	West	North	East	South
♠ 9 8 6 5 4 2	1♡	Pass	1NT	2♠
♡ A 3	Pass	Pass	Pass	
◇ K Q 7				
♣ K 3				

NOT VS. NOT	West	North	East	South
♠ Q 10 8 7 5	1♡	Pass	2♡	2♠
♡ A 8 3	3♡	3♠	Pass	Pass
◇ 8 6	Pass			
♣ A J 3				

NOT VS. VUL.	West	North	East	South
♠ A 10 3	1◇	Pass	2◇	2♡
♡ K 10 8 6 4 3	3◇	3♡	Pass	4♡ (Pass = 80)
◇ A 9 7	Pass	Pass	Pass	
♣ 3				

NOT VS. NOT	West	North	East	South
♠ A 10 3	1♣	Pass	2♣	2♡
♡ K 10 8 7 5 4	3♣	3♡	Pass	Pass (4♡ = 50)
◇ A 9 6	Pass			
♣ 4				

VUL. VS. NOT	West	North	East	South
♠ 10 8 6 5 4	1◇	Pass	2◇	2♠
♡ 4	Pass	3♠	Pass	4♠
◇ A Q 4	Pass	Pass	Pass	
♣ A K Q 8				

NOT VS. VUL.	West	North	East	South
♠ K 2	1♣	Pass	1♡	2♡*
♡ K Q 10 9 7 5	3♣	Pass	Pass	Pass
◇ A 8 5 3				
♣ 3				

*Since you rarely need to cue bid in this sequence, you might try playing it as natural.

NOT VS. NOT	West	North	East	South
♠ K J 8 4	1◇	Pass	1♡	2◇ (1♠ = 40)
♡ 4	2♡	Pass	Pass	2♠
◇ A Q 10 9 7 4	Pass	Pass	3♡	Pass
♣ 8 4	Pass	Pass		

VUL. VS. VUL.	West	North	East	South
♠ A Q J 8 4	–	Pass	1◇	1♠
♡ K 10 7 4	3◇	Dbl.*	Pass	4♡
◇ 8 4 3	Pass	Pass	Pass	
♣ 5				

*Responsive

NOT VS. VUL.	West	North	East	South
♠ A K J 8	–	Pass	1♣	1♠
♡ 9 2	2♣	2♠	Pass	Pass
◇ A 4 3 2	3♣	3♡	Pass	Pass
♣ 10 6 5	Pass			

NOT VS. VUL.	West	North	East	South
♠ 10 8 7 6 5	–	–	1◇	1♠
♡ K J 4	2◇	Dbl.*	Pass	3♣
◇ 2	3◇	Dbl.	Pass	3♡
♣ A Q 7 5	Pass	Pass	Pass	

*Responsive

VUL. VS. VUL.	West	North	East	South
♠ K Q 10 9 8 6 5	1♡	Pass	2♣	3♠
♡ 3	4♣	Pass	5♣	Pass
◇ Q J 9 5	Pass	Pass		
♣ 7				

Even though it's defined as weak, a vulnerable jump on this auction must show worthwhile values.

RESPONDER (*South*)

NOT VS. VUL.	*West*	*North*	*East*	*South*
♠ K 8 4	1♣	1♠	Dbl.*	2♠
♡ 4 3	3♡	Pass	Pass	Pass
◊ K 10 8 5 4				
♣ J 7 4				

*Negative

After a negative double you should raise partner whenever possible.

NOT VS. NOT	*West*	*North*	*East*	*South*
♠ K J 10 8 4	—	—	—	Pass
♡ J 5 4	1♡	2♣	2♡	2♠
◊ 8 4 2	Pass	3♠	Pass	Pass
♣ Q 9	Pass			

VUL. VS. VUL.	*West*	*North*	*East*	*South*
♠ K J 9 7 4	1◊	1♡	2♣	Pass
♡ J 3	2◊	Pass	Pass	Pass
◊ Q 10 7				
♣ J 7 3				

NOT VS. VUL.	*West*	*North*	*East*	*South*
♠ Q J 10 8 4 3	1♣	1♡	2◊	2♠ (3♠ = 60)
♡ Q 4	3♣	Pass	3◊	Pass
◊ 9 7 5 4	3NT	Pass	Pass	Pass
♣ 7				

VUL. VS. VUL.	*West*	*North*	*East*	*South*
♠ K Q 9 7 6 5 3 2	1◊	1♡	2♣	3♠
♡ J 4	4♣	Pass	4◊	Pass
◊ 9 4	5◊	Pass	Pass	Pass
♣ 3				

Jumps are pre-emptive after a two-over-one by RHO.

VUL. VS. NOT	West	North	East	South
♠ K Q 10 9 7 5	1♣	1♡	Pass	2♠
♡ Q 8	Pass	3♠	Pass	4♠
◇ A Q 5	Pass	Pass	Pass	
♣ 8 4				

NOT VS. NOT	West	North	East	South
♠ 7 2	1♣	1♠	2◇	3♡
♡ K Q J 10 8 7 5	4◇	Pass	Pass	Pass
◇ 9 7 5				
♣ 3				

VUL. VS. VUL.	West	North	East	South
♠ 8 6 2	1♠	2♣	2♡	4◇
♡ —	4♡	Dbl.	Pass	Pass
◇ K Q 10 8 7 6 4 3	Pass			
♣ J 9				

NOT VS. VUL.	West	North	East	South
♠ K Q J 8 7 5 4	1◇	1♡	2♣	4♠ (4♡ = 90)
♡ 10 7 5 3	5♣	Pass	Pass	5♡ (3♠ = 50)
◇ 3	Dbl.	Pass	Pass	Pass
♣ 4				

The important thing here is to buy the contract.

NOT VS. NOT	West	North	East	South
♠ Q 9 6 4	1♣	1♠	2♣	3♠
♡ A J 10 7 5	Pass	4♠	Pass	Pass
◇ K 4	Pass			
♣ 8 4				

NOT VS. NOT	West	North	East	South
♠ J 10 8 4 3	1♣	1♠	2♡	3♠ (4♠ = 70)
♡ 8	Pass	4♠	5♣	Pass
◇ Q J 9 3	Pass	Dbl.	Pass	Pass
♣ 8 5 3	Pass			

NOT VS. VUL.	West	North	East	South
♠ Q 8 6 5 4	1♡	1♠	3◇	5♠ (4♠ = 60)
♡ 8 5 4	Dbl.	Pass	Pass	Pass
◇ 9 2				
♣ Q 10 7				

They may or may not have a slam, but game is sure. Five spades shuts out Blackwood.

NOT VS. NOT	West	North	East	South
♠ J 2	1♣	1♠	Pass	Pass
♡ J 9 7 5	Dbl.	2◇	2♡	Pass
◇ Q 7 3	Pass	Pass		
♣ K 8 5 3				

VUL. VS. VUL.	West	North	East	South
♠ K Q 9 7 5	1♣	1◇	1♡	1♠
♡ 8 4	2♡	2♠	Pass	Pass
◇ K 10 4	3♡	Pass	Pass	3♠
♣ J 8 3	Pass	Pass	Pass	

Nothing wasted. Playing strength with a diamond fit.

VUL. VS. NOT	West	North	East	South
♠ K 10 7	1◇	1♠	2◇	2♠
♡ Q J 9 6	3◇	Pass	Pass	Pass
◇ K 8 5				
♣ J 5 4				

Bidding again would be hanging partner. You have a defensive hand, wasted values and only three trumps.

NOT VS. NOT	West	North	East	South
♠ 7 5 4	1♣	1◇	Pass	1♡
♡ A J 9 8 4	2♣	Pass	3♣	3◇
◇ Q J 4	Pass	Pass	Pass	
♣ 7 5				

NOT VS. VUL.	West	North	East	South
♠ 8 6 5 4 2	1◊	1♠	2◊	2♠
♡ K 10 7	3◊	Dbl.	Pass	Pass
◊ 7 5	Pass			
♣ K J 4				

In spite of the fifth spade, you have good defence.

NOT VS. NOT	West	North	East	South
♠ K Q 7 5	1♣	1♠	2♣	2♠
♡ 8 2	3♣	Pass	Pass	3♠
◊ Q J 8 7	Pass	Pass	Pass	
♣ 10 8 7				

When you raise a second time on your own, you need four or more good trumps, not scattered points.

NOT VS. NOT	West	North	East	South
♠ 8 7 4	1♣	1♠	2♡	Pass
♡ K J 6 4	3♣	Pass	3◊	Pass
◊ Q 9 8	3NT	Pass	Pass	Pass (Dbl. = 40)
♣ Q J 3				

VUL. VS. VUL.	West	North	East	South
♠ Q 9 8 7	1♣	1♠	2♡	3♠
♡ 3	Pass	Pass	4♡	Pass
◊ J 10 8 7 5 4	Pass	Pass		
♣ 9 7				

NOT VS. NOT	West	North	East	South
♠ 9 5 3	1♡	1♠	1NT	Pass
♡ K 8 5 4	2♣	Pass	Pass	Pass
◊ K 9 2				
♣ Q 10 7				

NOT VS. NOT	West	North	East	South
♠ 8 6 5 4	1♣	1♠	1NT	2♠
♡ 8	Pass	Pass	3♣	Pass
◊ K 10 9 6 4	Pass	Pass		
♣ 10 7 5				

NOT VS. NOT	West	North	East	South
♠ 8 6 5 3 2	1♣	1♠	1NT	3♠
♡ K J 9 7 5	Pass	Pass	Pass	
◇ —				
♣ Q 9 7				

NOT VS. NOT	West	North	East	South
♠ 8 2	1◇	1♡	Pass	2◇
♡ K Q 7	Pass	2♡	Pass	Pass
◇ K 9 5 4	Pass			
♣ A 9 8 5				

NOT VS. VUL.	West	North	East	South
♠ K J 7	1♣	1♠	2♣	3♣
♡ A Q 7 5 3	Pass	3◇	Pass	3♠
◇ Q 7 3	Pass	4♠	Pass	Pass
♣ 5 2	Pass			

VUL. VS. NOT	West	North	East	South
♠ 9 5 3	1♣	1♠	Pass	2♣
♡ A K 8	Pass	2♡	Pass	2♠
◇ A 10 7 3	Pass	Pass	Pass	
♣ J 7 3				

VUL. VS. VUL.	West	North	East	South
♠ K J 8 5	1♣	1♠	2♣	3♣
♡ K Q 7 5	Pass	3♠	Pass	Pass
◇ K 3 2	Pass			
♣ 7 4				

VUL. VS. VUL.	West	North	East	South
♠ 3	1♣	1♠	Pass	2♣
♡ A K J 8 5	Pass	2♠	Pass	3♡
◇ A K Q 8 4	Pass	3♠	Pass	4◇
♣ 8 5	Pass	4♡	Pass	Pass
	Pass			

VUL. VS. NOT	West	North	East	South
♠ Q 2	1♣	1♠	Pass	2♣
♡ A K 7	Dbl.	Pass	Pass	2◇
◇ K Q J 10 6	Pass	2♠	Pass	3♣
♣ J 10 5	Pass	3NT	Pass	Pass
	Pass			

NOT VS. VUL.	West	North	East	South
♠ Q 10	1♣	1♠	Pass	2♣
♡ A J 4	Pass	2♠	Pass	3◇
◇ A K Q 8 5	Pass	3♠	Pass	4♠
♣ 8 6 4	Pass	Pass	Pass	

VUL. VS. VUL.	West	North	East	South
♠ 8 4	1♣	1♠	2♣	Dbl.*
♡ K Q 7 4	Pass	2♡	Pass	Pass
◇ K 10 8 5 3	3♣	Pass	Pass	Pass
♣ 8 3				

*Responsive

VUL. VS. VUL.	West	North	East	South
♠ 3	1♣	1♠	2♡	Pass*
♡ K Q 10 8 4	2NT	Pass	3NT	Pass
◇ 8 6 5 3	Pass	Pass		
♣ 9 6 3				

*Would double here be for penalty, responsive, or showing a spade raise? What are your agreements? P.S.: If double is for penalty, you should pass.

VUL. VS. VUL.	West	North	East	South
♠ K 2	1◇	1♠	2◇	Dbl.*
♡ 10 8 5 4	Pass	2♡	Pass	2♠
◇ 8 4	Pass	Pass	Pass	
♣ A Q J 8 5				

*Responsive

This should show a good hand with two spades, four hearts, and four or more clubs. It is a useful exercise to work out the reasons.

VUL. VS. VUL.	West	North	East	South
♠ Q J 8 7 5	1♣	1♡	2♣	Dbl.*
♡ 5 2	Pass	2♠	Pass	Pass
◇ A 10 9 7 5	3♣	Pass	Pass	3♠
♣ 9	Pass	Pass	Pass	
*Responsive				

VUL. VS. VUL.	West	North	East	South
♠ K 8	1♣	1♠	2♣	Dbl.*
♡ A Q 9 8 4	Pass	2♡	Pass	3♡
◇ K 10 8 6 5	Pass	4♡	Pass	Pass
♣ 8	Pass			
*Responsive				

NOT VS. VUL.	West	North	East	South
♠ 8 2	1♣	1♠	3♣	Dbl.*
♡ K Q J 9	Pass	3♡	Pass	Pass
◇ K Q 7 5 2	Pass			
♣ 7 3				
*Responsive				

VUL. VS. VUL.	West	North	East	South
♠ 3	1♣	1♠	3♣	Pass
♡ K 8 6 4	Pass	Pass		
◇ K 10 7 5 4				
♣ 8 7 4				

NOT VS. NOT.	West	North	East	South
♠ K Q 10 9 6	1♠	2♡	2♠	Pass
♡ 3	Pass	Pass		
◇ K 4 2				
♣ Q 10 8 3				

NOT VS. NOT.	West	North	East	South
♠ Q J 8 6 4	1♣	1♡	Pass	1♠
♡ 8	Pass	2♡	Pass	Pass
◇ A 10 7 4	Pass			
♣ 8 3 2				

VUL. VS. NOT	West	North	East	South
♠ 10 3	1♣	1♠	Pass	2♣
♡ A Q 8 5	Dbl.	Rdbl.*	Pass	3NT
◇ A K J 7 4	Pass	Pass	Pass	
♣ J 8				

*Shows something in clubs and more than a minimum overcall. Probably a balanced hand.

VUL. VS. NOT	West	North	East	South
♠ 4 2	1♣	1♠	Pass	2NT
♡ Q 8 5	Pass	3NT	Pass	Pass
◇ K J 4	Pass			
♣ A Q J 9 5				

NOT VS. VUL.	West	North	East	South
♠ Q 8 7 5 4	1♣	1♠	2♡	4♠
♡ 7 3	Pass	Pass	Dbl.	Pass
◇ K 8 6 4	Pass	Pass		
♣ 4 3				

VUL. VS. NOT	West	North	East	South
♠ 3	—	Pass	1♣	Pass
♡ Q 4 3 2	1◇	1♠	Pass	1NT
◇ A 7 5 2	Pass	Pass	Pass	
♣ K Q J 7				

No game opposite a passed hand.

NOT VS. VUL.	West	North	East	South
♠ Q J 3	1♣	1♠	2♣	2♠
♡ 7 3	Pass	Pass	Pass	
◇ A 10 8 6 4				
♣ 9 6 3				

NOT VS. VUL.	West	North	East	South
♠ K J 7	1◇	2♣	2◇	3♣
♡ A Q J 4	Pass	Pass	Pass	
◇ 4 3				
♣ 10 8 7 5				

Just shy of a cue bid. The ideal would be to make a cue bid without stopping outside the three club zone. There's no way.

NOT VS. NOT	West	North	East	South
♠ 8 7 4	1♣	1♡	1♠	2♡
♡ Q 8 4	2♠	Pass	Pass	Pass
◇ K J 8 5				
♣ K Q 4				

NOT VS. VUL.	West	North	East	South
♠ K 10 8	1♣	1♠	2♣	2♠
♡ 4	3♣	Pass	Pass	3◇
◇ Q J 10 8 6 4	Pass	3♠	Pass	Pass
♣ 10 7 3	Pass			

NOT VS. VUL.	West	North	East	South
♠ 4	1♡	1♠	Pass	2♣
♡ 10 8 5 3	Pass	2◇	Pass	Pass
◇ Q 3	Pass			
♣ K J 10 7 6 3				

NOT VS. NOT	West	North	East	South
♠ 8 2	1♣	1♠	2♣	Dbl.*
♡ K J 9 7	Pass	2♡	3♣	3◇
◇ K J 10 8 6 3	Pass	Pass	Pass	
♣ 7				

*Responsive

NOT VS. VUL.	West	North	East	South
♠ A Q 10 8 7	1◇	1♡	2◇	Dbl.*
♡ 8 3	3◇	Pass	Pass	3♠
◇ 4	Pass	4♣	Pass	Pass
♣ K Q 9 6 3	Pass			

*Responsive

VUL. VS. VUL.	West	North	East	South
♠ 9 2	1♣	1♠	2♣	Dbl.*
♡ A Q 10 6	Pass	2◇	3♣	Dbl.
◇ A Q 9 7	Pass	3◇	Pass	Pass
♣ 7 5 3	Pass			

*Responsive

NOT VS. VUL.	West	North	East	South
♠ 2	1♠	2♡	3♣	3♢ (4♢ = 100)
♡ J 7 3	3♠	Pass	4♠	4NT*
♢ K Q 10 9 7 6 2	Pass	5♢	Dbl.	Pass
♣ 8 7	Pass	Pass		

*Unusual for hearts and diamonds.

VUL. VS. NOT	West	North	East	South
♠ 9 5	1♠	2♣	2♡	3♢ (4♢ = 40)
♡ 5 3	Pass	3NT	Pass	Pass
♢ K Q 10 7 6 5 3 2	Pass			
♣ 3				

Bad shape and unfavourable vulnerability. You have your bid, so there's no reason to run.

VUL. VS. VUL.	West	North	East	South
♠ 3	1♠	2♣	2♢	3♡
♡ K Q J 8 7 5 4	Pass	3NT	Pass	Pass
♢ 5 2	Pass			
♣ 10 7 5				

Likewise.

VUL. VS. NOT	West	North	East	South
♠ 10 5 3 2	1♡	2♣	2♡	3♢
♡ —	Pass	3NT	Pass	4♢
♢ K Q 10 8 7 6 5	Pass	Pass	Pass	
♣ 9 7				

On this sequence, you are expected to have a fair hand. You haven't, so you can't stand 3NT.

NOT VS. VUL.	West	North	East	South
♠ J 10 8 7 5 3	1♣	1♡	2♣	Pass (2♠ = 30)
♡ J 3	Pass	2♢	Pass	3♢ (Dbl. = 30)
♢ K 10 8 7	Pass	Pass	Pass	
♣ 4				

VUL. VS. VUL.	West	North	East	South
♠ 10 8 7 5 3 2	1♣	1♡	2♣	Pass
♡ Q 10	Pass	2◇	Pass	2♡
◇ Q 5	Pass	3♡	Pass	4♡
♣ 8 6 3	Pass	Pass	Pass	

NOT VS. VUL.	West	North	East	South
♠ 10 8 7	1♠	2♣	Pass	3♣ (2♡ = 60)
♡ K J 9 7 4	3◇	Pass	Pass	Pass (3♡ = 70)
◇ 7 3				
♣ A J 5				

VUL. VS. VUL.	West	North	East	South
♠ Q J 9 7 6 4 3	1♡	2◇	Pass	3♠
♡ A 9 3	Pass	Pass	Pass	
◇ K 7				
♣ 3				

VUL. VS. NOT	West	North	East	South
♠ K Q J 10 7 5	1♡	2◇	2♡	4♠
♡ 7 5	Pass	Pass	Pass	
◇ A 10 4				
♣ Q 7				

NOT VS. NOT	West	North	East	South
♠ 8 3	1♠	2♡	4♠	Pass
♡ K 8 4 3	Pass	Pass		
◇ Q 8 5 3				
♣ Q 10 7				

Never save if it's marginal.

VUL VS. VUL.	West	North	East	South
♠ J 3	1♠	2♣	2◇	Pass
♡ K 8 6 5 3 2	2♠	Pass	3♠	Pass
◇ Q J 8	Pass	Pass		
♣ 9 2				

VUL. VS. NOT	West	North	East	South
♠ 8 5 3	1♣	2◊	2♡	Pass
♡ Q 8 4	1♠	Pass	3♡	Pass
◊ —	4♡	Pass	Pass	Pass
♣ K Q 8 6 5 3 2				